HEIDEGGER'S POIETIC W

HEIDEGGER'S POIETIC WRITINGS

From *Contributions to Philosophy* to *The Event*

Daniela Vallega-Neu

Indiana University Press

This book is a publication of

Indiana University Press
Office of Scholarly Publishing
Herman B Wells Library 350
1320 East 10th Street
Bloomington, Indiana 47405 USA

iupress.indiana.edu

The paper used in this publication meets the minimum
requirements of the American National Standard for Information
Sciences—Permanence of Paper for Printed Library Materials,
ANSI Z39.48-1992.

Manufactured in the United States of America

Library of Congress Cataloging-in-Publication Data

Names: Vallega-Neu, Daniela, 1966– author.
Title: Heidegger's poietic writings : from contributions to philosophy
    to the event / Daniela Vallega-Neu.
Description: 1st [edition]. | Bloomington : Indiana University Press,
    2018. | Series: Studies in Continental thought | Includes
    bibliographical references and index.
Identifiers: LCCN 2017037201 (print) | LCCN 2017053046 (ebook) | ISBN
    9780253032140 (e-book) | ISBN 9780253032133 (cloth : alk. paper)
Subjects: LCSH: Heidegger, Martin, 1889–1976.
Classification: LCC B3279.H49 (ebook) | LCC B3279.H49 V274 2018
    (print) | DDC 193—dc23
LC record available at https://lccn.loc.gov/2017037201

ISBN 978-0-253-03388-8 (pbk.)
ISBN 978-0-253-03389-5 (MOBI)
ISBN 978-0-253-03391-8 (ePub)

1 2 3 4 5 23 22 21 20 19 18

In memory of my father,
   Helmut Neu (1920–1986)

Contents

Preface   *ix*

Acknowledgments   *xiii*

Key to Heidegger's *Gesamtausgabe* (When Applicable,
with English Translation)   *xv*

1   Introduction to Heidegger's Poietic Writings: The Regress
to the Source   *1*

2   *Contributions to Philosophy (Of the Event)* (GA 65)   *20*

3   Attunement and Grounding: A Critical Engagement with
Heidegger's *Contributions to Philosophy (Of the Event)* (GA 65)   *45*

4   *Besinnung* (*Mindfulness*) (GA 66)   *63*

5   Heidegger and History: A Critical Engagement with Heidegger's
Besinnung (GA 66), *Die Geschichte des Seyns* (GA 67), and the
Black Notebooks   *92*

6   *Über den Anfang* (*On Inception*) (GA 70)   *104*

7   Hovering in Incipience: A Critical Engagement with Heidegger's
Über den Anfang (*On Inception*) (GA 70)   *129*

8   *The Event* (GA 71)   *140*

9   At the Brink of Language: A Critical Engagement with
Heidegger's *The Event* (GA 71)   *167*

Conclusion   *182*

Bibliography   *195*

Index   *199*

Preface

THIS BOOK TRACES and engages critically the development of Heidegger's non-public writings on "the event" between 1936 and 1942. Heidegger held these manuscripts as well as the notorious *Black Notebooks* (another series of nonpublic writings) hidden from the public and directed that they be published as part of his collected works only after all his lecture courses had been published. The first of the nonpublic writings of the event is *Beiträge zur Philosophy (Vom Ereignis)* (*Contributions to Philosophy*) and is considered by many to be Heidegger's second major work after *Being and Time*. It appeared in German in 1989 and was first translated into English in 1989 and then again in 2012. The following volumes *Besinnung* (*Mindfulness*), *Die Geschichte des Seins* (*The History of Beyng*), *Über den Anfang* (*On Inception*), and *Das Ereignis* (*The Event*) were published in German between 1997 and 2009 and were translated into English between 2006 and now. The last volume of the series (*Stege des Anfangs*), dating to 1944, has not yet been published in German.

These volumes are not philosophical works in the traditional sense and read more like collections of notes, reflections, and expositions that are uneven in character, ranging from outlines and fragments to more elaborated developments of topics. In them, Heidegger searches for a language that would not simply speak *about* being but rather let a sense of being emerge in his thinking and saying. He attempts to open paths of thinking the occurrence of being in its historicality in terms of the event and to evoke a transformation of the sense of being in the West in order to prepare what he calls "the other beginning." This is why I call them Heidegger's "poietic" writings, with reference to the Greek word "ποίησις," which means, "to bring forth." In Germany, these writings are usually called Heidegger's "seynsgeschichtliche Abhandlungen" ("treatises pertaining to the historicality of beyng") but they are far from "treatises" in any conventional sense.

The sense of being that Heidegger seeks to evoke is without ground; it cannot be explained but may only be performatively understood (i.e., in the undergoing of this very sense of being in thinking). It escapes a thinking in terms of activity or passivity, subject and object. It might be thought as in some ways close to what resonates in the short poem "Der Cherbinische Wandersmann" [The cherubinic pilgrim] by the mystic Angelus Silesius: "The rose is without 'why'; it blooms because it blooms"; only that Heidegger's sense of being in transition from metaphysics to the other beginning, includes also (especially up to the end of the 1930s) a sense of loss marked by "shock" or "horror." What he calls "the truth of beyng" thus harbors an abyssal dimension that is for Heidegger at the same time revelatory in terms of other, fuller possibilities of being.

There are other nonpublic texts that Heidegger wrote at the same time, other notes that often take the form of attempts at thinking and engaging his times critically in view of his understanding of being as historical event. To them belong the *Black Notebooks* (that bear, among others, the titles "Considerations" and "Notes") that received and are still receiving major attention also outside academia, mainly because of a number of disturbing anti-Semitic remarks they contain. To the nonpublic writings belong as well two volumes of notes—roughly 1,480 pages—under the title *Concerning the Thinking of the Event*. Even if what I call Heidegger's poietic writings are to be distinguished from the *Black Notebooks* (the former are more strictly attempts at uncovering the most hidden aspects of historical being, whereas the latter contain far more polemical reflections on what Heidegger saw happening around him), there are some overlaps between them. Thus an engagement with Heidegger's poietic writings requires, at least to some extent, an engagement with the *Black Notebooks* as well.

In this book, I show how between the first and last published volumes of the poietic writings, all written shortly before and during World War II, striking shifts happen in the tonality and movement of Heidegger's thinking. In these years, a shift occurs from a more Nietzschean pathos in which Heidegger seeks an "empowerment" of being, to a more "mystical" attitude in which he seeks to be responsive to and follow what he calls "the silent call of being." At the same time, there are shifts in conceptuality and in the directionality of thought. Heidegger moves more and more away from the primacy of human being such that the origin of language is sought in historical beyng (written with a "y" to mark a more original sense of being). Thinking first comes to itself out of what is assigned to it in the word "of" (in the sense of belonging to) beyng. Especially the last published volumes of the poietic writings read like meditative exercises that abound with repetitive word-sound variations at the brink of the sayable. Heidegger meditates, directed toward silence and concealment, following attunements that he understands to arise from and to disclose historical beyng. Along with the shift in tonality a shift occurs as well in his attitude toward what he understands to be the last epoch of metaphysics (i.e., our epoch).

Heidegger's attempt at evoking a more primordial sense of being is necessitated (in his view) by what he calls the abandonment of beings by being that marks the way being occurs in metaphysics. In his reading, the history of being has evolved in the West in such a way that our relation to things and events is more and more predisposed by machination (*Machenschaft*), that is, by makeability and calculability, and by lived experience (*Erlebnis*), that is, by the integration of everything into a nongenuine and subjectively oriented sense of "life." Machination and especially lived experience are so dominant in our epoch that Heidegger sees the possibility of a deeper questioning of being to be in danger of disappearing. It is striking that, whereas in the earlier poietic writings Heidegger's stance toward the machinational deployment of being in our times is one of resistance, in the later poietic writings his stance changes: instead of resisting machination and the abandonment of beings by being, he lets them "pass by."

In my book I not only trace the shifts in tonality, conceptuality, and the movement of thought in Heidegger's poietic writings. Their unorthodox and intimate character also warrants an approach that differs from that required for traditional philosophical texts. I am separating, therefore, a more expository approach to the texts from a freer, more intimate, and also more critical engagement with them. I have, thus, expository or interpretative chapters in which I attempt to give the reader some "structures" for navigating these difficult texts, and in which I explain as much as possible some main concepts. A chapter in which I explore more freely various themes and issues relating to the previous chapter follows each of these more expository chapters.

Chapter 1 introduces Heidegger's poietic writings in view of his earlier project, *Being and Time*, paying special attention to the role of history and language; it introduces concepts that play a major role in his thinking of the 1930s and early 1940s, and ends with a presentation of the questions that guide my reading of Heidegger's texts. Starting with chapter 2, I begin an expository interpretation of each of the four volumes I discuss in the book. Chapter 2 is dedicated to *Contributions to Philosophy* (GA 65), chapter 4 to *Mindfulness (Besinnung)* and *The History of Beyng (Die Geschichte des Seyns)* (GA 66 and 67, respectively), chapter 6 to *On Inception (Über den Anfang,* GA 70), and chapter 8 to *The Event (Das Ereignis,* GA 71). As I have already pointed out, the remaining chapters take a more questioning and critical approach. In chapter 3 (relating to *Contributions*), I question the issue of grounding in the context of Heidegger's differentiation between beyng and beings, the questions of the body, decision, and the performativity of his writing. In chapter 5 (relating to *Besinnung* and *Die Geschichte des Seyns*), I engage the difficult question of Heidegger's thinking in relation to its historical setting in Germany during World War II. This includes the questions of his nationalism and anti-Semitism, which requires a look at the *Black Notebooks* from the same time. In chapter 7 (relating to *Über den Anfang*), I reflect on the major change that happens with this volume, the shift in attunement in this text, and Heidegger's move toward attempting to think the event as inception (*Anfang*). I inquire into the way he begins to understand his thinking in a movement of departure into the most inceptive, abyssal dimension of beyng, indeed even beyond beyng, as he introduces the difficult notion of the "beingless." Chapter 9 (relating to *The Event*) is dedicated to an inquiry into language and to how, after his descent into the most abyssal dimension of being, Heidegger will emerge with a new "cosmology" (the fourfold of gods, humans, earth, and sky) and a rethinking of things as sites of gathering and disclosure of a world—a world that, for him, is not yet there and has never been there. In my concluding chapter 10, I pull together the different interpretative strands that have emerged from my reading of Heidegger's poietic writings, focusing especially on the questions of attunement, language, body, and history in his thinking.

Acknowledgments

I WOULD LIKE to thank all those who inspired and helped shape this book, many of whom, I am sure, did so without my awareness. In particular, I thank Dee Mortensen and the staff of Indiana University Press as well as John Sallis for their support in making its publication possible. Perhaps the core questions of my book took shape when I was writing the lecture course for the Collegium Phaenomenologicum in 2013, titled "Heidegger's Reticence: From *Contributions* to *Das Ereignis* and toward *Gelassenheit*," and I thank the director of the Collegium of 2013, Drew Hyland, who invited me to give this lecture course, and all the faculty and participants at that Collegium for their questions and conversations. Among those who influenced or were present at my lecture course I would like to acknowledge in particular Andrew Benjamin, Robert Bernasconi, Bret Davis, Antonia Egel, Eliane Escoubas, Günter Figal, Andrew Mitchell, Jim Risser, Dennis Schmidt, Susan Schoenbohm, Charles Scott, Gert-Jan van der Heiden, Ben Vedder, Sanem Yazicioglu, and Krysztof Ziarek, as well as Sam Ijsseling, one of the founders of the Collegium who attended for the last time prior to his passing in 2015. An abridged version of the lecture course appeared in *Research in Phenomenology* in 2015. A New Faculty Award from the Office for Research, Innovation, and Graduate Education at the University of Oregon gave me a quarter off from teaching in 2013, and with it, precious time to make some progress on the book manuscript. I am also grateful for an author subvention grant I received from the Oregon Humanities Center and the College of Arts and Sciences of the University of Oregon, and to Joshua Kerr who did the indexing for the book. The publication of the first volume of Heidegger's *Black Notebooks* in 2014 and the heated discussions issuing from it complicated and enriched my book in many ways. I thank Jeff Malpass for inviting me to contribute to his and Ingo Farin's edited volume on the *Black Notebooks* from 1931 to 1941, which was an additional incentive to engage the *Notebooks* more deeply. Finally I would like to extend my special gratitude to David Farrell Krell, Andrew Mitchell, and Susan Schoenbohm who all read the whole manuscript, gave me valuable feedback, and made insightful comments that helped strengthen the book. So did Alejandro Vallega, who has sustained me in life and thought throughout the process of writing this book and to whom my deepest gratitude goes.

Key to Heidegger's *Gesamtausgabe*
(When Applicable, with
English Translation)

Heidegger, Martin. *Gesamtausgabe* (GA). 102 volumes projected. Frankfurt am
Main: Vittorio Klostermann, 1975–.

GA 2   *Sein und Zeit.* Edited by Friedrich-Wilhelm von Herrmann. 1977.
        Translated by Joan Stambaugh as *Being and Time*, revised by
        Dennis J. Schmidt. Albany: State University of New York Press,
        2010.

GA 4   *Erläuterungen zu Hölderlins Dichtung.* 2nd ed. Edited by Friedrich-
        Wilhelm von Herrmann. 1991. Translated by Keith Hoeller as
        Elucidations of Hölderlin's Poetry. Amherst, NY: Humanity Books,
        2000.

GA 5   *Holzwege.* 7th ed. Edited by Friedrich-Wilhelm von Herrmann.
        1994. Edited and translated by Julian Young and Kenneth Haynes
        as *Off the Beaten Track.* Cambridge: Cambridge University Press,
        2002.

GA 6.1 *Nietzsche I.* Edited by Brigitte Schillback. 1996.

GA 6.2 *Nietzsche II.* Edited by Brigitte Schillback. 1997.

GA 7   *Vorträge und Aufsätze.* Edited by Friedrich-Wilhelm von Herr-
        mann. 2000.

GA 9   *Wegmarken.* 3rd ed. Edited by Friedrich-Wilhelm von Herrmann.
        1996. Edited and translated by William McNeill as *Pathmarks.*
        Cambridge: Cambridge University Press, 1998.

GA 12   *Unterwegs zur Sprache.* Edited by Friedrich-Wilhelm von Herr-
        mann. 1985. Translated by Peter D. Hertz as *On the Way to Lan-
        guage.* San Francisco: Harper, 1971.

GA 24   *Die Grundprobleme der Phänomenologie.* 2nd ed. Edited by
        Friedrich-Wilhelm von Herrmann. 1989. Translated by Albert
        Hofstadter as *The Basic Problems of Phenomenology.* Rev. ed.
        Bloomington: Indiana University Press, 1982.

GA 29/30   *Die Grundbegriffe der Metaphysik: Welt—Endlichkeit—Einsamkeit.* 2nd ed. Edited by Friedrich-Wilhelm von Herrmann. 1992. Translated by William McNeill as *The Fundamental Concepts of Metaphysics: World, Finitude, Solitude.* Bloomington: Indiana University Press, 1995.

GA 39   *Hölderlins Hymnen "Germanien" und "Der Rhein."* 2nd ed. Edited by Susanne Ziegler. 1989. Translated by William McNeill and Julia Ireland as *Hölderlin's Hymns "Germania" and "The Rhine."* Bloomington: Indiana University Press, 2014.

GA 40   *Einführung in die Metaphysik.* Edited by Petra Jäger. 1983. Translated by Gregory Fried and Richard Polt as *Introduction to Metaphysics.* New Haven, CT: Yale University Press, 2000.

GA 44   *Nietzsches metaphysische Grundstellung im abendländischen Denken: Die ewige Wiederkehr des Gleichen.* Edited by Marion Heinz. 1986.

GA 45   *Grundfragen der Philosophie: Ausgewählte "Probleme" der "Logik."* 2nd ed. Edited by Friedrich-Wilhelm von Herrmann. 1992. Translated by Richard Rojcewicz and André Schuwer as *Basic Questions of Philosophy: Selected "Problems" of "Logic."* Bloomington: Indiana University Press, 1994.

GA 47   *Nietzsches Lehre vom Willen zur Macht als Erkenntnis.* Edited by Eberhard Hanser. 1989.

GA 50   *Nietzsches Metaphysik: Einleitung in die Philosophie—Denken und Dichten.* Edited by Petra Jäger. 1990.

GA 51   *Grundbegriffe.* Edited by Petra Jaeger. 1991.

GA 52   *Hölderlins Hymne "Andenken."* 2nd ed. Edited by Curd Ochwald. 1992.

GA 53   *Hölderlins Hymne "Der Ister."* 2nd ed. Edited by Walter Biemel. 1993. Translated by William McNeill and Julia Davis as *Hölderlin's Hymn "The Ister."* Bloomington: Indiana University Press, 1996.

GA 54   *Parmenides.* 2nd ed. Edited by Manfred S. Frings. 1992. Translated by André Schuwer and Richard Rojcewicz as *Parmenides.* Bloomington: Indiana University Press, 1992.

GA 55   *Heraklit.* 3rd ed. Edited by Manfred S. Frings. 1994.

GA 65   *Beiträge zur Philosophie.* 2nd ed. Edited by Friedrich-Wilhelm von Herrmann. 1994. Translated by Richard Rojcewicz and Daniela

Vallega-Neu as *Contributions to Philosophy (Of the Event)*. Bloomington: Indiana University Press, 2012.

GA 66   *Besinnung*. Edited by Friedrich-Wilhelm von Herrmann. 1997. Translated by Parvis Emad and Thomas Kalary as *Mindfulness*. New York: Continuum, 2006.

GA 67   *Metaphysik und Nihilismus*. Edited by Hans-Joachim Friedrich. 1999.

GA 69   *Die Geschichte des Seyns*. Edited by Peter Trawny, 1998. Translated by William McNeill and Jeffrey Powell as *The History of Beyng*. Bloomington: Indiana University Press, 2015.

GA 70   *Über den Anfang*. Edited by Paola-Ludovika Coriando. 2005.

GA 71   *Das Eregnis*. Edited by Friedrich-Wilhelm von Herrmann, 2009. Translated by Richard Rojcewicz as *The Event*. Bloomington: Indiana University Press, 2013.

GA 73.1   *Zum Ereignis-Denken*. Edited by Peter Trawny. 2013.

GA 73.2   *Zum Ereignis-Denken*. Edited by Peter Trawny. 2013.

GA 77   *Feldweg-Gespräche*. Edited by Ingrid Schüßler. 1995. Translated by Bret W. Davis as *Country Path Conversations*. Bloomington: Indiana University Press, 2012.

GA 79   *Bremer und Freiburger Vorträge*. Edited by Petra Jaeger. 1994. Translated by Andrew J. Mitchell as *Bremen and Freiburg Lectures: Insight into That Which Is and Basic Principles of Thinking*. Bloomington: Indiana University Press, 2012.

GA 90   *Zu Ernst Jünger*. Edited by Peter Trawny. 2004.

GA 94   *Überlegungen II–VI (Schwarze Hefte 1931–1938)*. Edited by Peter Trawny. 2014.

GA 95   *Überlegungen VII–XI (Schwarze Hefte 1938–1939)*. Edited by Peter Trawny. 2014.

GA 96   *Überlegungen XII–XV (Schwarze Hefte 1939–1941)*. Edited by Peter Trawny. 2014.

GA 97   *Anmerkungen I–V (Schwarze Hefte 1942–1948)*. Edited by Peter Trawny. 2015.

HEIDEGGER'S POIETIC WRITINGS

1 Introduction to Heidegger's Poietic Writings

The Regress to the Source

Volumes 65 to 72 of Heidegger's collected works contain his attempt at rethinking the question of being more radically than in *Being and Time*.[1] They were not conceived for public understanding and were written only in view of finding a language to think and speak of being in a more originary (*ursprünglich*) way.[2] *Contributions to Philosophy (Of the Event)* is the first of the series and many consider it to be Heidegger's second major work. According to the testimony of the editor of Heidegger's collected works, Friedrich Wilhelm von Herrmann, Heidegger said that *Besinnung* (1938/1939), *Über den Anfang* (1941), *Das Ereignis* (1941/1942), and *Die Stege des Anfangs* (1944) are all "especially closely connected with *Contributions to Philosophy* [1936–1938] insofar as these treatises rethink in its entirety and with a new approach the conjuncture [*Gefüge*] of *Contributions to Philosophy*" (GA 66, "Afterword of the Editor," 433–434). Furthermore, *Die Überwindung der Metaphysik* (1938/1939) and *Die Geschichte des Seyns* (1939/1940) are also closely related to *Contributions*. All these volumes (as well as further notes gathered in GA 73.1/73.2, and perhaps—at least to some extent—Heidegger's concurrently written *Black Notebooks*[3]) contain Heidegger's attempts at thinking being as and in its historical happening, which he now calls *Ereignis* ("the event"). Such thinking is *seynsgeschichtlich*, "beyng-historical," which means that its aim is not to objectify or represent being but rather to respond to being in its historical eventuation in such a way that in this response, historical being is opened up and articulated in an originary way.[4] If and when such thinking succeeds, it allows itself to be addressed by historical being in such a way that what is articulated in this thinking becomes a site of disclosure of being in its historicality. In other words, if a saying of the event succeeds, then it is historical being itself that comes to word and not simply a representation of "it" based on some form of subjective act or projection (Heidegger would call the objectifying representation of history *Historie* ["historiography"] in contrast to history as event, which he calls *Geschichte*). In order to mark this more originary sense of historical being, Heidegger writes "beyng" (*Seyn*) with a "y."

Because historical being is not something ready-made and only subsequently thought but rather occurs only in thinking, I speak of Heidegger's beyng-historical (*seynsgeschichtlich*) writings as "poietic."[5] Although such thinking is not poetry, in its approach it is very close to poetry.

Already in the early 1930s, when Heidegger begins to search for a new language to think and say being in its historicality, he reflects on the proximity of poetry and thought (*Dichten und Denken*).[6] As is well known, the poetry of Hölderlin becomes central to Heidegger and his quest for a new articulation of being. It is in dialogue with Hölderlin that Heidegger will begin to articulate beyng in its historicality and that he will frame the history of being in terms of a first and other beginning of this history. All this begins in the early 1930s, when Germany is being seized by a new resurrection after World War I, by a new promise for a great history, a fever that—as is well known—infected Heidegger's thinking and acting as well.

Impasses in the Project of *Being and Time*

Heidegger was led to conceive the necessity of a thinking (out) *of* the event—proceeding *from* an originary disclosure of being itself—due to impasses he encountered in the project of *Being and Time*. Here already the attempt was to think being out of time, that is, to resituate the metaphysical question "What is . . . ?" in the "is," such that being is understood temporally. The issue is no longer to think atemporal essences, but instead to question the "is," the be-*ing* of things. Philosophy was to be brought back from its entrenchment in neo-Kantian epistemology to the question of the meaning of being. Heidegger continuously points out how in traditional Western thinking, being as such (*Sein*) is always questioned on the basis of *a* being (*Seiendes*), such that when we ask "What is a living being," the answer to this question is framed as an atemporal essence on the basis of a particular living being we represent. Western thought develops as a representing (*Vor-stellen*) such that thought places (*stellt*) what is thought before (*vor*) itself. At the same time, Heidegger shows that while in ancient and medieval thought the thing—what shows itself to us—was conceived as the basis for a representation, with modern philosophy, the "I think" becomes the ground for all representation. Thus the question of being is conditioned by the "I think," which is an "I represent"; being is conditioned and objectified by a subjectivity and being as such is simply represented as the most general determination of beings with no meaning on its own, an empty husk hovering before the mind's eye.

The task then becomes to revitalize the notion of being as one that addresses us in our concrete temporal and historical existence. In *Being and Time*, Heidegger chose to approach the question of the temporal meaning of being through an inquiry into the being that each of us is, which he calls "Dasein," translated literally, there-being.[7] Rather than placing the question of being in human subjectivity, this entails decentering the concept of human subjectivity, since, as he shows, in our concrete everyday "there-being," we are precisely not first and foremost with ourselves, encapsulated in some self-conscious "I-thing," but rather "out there," engaged by things, tasks, and others. Dasein is being-in-the-world and only from there comes back *to* itself when it becomes reflexively self-aware. This reflexive return to oneself carries with it a distancing of I and thing, I and other, I and world. Pointing to our prereflexive being-in-the-world fulfills the double task of resituating our being in its engaged being with . . . and of bringing alive the question of being as one that addresses our very existence along with the being of things and events we find ourselves to be prereflexively engaged with. The discovery of our being as being-in-the-world becomes as well the discovering of the being of other beings, or, as Heidegger would articulate it in *Being and Time*, along with the being of Dasein, the being of beings as a whole is disclosed.

Heidegger shows how the meaning of being is temporal by again first considering Dasein's being. Dasein has the character of a thrownness into and projection onto possibilities of being; this thrown projection is rooted in temporality as the coming toward oneself (futurity) in retrieving one's having been (past), which opens up and structures the present.[8] In our being, future, past, and present appear in their indissoluble unity, with respect to which time, understood as the flowing by of moments of "now," is derivative.

The explicit discovery of the temporal character of our being requires that we are faced with our existence such that our daily engagement with things is interrupted, that we find ourselves exposed to our mortality and with it to being *as such*; that we endure this exposure as we face our finitude and thus *are* more authentically. This is made possible by fundamental attunements (*Grundstimmungen*), which are not simply feelings but dispositions that overcome us and expose us to what they reveal, moods in which we find ourselves exposed to our finitude. In *Being and Time* Heidegger shows this with the fundamental attunement of *Angst*. In later writings he will speak of other fundamental attunements.

The next step in the project of *Being and Time* is announced in section 8 of the book but was never carried out. The initial task entailed showing how the temporality of Dasein, the being each of us is, is rooted in the temporality of the being of beings as a whole. This latter temporality Heidegger articulated as the horizon into which Dasein always already transcends and from which it comes back to itself. Heidegger called this transcendental horizon the "condition of the possibility" for the disclosure of being, using a conceptuality that echoes Kant. Yet the project of Heidegger's fundamental ontology completely overturns the Kantian subjective approach. It overturns the Kantian project—almost in a new "Copernican Revolution"—in that the transcendental realm of the condition of the possibility for experience is not transcendental subjectivity but the temporal horizon of being as such *out of which* Dasein—our being—temporalizes and finds itself always already "there," in a world, and not "here" in a human consciousness.

However, Heidegger became dissatisfied with the transcendental-horizonal approach to being. He thought that the language of *Being and Time* failed in its attempt to say being in its truth,[9] and that it still borrowed too much from metaphysics. Although ultimately the task was also to show how our being is disclosed *out of* the temporal horizon of being as such, the notion of transcendence still invites one to think of a human subject that transcends *into* a horizon, thereby seemingly turning the horizon of being into an object of thought (GA 65: 450–451).[10] What was required, then, was to think and articulate being "directly" *out of* the horizon of its disclosure. Heidegger indicates this in a marginal note referring to the planned third division ("Time and Being") of the first part of the project of *Being and Time*: "The overcoming of the horizon as such. The return into the source [*Herkunft*]. The presencing out of this source" (GA 2: 53; BaT 37).

Presencing from out of the Source and the Withdrawal of the Source

To think being *out of* its disclosive, temporal horizon, means to understand being as a *presencing* rather than as some entity that is already present. Coming to presence occurs as a disclosure, which is how Heidegger rethinks the notion of truth. Reinterpreting the Greek notion of truth, ἀλήθεια, in terms of unconcealing, Heidegger understands the truth of being as the unconcealment of presencing. This presencing is not a thing; it is not *a* being but the presencing through which beings are revealed in their being. Let us say that on a sunny afternoon, sitting on a balcony, you find yourself suddenly caught by the slow movements of a caterpillar; you are struck by the *being* of this caterpillar; *that it is*. In Heidegger's thinking you would not have first a sensible representation of this entity that subsequently you identify as a caterpillar. All this—the representation, the identification, and "you"—comes "later"; it is already the result of the coming to presence of what then reveals itself to be a caterpillar and you looking at it.

For Heidegger, presencing needs to be thought in the middle voice, a verb form that is neither active nor passive, and that we find in Ancient Greek but not in contemporary Western languages (I emphasize "Western" because at least some African languages do have a middle voice). There is nothing that presences, presencing is not the activity of a subject or entity, but happens as rain happens, when "it" rains. Ultimately, presencing is groundless; we may say, the source of the presencing is "abyssal" (*abgründig*). We find this expressed in the lines of Angelus Silesius I quoted already in the preface: "The Rose is without 'why'; she blooms, because she blooms."

We will see how in the sequence of Heidegger's poietic writings, his thinking will move more and more into this abyssal dimension of being, into the concealment that goes along with unconcealing, into the unsaid that withdraws in what is said (the silence of the rose, as it were). Concurrently, he will think being not primarily as presencing but as self-withdrawal such that in this withdrawal things and events appear as what is present. In being present, however, beings (what appears) conceal the unitary occurrence of concealment and unconcealment through which their presencing happens. Things appear, so to speak, "flat"; they do not let their being resound "without why." They become objects, things opposing our gaze, things we can describe, count, classify, and reckon with. These certainly are all very useful attributes for the development of science and for our daily dealings, except that once we operate in the mode of objectivity, the *question* of being has no more place.

Truth of Being as *Ereignis*: The Event and the Turning in the Event

To think the truth of being from itself as that from which we, too, first come to ourselves would require that we do not objectify it in any way but rather attempt to articulate how being occurs *in the very moment* it occurs. Such thinking is utterly groundless, as it has nothing already there to hold on to. It requires a *Loswurf*, a casting oneself loose, as Heidegger says in an early *Black Notebook* (GA 94; Ü II, 108–110). In such casting loose Heidegger begins to experience and think the truth of being as appropriating event, as *Er-eignis*, in which the being of beings and we as well, first are appropriated (*ereignet*), come into our own being.[11] This new approach to the truth of beyng would not start with an analysis of Dasein and would involve an even further displacement of human being from subjectivity. Heidegger had planned a new work that would take this approach "from" the truth of being as event as early as 1932 (GA 66: 424),[12] as we can now see from the *Black Notebooks*, but it finds its first attempt at a configuration only with *Contributions to Philosophy: Of the Event*, written 1936–1938. Heidegger had to find a radically new approach and with it, a new conceptuality, a different language. The following elucidations of what he means by the event therefore are drawn from *Contributions*.

Thinking out of the event (when it succeeds) does not mean that we return to think from a somewhat "objective" horizon toward "us." Activity and passivity are insufficient for understanding the event, which occurs rather in the "middle voice" as I have already indicated above. Heidegger often articulates the middle voice character of the event in terms of a "turning" (*Kehre*). In this turning, being and thinking do not stand in an opposition such that one could relate to the other as somehow distinct. They emerge at once: thinking occurs as the thinking *of* being and being emerges as such only in thinking. Still, Heidegger suggests a certain priority of being when he emphasizes how thinking is always already a response, how it finds itself responding to a call (of being) that in turn discloses itself as call only in the response. We may approximate this with experiences in which an idea "comes to us" out of an attuned being toward some indefinite, not yet articulated "region." The idea is articulated as it comes to us and it is as if the idea itself beckoned the fitting word that we may eventually find (or not) such that only in this finding of the word the idea properly emerges. Moments of wonder bear the same middle voice character. The movement of wonder does not start with a sense of self but rather with a dispossessed exposure to some "thing" or event that comes to light. Poets and artists are familiar with this "middle voice" occurrence and cultivate it as they search for the fitting word or gesture or rather, as they cultivate a space in which the word or gesture can find its way.

Heidegger speaks of the turning as well in terms of the turning in the "between" of truth and being: the being of truth is the truth of being; or he articulates the turning as one between the truth of being and Da-sein: the truth of being occurs in Da-sein as Da-sein occurs in the truth of being. Let me comment on this latter turning.

The notion of Da-sein shifts in *Contributions* with respect to *Being and Time*, and the notion of the human being (*Mensch, Menschsein*) is reintroduced. Heidegger now plays with the two parts of the term "da" and "sein" and thinks even more explicitly than in *Being and Time* the "da" as the "here" or "there" (in German "da" means both), as the opening site of the truth of being. At the same time the "-sein" articulates the being of that opening: that it *is*. This being of the opening requires humans who sustain it, who *are there* (*da*), exposed to a time-space in which, rather than being with themselves, they are dispossessed (out there in the nameless, so to speak); and through word, gesture, or deed humans may "hold open" that opening, sustain it, endure the groundless eventuation of what comes to be instead of turning away from it. Thus, the truth of being occurs in being-there (Da-sein) at the same time that being-there occurs in the truth of being, that is, in the unconcealing concealment of being—while a word is spoken, a gaze encountered, a decision made, a melody written. There is, in other words, not a linear progression either from the truth of beyng to Da-sein or from Da-sein to the truth of beyng, that is, beyng thought as event (*Ereignis*) is nothing in itself that would then be revealed in a word; it occurs neither prior to nor after Da-sein but only through the eventuation or appropriation (*Ereignung*) of Da-sein.

In thinking of the truth of being as event, Heidegger's concern was always to think not the eventuation of this or that thing or event but being as such in its historicality. His concern was the history of being and the impossibilities and possibilities latent within this history, which leads us to the next point.

The Historicality of Being and Thinking

The new approach to the question of being would think beyng more radically in a historical way, both in the sense that to beyng belongs a history (that issues in different epochs of Western history) and (perhaps even more so) in the sense that thinking itself would belong to this history and contribute in paving its way. Thus the thinking of beyng becomes "seynsgeschichtlich," "beyng-historical" in this double sense.[13]

In order to better understand what Heidegger means by historicality with reference both to thinking and to being, we must try to set aside our preconceived notions of history as a series of events in a linear set of time. *Geschichtlichkeit* echoes both history (*Geschichte*) and occurrence (*Geschehen*). Just as we lose the sense of being as event if we objectify it and conceive of it in terms of a duality of thinker and thought, subject and object, we lose the meaning of the historicality of being if we conceive it in an objectifying way. Just as we find ourselves always already being, we are also always already historical, in the sense that, even if we fail to acknowledge our historicality, we occur historically and belong to a history of beyng. Being-historical thinking attempts to think *from within* the historicality of being that always-already determines who we are and prefigures how we encounter and interpret determinate things and events. Such historicality of being takes different guises in different epochs of Western history and yet—according to Heidegger—shares a common trait that emerges in Ancient Greek thinking.

It is with the Ancient Greeks that Heidegger finds emerging a way of thinking and a comportment toward being that would ultimately lead to a greater and greater distancing of thinking and what is thought, of thinking and being, such that beings (things and events) end up being merely disclosed to us as things to be calculated, mastered, used for enjoyment. In *Contributions to Philosophy*, he calls this the abandonment of beings by being (*Seinsverlassenheit*). At the same time, Heidegger continues to seek, in the beginning of Ancient Greek thought, other possibilities of thinking. The return to the source, to the (both disclosive and concealing) truth of being, is at the same time (for Heidegger) a return to the inception of the very historicality of being that determines our present age. This is why Heidegger calls being-historical thinking also inceptual thinking (*anfängliches Denken*). That being per se emerged primarily as presence such that we tend to orient ourselves in relation to what is present: things, events we can objectify—this, for Heidegger, has its roots in what happened in Ancient Greek thought. Yet at the same time, he finds in Presocratic philosophers a sense of withdrawal and concealment that allows for a different thought of being. The return to the source, to a concealment out of which possibilities of thinking and being emerge, requires, according to Heidegger, a constant dialogue with the oldest heritage of Greek thought, such that, in remembering the first (Greek) beginning, the possibility of another beginning might be prepared. Heidegger's thinking of the other beginning takes much of its impulse as well from his reading of Hölderlin.

Hölderlin, Language, and History

In the winter semester of 1934/1935 Heidegger gave a lecture course titled *Hölderlins Hymnen "Germanien" und "Der Rhein"* (GA 39).[14] Here, in dialogue with Hölderlin, Heidegger will find ways toward a different articulation of the question of being by rethinking our relation to language and history. Many of the themes in *Contributions to Philosophy* are already being expressed in this lecture course. I will highlight a few of them.[15]

Already here, in 1934, Heidegger announces Hölderlin as *the* poet who founds the place of our (in the lecture course this "our" addresses primarily the Germans) future historical beyng (GA 39: 147, 162, 184, 214). The poet can found this future historical sense through a fundamental attunement (or disposition) because he is exposed to beyng in a singular way. Heidegger further interprets (Hölderlin's) poetry as a passing on of the beckonings of the gods, linking the issue of historical beginning—or rather inception—to the gods (GA 39: 32).

The whole lecture course begins with a differentiation between *Beginn* and *Anfang*, which both may be translated as "beginning," but I will use "starting point" for "Beginn" and "beginning" or "inception" for rendering "Anfang."[16] Heidegger writes:

> Where something starts—that is something different from its "beginning." A new weather condition, for instance, starts with a storm; its beginning, however, is the anticipatory, complete transformation of the circumstances of air. A starting point is the onset of something, beginning that out of which it emerges. The world war had its beginning centuries ago in the spiritual and political history of the West. The world war started with fights at the outposts. The starting point is quickly left behind; it disappears in the carrying on of an occurrence. The beginning, the source, on the other hand, first comes into appearance in the occurrence and is only there fully at its end. (GA 39: 4; my translation)

For Heidegger, Hölderlin's poetry opens a possible historical beginning that has not yet appeared, whereas we still stand in the end of the beginning marked by Greek thinking. The whole thinking of *Contributions* and the volumes following this first "work," are situated in the transition from the first to the other beginning. It is noteworthy, however, that in the lecture course on Hölderlin's "Germanien" and "Der Rhein," the historical beyng that is founded concerns the German people. (*Contributions to Philosophy* is less explicit in this respect and refers to the history of the West [*das Abendland*] in a larger sense. The other beginning will fully begin only when it founds the being of a people, Heidegger writes here, but he does not specify that this concerns primarily the German people.)

We should keep in mind that Hölderlin's poetry can found a beginning only if it finds the right hearing, which is Heidegger's main concern. The right hearing requires that we understand our relation to language differently, more originarily. We need to experience and understand that it is not we who have language, but language that has us (GA 39: 23). This is what Hölderlin tells us, according to Heidegger, in the verses, "Full of merit, yet poetically, do humans dwell on this earth" (GA 39: 36).[17] Through fundamental attunements, we find ourselves exposed to beyng and experience that the discovering of beings, that is, the appearing of what is, occurs in language (GA 39: 62). This is precisely what Heidegger tries to demonstrate in his reading of Hölderlin.

Language here has a wider meaning than we would commonly attribute to it and requires the same move Heidegger makes when he situates the origination of thought not in the thinker but in a disclosive event that we find ourselves responding to when a word "comes to us." Already in *Being and Time* Heidegger has elaborated language as being at work at the most basic level of disclosure of being in Dasein. Discourse (*Rede*) is equiprimordial with attunement and project and constitutes the most basic articulation of being. For Heidegger, language does not consist in word-things that indicate a meaning arbitrarily attached to them; instead, meaning "comes to words."[18] At the same time, more basic than uttering is listening. "Listening to . . . is the existential being-open of Dasein as being-with for the other. Listening even constitutes the primary and authentic openness of Dasein for its ownmost possibility of being, as in hearing the voice of the friend whom every Dasein carries with it" (GA 2: 217; BaT 158). With Hölderlin, Heidegger will elaborate how the listening is already a response to a silent call. Language originates in silence such that language occurs even when no word is uttered or written: "Language itself originates in silence [*Schweigen*]. First something like 'beyng' must have gathered in this silence, in order then to be spoken out as 'world.' This preworldly silence is more powerful [*mächtiger*] than any human powers. No human for himself has ever invented language, that is, was strong enough in himself for shattering the might [*Gewalt*] of that silence, if not under the duress of the god" (GA 39: 218; my translation).

We may understand the original dimension of language as a basic articulation of what comes to appear that may be uttered in words or not. Heidegger's attempt will always be to articulate precisely this most originary coming to word, the *event* of the truth of beyng, and he finds in Hölderlin's poetry not only a disclosure of this occurrence of language but with it the disclosure of the possible destiny of a people.

According to Heidegger, for the listening readers of Hölderlin's poetry this requires that they let themselves be attuned to the basic attunement that speaks in the poetry such that they may understand what the poet reveals. This is, for instance, that the gods have fled and that we need to experience the flight of the gods first (GA 39: 80), since only then might a new site of decision be prepared for a future destiny of a people. In this lecture course, then, Heidegger already draws attention to the plight of a lack of sense of plight (*Not der Notlosigkeit*) (GA 39: 134) in our epoch. In *Contributions to Philosophy* he will repeatedly highlight how it is precisely the acknowledgment of this plight that needs to be experienced first, and that would allow the truth of beyng to resonate more originarily. When we experience and sustain the plight, we discover how beyng occurs as withdrawal. Keeping silence is responsive to this withdrawal and might allow (we may say this is Heidegger's hope) a word to be spoken out into the world such that the truth of beyng finds a worldly site.[19] Yet meanwhile, the thinking that responds to the plight of our epoch cannot do more than hold itself in the space of beyng's withdrawal, stay, as it were, in the draft of beyng's withdrawal.[20] This opens up an untimely place, an "in-between" where what might or might not occur stands in decision without being decided. This "between" is how Heidegger understands Da-sein in *Contributions to Philosophy*.

In the lecture course on Hölderlin, Heidegger will begin to articulate the "between" as a space of strife or decision that brings to an encounter gods and humans. Hölderlin's "Germanien" begins with saying that the poet is no longer allowed to call the old gods, the gods of Greece. Heidegger interprets this as the necessity of a renunciation (entering the plight). This opens up a space of contestation between the disclosure of a preparedness and the lack of a fulfillment, a space of withdrawal that needs to be sustained. The words Heidegger finds here, *Rufen* (calling), *Austragen* (carrying out or sustaining), *Ausbleib* (staying away), *Widerstreit* (contestation), all these are words that we find again in *Contributions*. In this later work he will say in different places how some few "creative ones"—disposed by the plight of the lack of plight—may respond to the call of beyng such that this call first discloses a space of decision regarding the advent or absconding of the gods. The creative ones, *die Schaffenden*, are (according to the lecture course on Hölderlin) poets, thinkers, and founders of states who, disposed by a basic attunement, that is, responding to the call of the gods, create the spaces for future historical beyng of a people. The emphasis on the necessity of founding history is what seems to be at the forefront of Heidegger's reading of Hölderlin in 1934–1935. He writes: "Only a historical people truly is a people. Yet historically it [a historical people] is only when it occurs out of the ground of the middle of beyng, when the 'between' is there, when the demigods, the creative ones, effect the occurrence of history" (GA 39: 284).[21]

The point I wish to make is not simply that we will find many of the same words and themes in *Contributions* as in Heidegger's earlier lecture course. The point is that through his reading of Hölderlin, Heidegger finds a basic disposition (*Grundstimmung*) that speaks to a sense of language and historicality that guide and frame the way he will begin to think being as event. It is a space of tension between lack and possibility, a gathering of a "no longer" and a "not yet," suffering the end of an epoch (the first beginning) and hoping for the possibility of another beginning, which, according to Heidegger, Hölderlin experienced and poetized.

Guiding Questions for Reading Heidegger's Poietic Writings

My reading of Heidegger's poietic writings attempts to stay with the dispositions that underlie his thinking and from there to trace shifts in his thinking and language along some guiding questions that seem to me relevant for the developments of his thinking throughout these writings. These developments are far from a progression. If anything, Heidegger attempts a further and further *regression* into "the" beginning, at least in one dominant strand of the developments I will be tracing. This regression into the beginning will turn out to be crucial in my engagement with Heidegger. This aspect will come to the fore especially when looking at GA 70–71. Earlier volumes, however, contain as well what one might call explorations into certain domains of inquiry, which includes a rethinking of the history of Western thinking along some major figures and an intense "critique" of our current epoch along notions such as machination and power.

Here are some questions that structure my reading of Heidegger. The first set of questions (A) guide an expository reading of the volumes, while the last set of questions (B) guide a more intimate and critical approach to the texts.

(A)
1. How do the later volumes relate to the first attempt at a thoughtful saying of the event in *Contributions to Philosophy (Of the Event)*?
2. What shifts are there in terms of structure and systematicity of Heidegger's thinking?
3. What are dominant concepts and themes Heidegger explores in each volume and what shifts are there in conceptuality and thematic emphasis?
4. How does Heidegger articulate the relation between or differencing of being and beings?
5. How does the notion of Da-sein change?

(B)
6. How can or should I engage Heidegger's thinking in his poietic writings?
7. What happens when I consider them in their historiographical and biographical context?
8. What appear as the limits or delimitation of Heidegger's thinking and how should I engage them?

Here are some indications concerning what these questions entail:

1. Many (including myself) have called *Contributions to Philosophy* Heidegger's second major work after *Being and Time*. The fact that it is the first of the series of Heidegger's poietic writings certainly gives it a special status and *Besinnung* and *Die Geschichte des Seyns* seem indeed to move within a certain structural articulation of *Contributions*, namely, its "division" into "fugues" (*Fugen*) comprising the structure (*Gefüge*) of the volume. This changes however, with GA 70 where Heidegger seems to make a new beginning in search of a language "of" the event. Furthermore, in later volumes he will so much criticize his first attempt in *Contributions* as not being originary enough that, viewed internally, that is, from within his attempts at speaking poietically, it becomes indeed questionable to call *Contributions to Philosophy* Heidegger's second major work. This issue is addressed as well by my second guiding question, concerning the systematicity of Heidegger's thinking.

2. One of Heidegger's retrospective critiques of *Contributions* will be that it is still too structural and too much oriented around a differentiation between guiding question and basic question (*Leitfrage und Grundfrage*). This differentiation concerns the difference between metaphysical questioning of the being (beingness) of beings and the more originary questioning of the truth of beyng. One can note, beginning with GA 70, how Heidegger attempts to stay away from any form of structure. Although his thoughts are grouped under a number of headings, these groupings do not comprise any representable structure. He lets go as far as he can, it seems, of any anticipatory order or structure and of representational thinking.

3. What "organizes" Heidegger's thinking are rather dispositions out of which arise words, themes, focal points of exploration. It is quite stunning how creative Heidegger is in his language, how he tries out new words and semantic fields, how certain concepts that first seemed central recede and how others emerge. We may conjecture that this is at least partly related to thinkers and poets he is reading. One can see a shift in language that reflects to some extent the shift in focus from lecturing on Nietzsche to lecturing on Hölderlin and then Parmenides and Heraclitus. Other thematic fields directly point to the war, and critical reflections on (Heidegger's) current times. This applies especially to *Besinnung, Die Überwindung der Metaphysik*, and *Die Geschichte des Seyns*, and since the *Black Notebooks* stand in close proximity to those poietic writings, we need to take them into account as well.

4. My fourth guiding question, the one addressing the difference between being and beings, has been for me a guiding question from the beginning of my engagement with Heidegger's *Contributions to Philosophy*, namely, the question of "grounding." In *Being and Time* Heidegger emphasizes the ontological difference between being and beings (*Sein und Seiendes*) in order to mark the difference

between traditional metaphysical thinking that questions being on the basis of beings from his own question of being as such. In *Contributions*, however, he will speak of the simultaneity of being and beings, yet in such a way that this simultaneity is thought *out of* the truth of beyng. There is no disclosure of being without a concrete site, an opening that is sustained only through beings like words, deeds, and works of art. In this context Heidegger speaks of a "sheltering" of the truth of beyng in beings. The issue of sheltering may be considered in two respects: first, Heidegger's attempt at speaking "of" the event, at letting being itself eventuate, is itself—if it succeeds—a sheltering of the disclosure of being. The sense of being that comes to language in his writings is there, sheltered in words, provided they find a responsive listening. Second, Heidegger understands his whole project of poietic writing as being transitional from the first to the other beginning. This other beginning would initiate a new epoch for a people and would require a sheltering that grounds this epoch. With respect to this historical grounding of a disclosure of being for a people, Heidegger's poietic writings remain transitional. They attempt to articulate and hold open the "between" I wrote about above, that space—or rather time-space—of a "no longer" and "not yet," that untimely space of decision for the possibility of another beginning, which opens up for Heidegger in his reading of Hölderlin. In the later poietic writings (beginning with *Über den Anfang*), Heidegger will articulate this "in-between" with recourse to the differencing of being and beings, playing with the semantic overlapping of *Unterschied*, *Unterscheidung*, and *Abschied*, that is, "difference," "differencing," and "departure." The centrality of these concepts is another reason that it appears important to trace Heidegger's articulation of the difference between being and beings.

5. What names the "between" is the notion of Da-sein, which undergoes a shift in *Contributions* with respect to *Being and Time* and which Heidegger attempts to think ever more radically after *Contributions* in the sense that he will think Da-sein less and less with primary orientation to the human being. In *The Event* he criticizes the notion of Da-sein in *Contributions*, and says, "Da-sein is certainly thought essentially out of the event, and yet it is thought too one-sidedly with reference to the human being" (GA 71: 5). This and the fact that Dasein in *Being and Time* designates primarily human being so much that it invited a misinterpretation of Dasein as subject, are the reasons that I believe one ought to translate Da-sein with "being-there" or "there-being." Being-there is the open site, the time-space of the unconcealing concealment of being, of withdrawal and eventuation of the event. All this does not occur without the human, without an attuned, steadfasness (*Inständigkeit*) or ek-sistence, a "being" in the openness of the "there" of beyng. To speak "of" the event is an effort to speak what gives itself in a responsive listening to what addresses thinking. In this dimension of creative thinking, there is no differentiation of thinking and what is thought, no

differentiation of subject and object but a turning event in which differencing and encounter of various dimensions come to be. In *Contributions*, Heidegger highlights in Da-sein sometimes the "Da-," that is, the disclosure of the truth of being, and other times, the "-sein," the being of the there, which is how humans *are* when they stand in the openness of the truth of being. But nowhere in *Contributions* can we find Heidegger saying what he says in *The Event*: "Experienced in terms of the historicality of being, 'Da-sein' is the name for beyng which is thought out of the essential occurrence of its truth" (GA 71: 140). In this later volume, Heidegger thinks Da-sein more radically out of the truth of beyng and not primarily in relation to human being.

A careful look at how Heidegger thinks Da-sein is important especially in view of the regress into the beginning, which is performed in his poietic writings, a regress that seeks words at the limit of words and maybe even beyond that limit (the notion of the *Seinlose*, the "beingless," that he introduces in 1941, suggests this). In this regress it appears as if all "activity" of thinking sought to efface itself in the response to the word of being itself. It is as if one did not allow an awareness of one's own thinking to emerge and stayed oriented to the giving of what comes to thought. One might venture to say (alluding to Heidegger's "Letter on Humanism") that he "dehumanizes" Da-sein. At the same time, however, he would say that it is precisely in dehumanizing Da-sein that humans find a more originary being.

* * *

So far I have addressed questions that guide my expository interpretation of Heidegger's poietic writings. I am demarcating my remarks regarding the remaining guiding questions spatially in order to highlight a different approach I intend to take here, an approach that is less academic in the traditional sense, and this for specific reasons. These questions will be addressed in the chapters following each of the chapters in which I offer an expository interpretation of the different poietic writings.

6. Especially when reading *Das Ereignis* I was struck by the sense that a structured reading of the text cannot really penetrate into what is happening here. One can certainly attempt to find structures, relate what Heidegger writes here to the previous works and the published lecture courses and thereby gain insight into some of his developments as a thinker. I do some of this work in the expository chapters of my book and hope it will be useful for academic reception and discussions of Heidegger's thinking. But his thinking in *Das Ereignis* does not really lend itself to academic readings. The work with language this volume performs is so far removed from academic discourses, so daring and strange, so solitary and intimate, that any "finding of structure" appears like looking for empty shells washed to the shore; it is like missing what it is all about. Consider what

Heidegger writes in the volume: "Any discovering, any teaching, but also any awakening, any thrusting must stay away; in the same manner any 'ordering' of 'contents.' Only the pure word that rests in itself must resonate. No listener must be presupposed and no room for the listening-belonging [*Gehören*]" (GA 71: 297).

Since ordering contents and writing with someone in mind is precisely what is to be avoided in this poietic saying, how is one to respond as a reader of this work? Heidegger would say that one ought to be engaged by "the pure word that rests in itself." The word in question, he would advise, is not a word we should attribute to him. It is, rather, the word of beyng as it emerges in Heidegger's engagement with the beginning;[22] a word, moreover, that speaks through silence, and a word spoken for no one.

At this point, I find a recoil happening in my reading of Heidegger, since I find myself perpetually thrown back to the question as to how to read what he writes. In this recoil, spaces of interpretation open up that are at once in the draw of his text and removed from it. An "in-between" of a different kind than Heidegger's in-between of beginnings opens up, and I find myself drawn to consider what I customarily do not bring into play when reading Heidegger: His life and the historical context in which he writes.

7. *Das Ereignis* was written in 1941–1942. The renewed approach to the question of the truth of beyng as event he takes here begins already with the previous volume *Über den Anfang* (*On Inception*) (1941). The event is now approached in terms of *beginning* or *inception* (*Anfang*) and Heidegger works at staying close to the beginning as the silent source out of which the word of beyng might eventuate. It is striking how these volumes contain only minimal references to the markers of the end of the epoch of metaphysics, unlike *Besinnung* (1938/1939), *Die Überwindung der Metaphysik* (1938/1939), and *Die Geschichte des Seyns* (1938–1940), where references to machination, lived experience, and power are dominant. Instead, in the later volumes Heidegger repeats over and over the *downgoing* into the abyss, into the silent source of being. When we consider that, at the same time, World War II is raging over Europe, this retreat seems particularly striking.

I do not intend to "psychologize" Heidegger, or to reduce his thinking to reactions to the situation of his times. And yet, the war and the National Socialist movement must have had an effect on him. How should we interpret his writings in light of the war? I do not believe that one can come to real conclusions in this respect and so I separate this inquiry from a more immanent reading of Heidegger's poietic texts. Maybe all one can ask here are questions, but questions already envision a horizon out of which they emerge. This horizon is constituted in part by one's own lineages and circumstances. In my case, I was born as a German in Italy and went to study in Germany in 1985. Growing up in Italy gave me some distance from the events that stained the German people and I began to have a more lively sense and a stronger consciousness of the effects of what happened in German national socialism only during my studies in Freiburg. Only then did it strike me how little my father said about those times. He was born in 1920 and was spared active fighting at the front due to his very bad eyesight. He died before my awareness of the German past grew strong enough to have the desire to break the silence around this issue. Bits and pieces of stories he told remain in my memory but never did we engage in a conversation about the deeper issues related to the war, like the feeling of guilt even I and my brother and sister have with respect to a past that happened before we were born. It was later revealed to us that my father (supposedly) had Jewish parents and that the family hid their Jewish roots not only from the government but also from their son (my father) until he was about to get married—this did not help with respect to my feeling of uneasiness regarding the events surrounding German national socialism. I now believe that there is no solution to this uneasiness and that it must be sustained as part of one's history. I bring it up not because I want to perform a public self-exploration but in order to let the reader be aware that I am bringing my uneasiness to bear in my reading of Heidegger, in the question of how to read Heidegger in light of the historical times in which he lived.

8. I will not limit my question of how to read Heidegger's poietic writings to their relation to historiographical and biographical events, since there is another (not unrelated) dimension of questions that I wish to develop, which concerns language and thought and the limit at which Heidegger situates them. Here, some strands I explore in the expository chapters of this book will converge, particularly the difference between being and beings and the issue of grounding. I would like to further pursue a critique I brought up in earlier articles and that I partly share with other Heidegger scholars, namely, the framing of the question of being in terms of the history of being.[23] The "in-between" of the first and the other beginning in which Heidegger's thinking moves in his poietic writings is opened up in the attunement to a sense of plight and withdrawal that calls for another beginning that is not yet there, the possibility of another beginning he finds opening up—as pointed out above—in Hölderlin's poetry. This is a space of tension, of in-decision in the double sense of finding itself in the midst of a decision and not being able to make any decision. Heidegger situates language in this tension and his search for a word, for a being that holds open this space, at the same time appears to resist a "letting loose" (*Loslassung*) of something. The "letting loose of beings" is a phrase we find Heidegger using in relation to "machination," a mode of disclosure of being that characterizes the end of the first beginning (the end of metaphysics) where beings are abandoned by being, lost in the self-perpetuating circulation of productivity. For Heidegger, the possibility of grounding the truth of beyng in beings seems to be bound precisely to not "letting loose" but to holding on to the field or resonance of the abyssal reverberations of beyng in its with-

drawal. Although he speaks of the simultaneity of being and beings, although the truth of beyng cannot find any open site without beings, without concrete spoken or written words, gestures, deeds, things, his quest is always to hold open the abyssal dimension of being, the *not yet* spoken word.

The issue then, for Heidegger, is to stay near to the source. Something a Chinese friend of mine once said to me keeps coming to my mind in this context. We studied in Freiburg together and she was not much of a friend of Heidegger; something in his thinking very much disturbed her. One day she said approximately the following: "Heidegger always wants to go against the stream of the river, fighting to get back to the source from which the river flows. Why does he not just let go and follow the stream of the river into the open sea?"[24] Indeed, why not? What if Heidegger had let go? Could he let go? Maybe at some point he did let go and what emerged was his thinking of *Gelassenheit*, which is often translated as "releasement." This happens at the end of the poietic writings and can be read, as I will show, as a development of them. In some way, Heidegger appears to emerge from the silent retreat into the imageless source of beyng with a cosmology, the fourfold of gods and mortals, earth and sky. Does he manage here to shelter a world in words? And do things emerge in their singularities and the uniqueness of their being from his saying of the fourfold?

Uniqueness and singularity are words that in his nonpublic writings Heidegger reserves to beyng thought as event. Although this does imply beings, their being is always sought out of the withdrawing source of being. It seems to me Heidegger could never "let go" of the listening/belonging to the silent source of the event in a way that would open being to a plurality in the sense of the eventuation of things in *their* unique constellations. Yet this limit of his thinking is at the same time constitutive of its strength, of a power of thought that continues to address many of us in ways ranging from an enthusiastic desire to follow to almost visceral aversion. Thinking with Heidegger is not easy.

Notes

1. An exception is GA 68, which contains a number of texts written between 1938 and 1942 in which Heidegger discusses Hegel.

2. The German word *ursprünglich* carries a sense of origin that the word "original" in its current use does not necessarily imply. Hence the neologism "originary."

3. The *Black Notebooks* so far published in German comprise GA 94–97. GA 94–96 are titled *Überlegungen* (*Ponderings*), GA 97 *Anmerkungen* (*Notes*); GA 98–102 have yet to be published. *Ponderings II–VI* have been translated by Richard Rocewicz and published by Indiana University Press in 2016. Other volumes have yet to be published.

4. I am indicating here what Heidegger calls "the turning in the event."

5. See the preface, p. ix.

6. See Heidegger's notes in "Winke und Überlegungen (II) und Anweisungen" (hereafter cited as Ü II) in GA 94: 14–15, 30, 52, 88, 115. These early notes of the *Black Notebooks* testify to Heidegger's search for a new approach to being in 1932, which would eventually result in *Contributions to Philosophy* (1936–1938).

7. As David Farrell Krell points out, etymologically, Dasein goes back to "Dass-sein," which means "that one is," that is, the fact of being or existence in an emphatic sense. See Krell's introduction to *Being and Time* in Martin Heidegger, *Basic Writings*, 2nd ed., ed. David Farrell Krell (San Francisco: Harper San Francisco, 1992), 38.

8. "Coming back to itself, from the future, resoluteness brings itself to the situation in making it present. Having-been arises from the future in such a way that the future that has-been (or better, is in the process of having-been) releases the present from itself. This unified phenomenon of the future that makes present in the process of having-been is what we call *temporality*." (Martin Heidegger, *Being and Time*, trans. Joan Stambaugh, rev. Dennis J. Schmidt [Albany: State University of New York Press, 2010], 311 [hereafter cited as BaT].)

9. Martin Heidegger, "Letter on Humanism," in Krell, *Basic Writings*, 231; GA 9: 328.

10. For a more detailed discussion of this, see Daniela Vallega-Neu, *Heidegger's* Contributions to Philosophy: *An Introduction* (Bloomington: Indiana University Press, 2003), 9–29.

11. The translators of the first English translation of *Contributions to Philosophy* translate *Ereignis* with the neologism "enowning" in order to render the sense of "eigen," which means "own," and the prefix "er-," which in German has the sense of initiation or achievement of an occurrence.

12. In the *Black Notebooks*, we find this telling entry that I believe marks something like a "new beginning" in Heidegger's thinking: "Today (March 1932) I am in a clear place from which the whole previous writings (Being and Time; What Is Metaphysics?; Kant-book and On the Essence of Ground I and II) have become foreign to me. Foreign like a path that has been set still and that overgrows with grass and shrubs—a path, however, that leads into Da-sein as temporality" (GA 94; Ü II, 19).

13. In their translation of *Contributions*, Rojcewicz and Vallega-Neu render *seynsgeschichtliches Denken* with "a thinking that pertains to the historicality of being." Other scholars translate it as "ontohistorical thinking."

14. English translation: Martin Heidegger, *Hölderlin's Hymns "Germania" and "The Rhine,"* trans. William McNeill and Julia Ireland (Bloomington: Indiana University Press, 2014).

15. It is not my aim to give an interpretation of Heidegger's reading of Hölderlin but only to trace some themes that will continue in Heidegger's poietic writings.

16. Another possible translation of *Anfang* is "inception." This translation would free "beginning" for translating *Beginn*. "Inception," if we trace the word to its Latin roots, has the same meaning, since the Latin "capere" means to catch, just as the German "fangen." However, scholarly writing of Heidegger customarily speaks of Heidegger's notion of a first and other beginning (*Anfang*) and for this reason I chose to translate it just this way. McNeill and Ireland translate *Beginn* with "beginning" and *Anfang* with "commencement."

17. Hölderlin's verses in German are: "Voll Verdienst, doch dichterisch wohnet / Der Mensch auf dieser Erde" ("In lieblicher Bläue . . .").

18. "Words accrue to significations. But word-things are not provided with significations" (*Being and Time*, 156). "Den Bedeutungen wachsen Worte zu. Nicht aber werden Wörterdinge mit Bedeutungen versehen" (GA 2: 214).

19. See the sections on *Erschweigen* (keeping-silence) in *Contributions* (GA 65: 78–80).

20. Charles Scott uses this expression in *Living with Indifference* (Bloomington: Indiana University Press, 2007), 41.

21. It should be noted that Heidegger's interpretation of Hölderlin should be distinguished from Hölderlin's poetry. The later, for instance, makes no reference to "a historical people."

22. One is reminded, here, of Heraclitus B 50 in which he admonishes that one should listen not to him but to the Λόγος. See G. S. Kirk, J. E. Raven, and M. Schofield, *The Presocratic Philosophers*, 2nd ed. (Cambridge: Cambridge University Press, 1983): "Listening not to me but to the Λόγος it is wise to agree that all things are one" (187).

23. I am referring especially to my article, "Thinking in Decision: On Heidegger's *Contributions to Philosophy*," *Research in Phenomenology* 33 (2003): 247–263, 281–283.

24. Gadamer makes a similar observation in his essay, "Destruktion *and Deconstruction*." Referring to some of Heidegger's unusual ways of understanding certain words or phrases Gadamer writes: "All of these interpretations are clearly acts of violence committed by a swimmer who struggled to swim against the current." (In Diane P. Michelfelder and Richard E. Palmer, eds., *Dialogue and Deconstruction* [Albany: State University of New York Press, 1989], 108.)

2 Contributions to Philosophy (Of the Event) (GA 65)

T HIS CHAPTER IS limited to an exposition of aspects and themes of *Contributions* that I find relevant with respect to developments and changes in Heidegger's thinking and language in his nonpublic writings of the event between 1936 and 1942 (see my guiding questions in chapter 1) as well as with respect to my own critical approach to his work. It cannot do justice to all the themes and basic words Heidegger introduces in *Contributions to Philosophy*. For a more "even" introduction to *Contributions* I would like to refer readers to my earlier book: *Heidegger's* Contributions to Philosophy: *An Introduction*.[1] For my more critical engagement with Heidegger's thinking in *Contributions*, see chapter 3.

The Structure of *Contributions*

Long before its publication in 1989, Otto Pöggeler announced *Contributions to Philosophy (Of the Event)* as Heidegger's major work and Friedrich-Wilhelm von Herrmann agreed with the small correction that it is Heidegger's *second* major work (the first being *Being and Time*).[2] There are good reasons to think this, but the latest of Heidegger's poietic writings might lead us to think otherwise.[3]

Contributions to Philosophy is the first of Heidegger's poietic writings and takes a more radical approach to the question of being with respect to *Being and Time*. This alone grants it a special status. If we compare it with the volumes that follow it, we can readily see that it is also the most structured of those volumes: the six parts, or rather "junctures" (*Fugen*) into which it is divided invite the reader to take them as a journey through the realm of the truth of beyng in its transitional historical unfolding (from "The Resonating" to "The Last God"). According to the editor, von Herrmann, the original manuscript that was prepared by Fritz Heidegger culminated with the section titled "The Last God" and what is now the last part of the volume ("Beyng") was originally placed after the "Prospect." Since Heidegger made an annotation that he found the part titled "Beyng" "not well placed" since it is "an attempt to grasp the whole once again" and was written later than the rest of *Contributions*, von Herrmann made the editorial decision to place it at the end of the volume, a decision that has been criticized by a number of Heidegger scholars who (I believe rightfully) insist that *Contributions* should have ended with "The Last God."[4]

Despite the difficulty of the language and thought of *Contributions*, this "structure" renders the volume to some extent more readily approachable for the academically trained mind and provides a "grid" or "order" that allows a more structured reading of a book that, by "normal" standards, has no proper structure but appears instead as a compilation of reflections and notes.

Heidegger explicitly situates the thought of *Contributions* in a path from the first beginning to the other beginning of Western philosophy and history, a path that is first opened up in this thought. It is a transitional thought, a "preliminary exercise" in saying the conjuncture (*Fuge*) of the truth of beyng, that is, of the way being conceals and unconceals itself historically (GA 65: 4; C: 6).[5] It is also an attempt to provide "a first elaboration of the conjuncture (The resonating—The last god)" (GA 65: 59; C: 48). The German word for elaboration is *Durchgestaltung* and has the strong sense of shaping something throughout, so that one does get the sense that *Contributions* at least attempts a thorough articulation of the dimensions that make up the realm of the truth of being in its historical and transitional unfolding.[6] This may also allow us to speak of *Contributions* as a "work," albeit not a systematic work in the traditional sense. Furthermore, Heidegger writes: "The focusing on individual questions (the origin of the work of art) must dispense with a uniform opening up and elaboration of the entire domain of conjuncture" (GA 65: 60; C: 48). Von Herrmann takes this as contributing to the evidence of the fundamental importance of *Contributions* as Heidegger's second major work. *Contributions* provides something like a "mapping out" of Heidegger's thinking of the historicality of beyng (I would add: at a certain time) to which other published essays and lecture courses implicitly refer. This "mapping out" certainly does not occur in the manner of a systematic work that provides categories into which other works would fit, but rather in the manner of the opening up of the fundamental dimensions of the truth of beyng Heidegger explores.[7] (It is true that especially Heidegger's famous essay "On the Origin of the Work of Art" stems from the time of *Contributions* and develops further than *Contributions* the question of the sheltering of truth in beings.[8] The concurrent lecture courses on Nietzsche and the lecture course *Basic Questions of Philosophy* also clearly speak out of Heidegger's explorations in *Contributions*, although the lecture courses leave much unsaid.[9] Whether it is appropriate to include even the later poietic works of 1941–1942 within the "domain" of *Contributions* is another matter.)

The conjuncture of the truth of beyng has six junctures: the resonating (*Anklang*) of the truth of beyng as refusal in the acknowledgment of the abandonment of beings by being; the interplay (*Zuspiel*) between the first and the other beginning; the leap (*Sprung*) into being-there (*Da-sein*), that is, into the disclosure of beyng; the grounding (*Gründung*) of this openness through its sheltering in words, works, deeds, things; the future ones (*die Zukünftigen*) who are creatively involved in this grounding; and the last god (*der letzte Gott*) whose passing by grounds another beginning of history for a people. These are domains of the truth of beyng in its historicality as they are undergone and opened up in the transitional thinking of *Contributions*.

These six junctures have to some extent a sequential character that relates to how the question of the truth of beyng unfolds in Heidegger's path of thinking and also to how he believes the truth of beyng opens up historically. I will try to outline the quasi-sequential character of the junctures of *Contributions* in the awareness that much has to remain unexplained.

The whole domain of the truth of beyng opens up only for those who have a sense of plight in our epoch, who face this plight and are unsettled by it. The plight is constituted by the fact that beings (things and events in the largest sense) are abandoned by being; that they do not shelter any truth. Only when this abandonment is experienced as such, does the truth of beyng *resonate* in its refusal, and it resonates precisely in terms of lack and withdrawal. At the same time, meditating on what happened in the first (Greek) beginning of the history of beyng leads to understanding this abandonment of beings by being to have its roots in how the truth of beyng occurred inceptively. This in turn brings into play the intimation of another beginning. All this prepares for the leap in which the full expanse of the truth of beyng opens up. Heidegger writes: "The *interplay* [*Zuspiel*] commences with the first beginning playing over to the other beginning, in order to bring the latter into play such that *out of* this mutual interplay, the *preparation for* the leap develops" (GA 65: 9; C: 10; emphasis added). Only in the leap does thinking reach the domain of the other beginning more fully. Although the other beginning is not yet happening (this would imply a historical change in how being determines the history of a people, an event comparable to the beginning of metaphysics in Greek thinking) thinking is already determined by the intimation of the other beginning. In the leap, thinking experiences itself as being thrown and responding to the "throw" or "call" of beyng. Thinking experiences itself as appropriated (*ereignet*) out of the event (*Ereignis*) in *being* there (Da-*sein*) in the openness of the truth of beyng that is experienced as the disclosure of being's withdrawal (leaving whatever "is" empty and abandoned) and the disclosure that truth occurs not simply as unconcealing but more fundamentally as concealing beyng. The truth of beyng discloses itself in the turning relation (*Kehre*) of call and response. At the same time, thinking experiences the necessity to ground, that is, to sustain and hold open the abyssal "there," the disclosure of beyng's truth and thus to prepare a space of possibility, such that the other beginning may occur historically for a people. For Heidegger, the other beginning is made possible through the grounding of Da-sein (being-there) to which belongs the sheltering of the truth of beyng in beings (words, deeds, things). The grounding of Da-sein requires grounders. Heidegger calls them "the future ones" (*die Zukünftigen*), which literally means those *toward whom comes* "the intimation and intrusion of the absconding and nearing of the last god" (GA 65: 395; C: 313) and who ground Da-sein through words, works, and deeds.[10] The last god (this is *not* the Christian God) marks the most inceptive moment in the other beginning. His passing would mark the decision over the essential occurrence of the gods and another beginning of the history of beyng for a people.[11]

This "sequence" of the junctures or "fugues" of the truth of beyng in transition from the first to the other beginning cannot simply be understood as sequential in a linear sense. Heidegger says explicitly that the conjunctures should not be read as a linear sequence constituting "a step-by-step ascent from the low to the high" (GA 65: 6; C: 7) and that "in each of the six junctures, a saying of the same about the same is attempted, but in each case out of a different essential domain of that which is called the event" (GA 65: 81; C: 65). And yet, particularly the leap seems to suggest some kind of linearity and places the first two junctures "before" the full disclosure of the truth of beyng as event. Consider, for instance, that Heidegger speaks of the first two junctures as constituting the run-up to the leap (GA 65: 82; C: 65) and that he speaks as well of fundamental ontology (*Being and Time*) as constituting a "run-up" to the leap (GA 65: 228; C: 180). But once we enter into the dimension of the grounding of the truth of beyng, the quasi-linear aspect does not hold any longer. The sequential character can rather be found in the differentiation between the preparatory task of *Contributions* (grounding Da-sein as the site of the disclosure of truth) and the presentiment of a possible historical grounding of another beginning of the history of beyng (marked by the passing by of the last god).

Later Heidegger will let go of the notion of "leap" and criticize *Contributions* for being "too doctrinal" (GA 71: 4–5). Indeed, his attempt to speak out of the event is intermingled with explanations of concepts and reflections on the difference between the transcendental thought of *Being and Time* and the inceptive thought of *Contributions*, which suggests some attempt at guiding potential readers to his "new" thinking. Furthermore, in his public lectures and lecture courses of the time he stays within the domains of the first two junctures, seeking to ignite a sense of plight in his audience as well as a reflection on the first beginning and its ending (metaphysics) in order to prepare those who can listen for the "leap" into the other beginning.[12]

The main attempt in *Contributions* remains, however, to speak out of the event. I would like to note that already in the last part of *Contributions* (which was added to the six junctures by the editor of the volume) we find (for instance, in section 267) the attempt to say the truth of beyng as event in its manifold dimensions of appropriation without taking recourse to the six junctures as before, but rather by beginning with the plight of the gods.

Heidegger is aware of the "danger" of taking the conjuncture of the truth of beyng (with its six junctures) to be a "system" and he reflects on this issue in a number of places in the "Prospect" (GA 65: 5, 59, 65, 81; C: 6, 48, 52, 65). He is also explicit about the impossibility for beyng-historical thinking to take the form of a system: "The age of the 'systems' has past. The age that would elaborate the essential form of beings from out of the truth of beyng has not yet come. In the interim, in the transition to the other beginning, philosophy needs to have accomplished something essential: the projection, i.e., the grounding and opening up, of the temporal-spatial playing field of the truth of beyng [Da-sein]" (GA 65: 5; C: 6).

For Heidegger, the age of systems has passed because such systems presuppose metaphysical thinking in terms of represented ideas that can be ordered just as building blocks of a house. This does not preclude the fact that systematic works in the academic field of philosophy continue to be produced. Heidegger, however, would say that these academic works do not really respond to our historical situation, or particularly to how being occurs, or rather, withdraws, in our epoch. The age of system begins for him with Descartes and the dominion of mathematical thinking in the largest sense. It presupposes the notion of truth as certainty (GA 65: 65; C: 52). By contrast, Heidegger's attempt at speaking *of* the event, at letting his thinking be guided by a response to how beyng eventuates, is fundamentally exposed and without fundament in the metaphysical sense. This thinking attempts to respond not to a general idea of being or history, but to the uniqueness of a historical moment in which thinking *finds* itself. What emerges in this moment comes to be in this very emerging. What emerges in our historical times is, according to Heidegger, a sense of abandonment, of lack or withdrawal.

The notion of the uniqueness or singularity (*Einzigkeit*) of the event recurs throughout *Contributions* and is decisive in this respect.[13] The uniqueness of the essential occurrence (*Wesung*) of beyng does not mean an idea of only one being such that we understand this being as having a nontemporal essence, nor does it refer to a unique event in chronologically conceived time. Singularity should rather be understood in contrast to "the general."[14] The essential occurrence of the truth of beyng occurs in the singularity of a moment as it unfolds in thinking, and not in or as the generality of a thought. Whatever unfolds in the moment and takes shape in words, whatever fundamental words arise and domains open up should be understood out of this singularity of the moment, in *being* there in the "temporal-spatial playing field" (*Zeit-Spiel-Raum*) of the truth of beyng. It is in this sense, then, that we ought to understand the six junctures of *Contributions* as opening up in the temporal-spatial playing field of the truth of beyng. What appears as structure "ideally" would be more like the structures of a leaf growing on its own (in the manner of middle-voice occurrences) than like the rational projection of order and causation. To think in such a manner remains a struggle for Heidegger. He believes that, if once a saying can join the "free conjuncture of the truth of beyng" out of the event itself, then the essential occurrence of beyng itself would determine the "structure" (*das Gefüge*) of the work (GA 65: 4; C: 6).

The struggle for Heidegger is always to push away manners of understanding determined by modern rationality; and it is the Greeks, and more specifically the Presocratics, who help him retrieve a sense of being as self-emerging (this is how he reads the Greek notion of φύσις). Hence the necessity for the transitional thinking, of the interplay between the first beginning (Greeks) and the not yet (historically) begun but intimated (and thus initiated) other beginning. In *Contributions*, Heidegger is still searching, but he tries to speak "in the manner of a preliminary exercise" (*Vorübung*) as in the other beginning (GA 65: 4; C: 6).

Grounding Attunements of Thinking

How does one think in such a way that what is thought emerges "on its own"? How does one put thinking to the service of the truth of beyng in its historical eventuation? Heidegger would say that it requires "rigor" (*Strenge*) (GA 65: 65; C: 52). What allows for this rigor and for a direction in thinking are fundamental attunements or dispositions (*Grundstimmungen*) of thought that are not grounded in human subjectivity but rather arise from "what" calls to be thought. One may think of fundamental attunements as affective bodily dispositions that keep the body open, vulnerable to what calls for thinking. As we undergo such exposedness, we do not think of the body as an organism or experience the body as "ours"; rather, we experience our bodily *being* as ecstatic and responsive, as alien and intimate at once.[15] Fundamental attunements displace us from our everyday involvement with things and events and open up a finite sense of being. A grounding attunement is ungrounding and abyssal in relation to customary everyday being, and yet it is grounding in the sense of letting a sense of being, indeed a moment of truth (in the sense of unconcealing-concealing) emerge that otherwise remains concealed.

In *Being and Time* (1927), Heidegger's exemplary grounding attunement is *Angst*. In *Contributions* (1936–1939), the one he mentions most is "restraint" (*Verhaltenheit*).[16] The truth of being that restraint discloses belongs, according to Heidegger, to the other beginning, even if in terms of a history of a people or an epoch, this other beginning has not yet begun.[17] Still, he conceives the opening into which thinking is unsettled, that transitional time-space that is to be sustained in Da-sein, as an inceptive moment for the other beginning. In it, thinking is no longer caught in the dominant modes of being in our epoch; it finds itself in an untimely situation.

Grounding attunements are complex. In section 5 of *Contributions*, Heidegger meditates in more detail on the grounding attunement of restraint that is intrinsically tied to both shock and diffidence. Following Heidegger's analysis of these grounding attunements gives some insight as to how he came to articulate the first junctures of *Contributions* (the resonating, the interplay, and the leap). The attunement he names first is *shock* (*Erschrecken*). In shock, thinking is drawn back and unsettled from the customary such that what was customary now appears as alienating and as what fetters (*Fesselung*). In shock, humans are "taken aback by the very fact that beings *are* (whereas, previously, beings were to us simply beings), i.e. by the fact that beings *are* and that being has abandoned and withdrawn itself from all 'beings' and from whatever appeared as a being" (GA 65: 15; C: 14). While the notion of abandonment resonates with the notion of "being left empty," the notion of fettering reminds us of Plato's cave allegory: liberated from his shackles, the prisoner ascends to the truth of being. Except that in Heidegger's thought the movement is one of downgoing, since being discloses as withdrawal and the primary moment of truth is the concealment and not the unconcealment of being as presence (the latter discloses in wonder). In shock, concealment is unconcealed; withdrawal is disclosed; an abyss opens up. Being *resonates* as withdrawal. For Heidegger this is the first juncture of the conjuncture of the truth of being; or—if we highlight the musical connotation of the German word for conjuncture: *Fuge* (as in Bach's fugues)—it is the first theme of the grand fugue of the truth of being in the other beginning. It occurs in an acknowledgment of what he calls the plight of the lack of plight (*Not der Notlosigkeit*) and reveals that in our epoch we are without a sense of need—we are both needless and heedless. It reveals that beings have been abandoned by being. With this notion of abandonment, Heidegger rethinks what Nietzsche experienced as nihilism. And just as Zarathustra did not find any ears when he descended from his cave and announced the death of God, Heidegger finds people to be deaf to the plight.

Shock by itself is not enough to allow thinking to dwell in the truth that is opened up in it. Just as the unshackled prisoner in Plato's cave has to be forced into the ascent, another impetus is required for thinking to be there in the abysmal opening of the other beginning. (There are many modes of escape from the groundlessness of being, and what Heidegger writes in *Being and Time* about the ways in which Dasein seeks to escape facing its own mortality applies here as well. There is an internal connection between the disclosure of beyng as withdrawal and being open to one's own finitude.)[18] Heidegger writes: "Because in this shock it is precisely the self-concealing of beyng that opens up, and because beings themselves as well as the relation to them want to be preserved, this shock is joined from within by its own most proper 'will,' and that is what is here called *restraint*" (GA 65: 15; C: 14).[19] An abyss opens up and at the same time "beings themselves as well as the relation to them *wants* to be preserved" (GA 65: 15; C: 14; emphasis added). This moment of preserving the relation to beings while being unsettled from them is what in the 1929/1930 lecture course Heidegger addresses as "being held in limbo" (*Hingehaltenheit*, GA 29/30: 149) A tension is sustained here, between withdrawal and concealment on the one hand, and beings on the other hand, a space of differencing and differing of beyng (refusal) and beings.

I will say more about the differencing of beyng and beings later. For now, I would like to indicate how this space of differencing is a temporal spacing: it is the time-space Heidegger calls the Da of Da-sein (the "there" of being-there) in which is disclosed truth in its more original dimension (unconcealing concealing).

Heidegger addresses the temporal dimension disclosed in the fundamental attunement of *Contributions* more explicitly when he speaks of presentiment (*Ahnung*) as a grounding attunement. "Presentiment is in itself at once shock and exaltation."[20] It "traverses and measures up the whole of temporality: the temporal-spatial playing field of the 'there'" (GA 65: 22; C: 19). In section 34 he relates presentiment to "primordial temporality" (*Temporalität*), that is, not to the ecstatic temporality of Dasein (*Zeitlichkeit*) in the project of *Being and Time*, but to the more original temporality in which the temporality of Dasein (of human being) is grounded and that in *Contributions* he rethinks as the truth of beyng.[21]

In traditional thinking, intimations have been conceived as "subjective" and the primordial temporality of which Heidegger speaks would have been interpreted as an "interior temporality." One can say that his sense of ecstatic temporality is in some way related to what Augustine unfolds in Book XI of his *Confessions* as "distentio animi," as a stretching of the soul. Yet one of the accomplishments of Heidegger's *Being and Time* is that in understanding our being as being-in-the-world, as Dasein, he does away with the distinction between inner and outer. This allows us to conceive ecstatic temporality or time-space not on the basis of subjectivity, not in the sense of interiority, but rather in a sense of an exposedness and opening up of a relatedness to historical dimensions that exceed the individual and even the strictly human dimension. Thinking of presentiment as an "opening up to," however, still emphasizes a primacy of subjectivity because of the directionality of thought it suggests. In following Heidegger's move from *Being and Time* to *Contributions*, we ought to think presentiment rather as an attunement coming to thought.

Presentiment is one of the many names Heidegger gives to the grounding attunements of the other beginning, and in each name, a specific aspect is highlighted. Most often, Heidegger will, however, speak of restraint. This goes along with a certain emphasis he places on the necessity of withstanding (*ausstehen*) the abyssal opening of truth. This highlights a certain tension that resonates as well in the notion of *Inständigkeit*, which replaces the notion of existing or ecstasies in *Being and Time*. *Inständigkeit* literally means "standing in" and may also be translated as "steadfastness" or (more fittingly for Heidegger's thinking in the 1940s) "indwelling." Out of this steadfastness, thinking draws its rigor. Attuned by restraint, humans are called (are appropriated) to be steadfast in the groundless opening of the truth of beyng as the unconcealing-concealment of beyng as refusal. Thus they become grounders of the truth of beyng or "grounders of the abyss."[22]

Withstanding (like shock) is only one moment of restraint. There is also another moment Heidegger discusses in section 5, a moment that marks a "being-turned-*toward*" the withdrawal in the hesitation of the withdrawal: *Scheu*. *Scheu* normally means shyness, but Heidegger does not want us to understand the word in that sense. Rather it is an attitude of hesitant openness toward the withdrawal. *Scheu* has often been translated as "awe" but may be more appropriately translated as "diffidence" whereby we want to blend out the connotation of shyness, just as Heidegger did, and highlight more the sense of humility and hesitancy. Diffidence relates to the dimension of the last god (the last juncture of *Contributions*). Following Hölderlin, who poetizes this dimension in terms of the flight of the gods, Heidegger thinks the gods as those who abscond themselves and beckon in this absconding. They are what is farthest and *at the same time* may become nearest such that the passing by of the last god might occur: "Diffidence is the way of drawing near and remaining near to what is most remote as such (cf. The last god). Yet the most remote, in its intimations, provided theses are held fast in diffidence, becomes the closest and gathers up into itself all relations of beyng" (GA 65: 16; C: 15). Diffidence marks an intensification of restraint, a gathering, as in the tension of a string whose oscillation becomes so intense that it reaches a moment of stillness.

Later in *Contributions* Heidegger will not speak of diffidence often but rather of keeping silence (*Verschweigung*), which (he says in section 5) grows out of diffidence. Keeping silence prepares for "the great stillness" for the passing by of the last god (GA 65: 34; C: 29). Silence is at the same time the originary dimension of language. The saying (*Sagen*) of the event needs to be differentiated from speaking or uttering words about something.[23] It arises from an attuned listening and belonging (*gehören*) to the most concealed and abyssal dimension of beyng. It is a poietic, originary saying that bears the inceptive silence in which resonate refusal and concealment. Poietic saying is intrinsically an *Erschweigen*, a bearing silence and Heidegger refers to this bearing silence as the "logic" of inceptive thinking and as emerging from the originating of language.[24] In section 13 we find an expression of this dimension of silence that recalls his much later reading of Stefan George's poem "The Word."[25] Heidegger writes: "Words fail us. . . . Words do not yet come to speech at all, but it is precisely in failing us that they arrive at the first leap. This failing is the event as intimation and incursion of beyng" (GA 65: 36; C: 30). Thus, keeping silence responds to the refusal of beyng, to how thinking is not (yet?) granted a simple saying of beyng. Yet keeping silence relates as well to the most inceptive moment of the event that bears in it the possibility of the decision over the gods. This decision is marked by the stillness of the passing by of the last god. In *Contributions* Heidegger does not write much explicitly about language and silence, yet at the same time the struggle of this book is precisely the saying of the event.

The Plight of Our Age: Machination and Lived Experience

That thinking is not yet granted a proper saying of the event has, for Heidegger, historical reasons. That it finds itself at the same time necessitated to attempt a saying of the event, also has historical reasons; historical reasons not in the sense of historical facts (Heidegger would say) but in terms of determinations directing how a world and worldly relations unfold. The whole discussion of grounding attunements in Heidegger remains somewhat undetermined, then, as long as one does not look deeper into the plight of our age.

Heidegger addresses the plight of our age especially in the juncture "resonating," and he meditates on it in relation to the whole history of Western philosophy. The roots of machination are to be found, for Heidegger, already in Ancient Greece. They are marked by the moment in which the notion τέχνη overpowers φύσις, when being comes to be addressed in terms of makeability. Concurrently a sense of truth (ἀλήθεια) as unconcealing "collapses" and gives way to the notion of truth as correspondence—the correspondence between thing and intellect. Being is experienced and understood on the basis of present beings (the being of this or that thing) and becomes merely something represented that the intellect either grasps truly or fails to grasp. Being (in the first beginning the presencing, the coming to presence of something) withdraws "behind" present and presented beings that thus remain "abandoned" by being.[26]

The history of the first beginning is the history of the abandonment of beings by being, which corresponds to the history of machination in a larger sense. Heidegger addresses this especially in section 61, "Machination." Here he tells us that machination names a mode in which being occurs essentially. The name machination (*Machenschaft*) refers to making (*Machen*), which in turn addresses the Greek notions of τέχνη and ποίησις. Φύσις (the way being was experienced by the Greeks) begins to be understood in relation to τέχνη as a "making itself by itself." In the Middle Ages this understanding of being is reinforced insofar as being is understood as God's creation and all beings are essentially understood as created beings. Only in modern times, however, does the dominance of machination properly come to the fore (machination in the more narrow sense), now on the basis of subjectivity and modern rationality. All disclosure of beings (the being of beings) now stands under the spell of makeability, of calculability (modern science and the mathematization of nature) and productivity of the rational mind.

Heidegger does not think that the dominion of machination is our human fault but rather that this is a necessary consequence of how being initially took place in Western history.[27] In our times, *we are drawn* to think in terms of makeability and productivity. We find ourselves responding to the urge to produce more efficiently and rapidly. We are drawn to plan and calculate more and more in advance. This state of being is so obvious and overwhelming in our times that we hardly need to be convinced about it. Section 58, where Heidegger writes about the ways in which the abandonment of beings cloaks itself, speaks to our times even more than to Heidegger's. He names calculability, the prevalence of organization (instead of a free-growing change), constant increase of speed, the "burgeoning of the massive" (making everything available to everybody). All these, for Heidegger are symptoms of a deeper-seated event that withdraws from representational grasp, namely, beyng's refusal.

The basic trait of machination in which beings always already address us is (according to Heidegger) reinforced and at the same time veiled by "lived experience" (*Erlebnis*). Section 63 gives a concise indication of how we should understand this.

> To relate beings as represented *to oneself* as the relational center and thus to incorporate them into "life." . . .
> What can count as actually "being" is only what is or can be the object of a lived experience, what presses forth in the realm of lived experience, what humans can bring to themselves and before themselves. (GA 65: 129; C: 102)

Heidegger understands lived experience on the basis of a representational (*vorstellungshaft*) relation to things. The German word *Vorstellung*, literally translated, means to place something before oneself. This emphasizes a subject–object differentiation that becomes increasingly marked in Western metaphysics such that finally, in modern philosophy, the self-conscious subject understands itself in opposition to the world. The world becomes an "other" in relation to the thinking subject; it becomes calculable, explainable, makeable (machination), but it also becomes a means for one's own enjoyment. Lived experience is a way of experiencing that, just as machination in its final stage, remains trapped in subjectivity. What is experienced is incorporated into the experiencing subject. Experience is in fact viewed as a subjective matter, as something happening "in us" and "to us," yet in such a way that we are the "relational center" for all experience.

Lived experience reinforces the plight of the abandonment of beings by being because, in lived experience, humans think they are in fact closest to life, they feel most alive and thus do not experience any plight. This closes off any necessity of questioning, any possibility of being shocked and unsettled into a deeper relationship with truth, now understood as unconcealing concealment of beyng in its withdrawal.

In order to open up other possibilities for the unfolding of history, ways in which beings are no longer abandoned but let a fuller and more original sense of being resonate, in other words, in order to open the possibility of another beginning, the plight of our times (the abandonment of beings by being) needs to be experienced and acknowledged, such that—in shock—thinking is unsettled into the untimely situation of being there in the openness of beyng's self-concealment. This openness is intrinsically the openness of a time-space of decision.

Being in Decision

"Decision" is one of the predominant concepts especially in the "Prospect" of *Contributions*. The fundamental task of *Contributions* as Heidegger articulates it explicitly, is to prepare a (ground), a site (the time-space of Da-sein) for the decision over the other beginning, which would be marked by the stillness of the passing by of the last god. For Heidegger, this is a decision over the possibility of another history in the sense of the history of being, since the abandonment of beings by beyng is reaching the final stage such that it becomes questionable whether beyng can once again eventuate inceptively and find an earthly-worldly site through the sheltering of the truth of beyng in beings. This alone would open up a new era of a historical world.

The untimely thinking of *Contributions* that finds itself unsettled into an experience of beyng in its refusal, finds itself unsettled precisely into a space of decision over the history of beyng. Thinking is inceptive in that sense, although it alone cannot initiate the inception of another epoch. The decision over another beginning of history is tied, says Heidegger, to "the *bestowal* or *withholding* of those eminent and distinctive ones whom we call 'the future ones'" (GA 65: 96; C: 77). The future ones range from the first pioneers who "ground in advance the sites and moments for the realms of beings" (poets and thinkers like Hölderlin and Heidegger), to "those numerous affiliated ones" who follow the pioneers and make visible their discoveries, to a people bound by their common earthly and worldly origin. Heidegger does not explicitly speak of the Germans here (whereas he does in his 1934/1935 lecture course on Hölderlin) and perhaps the disillusionment with the National Socialist movement has something to do with this. For sure, as Heidegger's *Black Notebooks* make evident, the Germans are not yet the people to whom the grounding of another beginning is bestowed (GA 94: 317, 329–330, 501, 521).

In section 44, Heidegger lists many decisions that come with the decision of another beginning. I will refer only to a few of them: "Whether the human being wishes to remain the 'subject,' *or* whether the human being grounds Da-sein" (GA 65: 90; C: 72). It is noteworthy that Heidegger names this decision first. In some way he seems to reconfirm the necessity of his earliest approach (*Being and Time*) to the question of being. As long as we experience ourselves and think of ourselves as subjects, agents, as willing entities acting upon a world that is conceived as being outside of us, the whole domain of the event remains closed off. It is only when we are unsettled into the groundless disclosure of beyng as refusal and experience our being as both exposed and appropriated, only then can we respond—attuned by restraint—to the appropriating call to be there (Da-sein) and thus ground another space of being.

"Whether truth as correctness deteriorates into the certainty of representation and the security of calculation and lived experience, or whether the initially ungrounded essence of ἀλήθεια comes to be grounded as the clearing of the self-concealing" (GA 65: 91; C: 72). I am highlighting this decision as well because of its centrality in Heidegger's work. It concerns especially the interplay between the first (Greek) and other beginning. Heidegger's reading of the notion of ἀλήθεια as unconcealment is an important step for thinking being in terms of a disclosive event (temporalizing, presencing) and also opens the thought of the concealment belonging to being. Furthermore, Heidegger's essay "On the Essence of Truth" foreshadows the shift ("turn") from the transcendental approach to beyng (in the project of Being and Time) to the thinking of beyng in its historicality.[28] To understand truth as correctness means to remain in the realm of representational thinking, in the duality of subject and object, thinking and thought. That people tend to think this way is, according to Heidegger, historically determined and a consequence of beyng's refusal, of its withdrawal "behind" the representation of beings (entities in the largest sense). It is a mode of alienation that distances us from the world yet in such a way that we do not notice the alienation but believe ourselves certain in the proximity of things as we reckon with them and enjoy them (lived experience), as we think "pragmatically" and "realistically" and try to solve our daily problems. To experience truth as unconcealing-concealing that has no ground and is no solid foundation is difficult to endure; it completely transforms our relation to the world. Indeed the occurrence of truth as unconcealing-concealment is itself a space of decision, as I will highlight below.

"Whether nature is debased into an exploitable domain of calculation and organization and into an occasion for 'lived experience,' or whether, as the self-secluding earth, it bears the open realm of the pictureless world" (GA 65: 91; C: 72). I am highlighting this decision despite the fact that Heidegger speaks very little of nature and earth in Contributions. He does mention the earth in its relation to the world more often than nature,[29] and we should keep in mind that the important essay "On the Origin of the Work of Art" was written at the same time as Contributions and should be read as developing a certain aspect of this thinking (the task of the work of art to put truth into work and thus ground Da-sein). I highlight this decision because the destruction of nature (and I am taking nature in the rather vague sense of everything that grows and decays and not in terms of nature scientifically viewed) and the part we humans play in it becomes more and more visible and because Heidegger enables a reflection on the roots of this occurrence.

"Whether the absence of the divine from beings celebrates its triumphs in the Christianization of culture, *or* whether the plight of the undecidability regarding the nearness and remoteness of the gods prepares a space of decision" (GA 65: 91; C: 72). For Heidegger, the thought of grounding (the decision of another beginning) is inextricably tied to the divine. Understanding the "advent and absconding of the gods" as well as "the passing by of the last god" remains one of the most difficult issues and I will approach such an understanding mostly negatively, that is, in terms of what Heidegger does not (cannot) mean. The gods and the god are no entities and no form of presence; in fact, they lack being, they *are* not. Any form of representation must fail. As I wrote in chapter 1, Heidegger finds a sense of them in his reading of Hölderlin. The poet is for Heidegger the one who receives the hints of the gods and passes them on in poetic speech. What Hölderlin writes of is the loss of the old gods (the gods of Greece but perhaps also the Christian God) and this loss or lack is what also prevails in Heidegger's thinking, although precisely the experience of the "flight" of the gods bears a sense of their possible arrival. This is how I understand why Heidegger always writes "flight *and* arrival" or "nearness *and* remoteness" and never "flight *or* arrival," "nearness *or* absconding." One could also add how Nietzsche's announcing of nihilism goes along with the "news" of the death of God. According to Heidegger, Nietzsche shares the experience of the abandonment of beings by being and in some way reaches into the domain of decision, but is not yet able to "leap" into another thinking and remains trapped in metaphysics (GA 65: 85, 182; C: 68, 143).

* * *

When thinking of decision in terms of the decision of another beginning of history for a people, it is hard not to think again in a sequential, almost linear way. Section 45 of *Contributions*, which speaks of the necessity of the future ones (and a people), inevitably leads the reader to do so. But if we follow Heidegger's thinking of decision into its core, it leads us into another space of thinking, a being-in-decision that must remain "blind" or unable to project what will happen, just as it happens to us when we find ourselves in the space of a decision that inevitably, and at least to some extent, is not up to us. There are moments when all we can do is to endure the space of undecidedness. Of course this comparison to more common modes of being-in-decision from a Heideggerian perspective holds only to a certain point. Heidegger's thinking has a historical "task"; when it becomes inceptive, it follows a necessity (*Not*), namely, that of thinking beyng out of the truth of beyng. Thinking of the event is not passive but a rigorous adhering to "what" necessitates thinking, to what calls for thinking, to "what" wants to be spoken and only *is* in this being spoken.[30]

Following Heidegger's thinking to the space of being-in-decision takes us right to the heart of the event. Here decision is not yet articulated into an either-or but is the time-space where these articulations emerge. Heidegger thinks the event in and as a turning. If we approach it (as Heidegger suggests, for instance, in section 122) with a meditation on what occurs in thinking, when the turning of the event is "discovered" we may say the following: unsettled by a plight, thinking occurs in the experience of a refusal that necessitates (calls for) a withstanding or enduring of this refusal. Thus, thinking already finds itself responding to beyng in its refusal. (There is a turning relation between call and response such that there is not one moment preceding the other in time.) The enduring of the withdrawal and the response of thinking to the necessity of beyng, allows the refusal to be retained in some way, such that it becomes a *hesitating* self-refusal (*zögerndes Sichversagen*). In this hesitation, truth discloses as unconcealing-concealment. There is then, a turning relation between the truth of beyng and the beyng of truth. The opening of this event is Da-sein: being-there. Da-sein requires that thinking *be* (in) the *there* of unconcealing-concealment, and thinking experiences itself as being appropriated to *be* there. Da-sein is the moment, the appropriated (*ereignet*) time-space that discloses and holds open the event of truth. It is thus the pivotal point of the turning in the event, the place of decision (*Entscheidung*) in the sense of scission, differentiation, but also of encounter and belonging.[31]

The de-cision as which the truth of beyng occurs in Dasein de-cides humans and gods in their encounter and opens what Heidegger calls the strife of world and earth (we have here a precursor to the later fourfold of mortals and divinities, sky and earth).[32] The encounter of gods and humans and the strife of world and earth name the full articulation of the truth of beyng as event. This means that it is not sufficient to think of the event as the turning relation between beyng and humans. Beyng's self-refusal bears in it the flight of the gods (in section 267, Heidegger even speaks of the plight—*Notschaft*—of the gods), yet when held in a hesitation, it becomes a site of decision over absconding *and* advent of the gods. There are many places where Heidegger approaches the necessity of grounding Da-sein not by speaking simply of beyng's self-refusal or the abandonment of beings by being, but rather by setting out with the gods, that is, with their flight and with how they necessitate Da-sein.[33]

In section 7, Heidegger differentiates between the opening of the site of decision over the gods from the occurrence of the event that brings humans and gods to an encounter. First he writes: "If, through [a] dislodging, humans come to stand in the event and remain steadfast there in the truth of beyng, then they still stand first only on the verge to the leap to the decisive experience as to whether in the event the remaining absent or the intrusion of the god decides for humans or against them" (GA 65: 26; C: 23). Heidegger here speaks of how the truth of beyng first discloses in a transitional way that does not yet involve the decision over the god. A little later in the texts he writes: "The event consigns [*übereignet*] god to the human being by assigning [*zueignet*] the human being to god. This consigning assignment is the appropriating event [*Diese übereignende Zueignung ist Ereignis*]; in it, the truth of beyng is grounded as Da-sein (and the human is transformed, set out into the decision of being-there [*Da-sein*] and being-away [*Weg-sein*]), and history takes its other beginning from beyng" (GA 65: 26; C: 23). Here Heidegger seems to think ahead toward how the event takes place historically *if* it takes place. The consignment of god and assignment of humans (another turning relation) are, we might say, intimated as a possibility out of a sense of necessity.

Heidegger continuously speaks in these different registers in *Contributions*. On the one hand, he articulates the transitional, albeit already inceptive, opening of the truth of beyng where beyng remains in its refusal and beings are abandoned by being; here the refusal is endured such that Da-sein and in it the truth of beyng discloses; on the other hand, he thinks ahead into the occurrence of the event in terms of the beginning (grounding) of another history when beings would no longer be abandoned by being. With the passing by of the last god the truth of beyng would be "sheltered" (*geborgen*) in beings. Truth would find a worldly earthly site.

Beyng and Beings: Grounding and Sheltering

This brings us to the problematic of *grounding* (*Gründung*) in relation to the inceptive and yet still preparatory character of Heidegger's own thinking. For the event to occur inceptively and initiate a new epoch of the history of beyng, the truth of beyng needs to be grounded in Da-sein. This would bring truth into the open of a world and set it into the earth. In order to be grounded in Da-sein, truth needs to be sheltered in beings. The latter requires that humans, responding to the appropriating call and thus taking the directive from the event itself, shelter truth in words, works, or deeds.[34] The attempt to speak of the event is an attempt to shelter truth in words. Whether and the extent to which Heidegger succeeds in this endeavor remains a question I will address later. For now I would like to highlight that inceptive thinking, when it is a grounding thinking, shelters truth by bringing beyng and beings into their "simultaneity," not in the sense of their occurring at the same time in a linear sense but in terms of their occurring together in the event.

The simultaneity of beyng and beings marks a decisive difference between how Heidegger approaches the question of being in *Contributions* and how he approached it in *Being and Time*. The earlier work approaches being not only through Dasein's (and here Dasein designates more narrowly the being of humans) transcendence but also through the articulation of the ontological difference. Heidegger distinguishes the ontic relation to being, that is, how being is factually experienced (and mostly forgotten in everyday life), from the ontological

approach (questioning and laying bare fundamental structures of being underlying all ontic modes of being). At the same time, he makes clear that the ontological approach to being, that is, asking the question of being, is itself an ontic
possibility of human existence, a possibility that is opened up ontically only in
the grounding attunement of anxiety. Heidegger criticizes all previous Western
philosophy (metaphysics) for not questioning being as such, that is, for never
reaching the ontological question of being explicitly. Metaphysics remains ontic
insofar as it remains oriented by the presence of what shows itself: beings. Metaphysics thinks being only as the most general determination of all beings, that is,
as "beingness" (*Seiendheit*) and not out of its temporal horizon (the coming to
presence, the truth of being). It is at once determined by and unable to question
the ontological difference between being (in its temporal horizon) and beings.
But Heidegger's own fundamental ontological approach also remains structured
by the ontological difference when he distinguishes existential ontological structures from concrete ontic modes of being.

In *Contributions* Heidegger merges these two foundational "layers" (the ontic and the ontological) and attempts to stay in an authentic experience of being
and speak from out of this experience.[35] There is, then, no structural difference
operative between ontic and ontological modes of thinking.[36]

This, however, does not abolish the difference between beyng and beings. In
section 266 of *Contributions* (toward the end of the last part of the book), Heidegger reflects on the ontological difference, on how it is necessary for paving a way
from the guiding question of metaphysics (what are beings) to the grounding
question (of the truth of beyng), but then hinders precisely a thinking out of the
event. Then he reaffirms a difference between being and beings (not in terms of
the ontological difference, though) by saying: "As grounded, the relation to being
[*Sein*] is steadfastness in Da-*sein*; it means to stand within the truth of beyng (as
event). . . . The relation to beings [*Seiendes*] is the creative conservation of the
preservation of beyng in the beings which, in accord with such preservation, place
themselves as beings into the clearing of the 'there'" (GA 65: 467; C: 368). In both
these sentences, the relation should be understood out of the relatedness that
is constitutive of human being and not as a link between discreet entities. For
humans, being discloses in *being* there, in the openness of truth; whereas the
relation to beings emerges *out of being* by creating and preserving in speaking,
acting, caring and thus sheltering the disclosure and concealment of being in
words, deeds, and things. The relation to beings occurs within (the relation to) being in being-there.

We may, however, take another approach to the difference between beyng
and beings in *Contributions* by thinking it out of the decision (in the literal sense
of a scission or differencing) as which the truth of beyng unfolds inceptively and
yet transitorily. This requires alertness to the emerging of a space of decision in

which one finds oneself as a participant rather than as an agent, an alertness that objectifies neither the space of decision nor oneself. The space of decision, in which Heidegger thinks, is also the space of differencing of beyng and beings. The in-decision, the being in decision of inceptive thinking means that it is not yet grounding in a fuller sense, and words (beings) do not fully say of the event (*vom Ereignis*). Heidegger indeed attempts to articulate the inceptive opening up of the there of Da-sein, the coming to be sheltered, the not yet being of beings in a fuller sense. This leads to one of the most difficult and central passages in *Contributions*, section 242, "Time-Space as the Abyssal Ground."

The "there" of being-there first discloses as abyssal ground, as the "staying away of the ground" (GA 65: 379; C: 299). This staying away refers to the abandonment of beings by beyng, which is experienced as a mode of leaving unfulfilled, empty. (Heidegger began to think this as the being-left-empty constitutive of deep boredom in 1929/1930.) This emptiness is also an opening that is attuned and disposed in a singular way by the emptiness. We may approach this thought through an analogy, for instance, the emptiness left by the death of someone who was close to us, or else the emptiness left when one's children leave home, or when moving to a new place. In each case, there is a sense of "loss," of "emptiness," a specific emptiness that has, so to speak, a "feel" to it. We are in the draw of what or who is no longer there. One may also think of the process of creative writing, when one has a sense that there is "something" (that is, no yet some thing) that wants to be said, but "it" withholds itself and leaves us searching as we remain attentive to this withholding.

In an analogous way, then, the thinking of *Contributions* finds itself in the draw of the historically determined self-withholding of being and in this draw a clearing of the abyssal ground occurs, a clearing (*Lichtung*) of concealment. This clearing of concealment (truth) is the hesitant refusal of beyng. The notion of hesitance is decisive here since there occurs not sheer refusal (which would disappear) but a tension and "spacing" in relation to the refusal in which lies an intimation (*Wink*) that beckons (appropriates) the *being* of the there (Da-*sein*), the sustaining and (through such sustaining) the constancy of the clearing concealment. It is thus that the truth of beyng is grounding of Da-sein and Da-sein is grounded in the truth of being.[37] We find ourselves called to withstand the draw of the emptiness and thus the refusal of beyng clears and finds a site, a moment of constancy, in being-there (Da-sein).

The clearing of beyng occurs out of an emptiness that disposes thinking (and I would add, that disposes our bodily being). Heidegger meditates further on this disposing emptiness as constituting the clearing or gaping open of time-space. He speaks of "an originary yawning open in hesitant self-withholding" (GA 65: 381; C: 301) that reminds one almost of the Chaos at the beginning of Hesiod's *Theogony*. The clearing of time-space is a temporalizing and spatializing *at once*.

Heidegger writes that the self-withholding creates an emptiness "that is in itself transporting [*entrückend*], i.e., transporting into the 'to come' and thereby simultaneously bursting open what has been. The latter, by making an impact together with what is to come, constitutes the present as a move into the abandonment that remembers and expects" (GA 65: 383; C: 203). A sense of time clears that is not a linear time but rather the ecstatic and suspended temporality of a moment (*Augenblick*), a moment of decision. This moment has also a spatial aspect, yet not in the sense of extended measurable space, but more like a space one would commonly interpret as "interior."[38] Insofar as it is held in hesitation, the self-withholding of beyng is originary "captivation" (*Berückung*) into an "embrace" (*Umhalt*). Heidegger writes: "This captivation is the *embrace* in which the moment and thus the temporalization are held fast. . . . This captivation also makes possible a bestowal as an essential possibility, grants bestowal a space. The captivation is the spatalization of the event. Through the captivation, the abandonment is an established one that is to be with*stood*" (GA 65: 384; C: 303).

One could say that for Heidegger the temporalizing marks more the ecstatic aspect of time-space, that is, the opening up of refusal and the transport into this refusal; whereas spatializing marks more the "holding open" that occurs in a withstanding that allows for the clearing of time-space to have constancy.

In the transport into beyng's refusal and captivation into the embrace (that entails withstanding and thus holding open of the refusal), a time-space of decision opens up, the decision over the possibility of another beginning. It is here that the thinking of *Contributions* is inceptive (*anfänglich*), that thinking fathoms (*ergründen*) the time-space of truth and inventively thinks (*erdenken*) and says this very occurrence, every time anew, every time in the singularity of an experience of beyng. At least this is what Heidegger attempts to do. If he succeeds, "his" words (the words arising out of the event) shelter truth, "his" words provide a site for the occurrence of truth as unconcealing-*concealment* (and not simply as presence of something).

The Performative Aspect of Heidegger's Writing

I would like to conclude my expository sections on *Contributions* with a few remarks concerning the more performative aspect of Heidegger's writing. My emphasis on trying to explain what he attempts to do does not quite allow the tentative and searching character of his writing to come through, the many question marks and interpolations that he inserts in the text, and the countless repetitions of thinking especially in relation to concepts such as event, truth, Da-sein, inceptive thinking, decision, resonating, abandonment by being, machination and lived experience, interplay, first and other beginning, leap, beyng and beings, essential occurrence (*Wesung*) of beyng, time-space, philosophy.

More would have to be said on the parts titled "Resonating" and "Interplay," but the themes related to these junctures recur as well in *Besinnung*, the next of his poietic writings, and I will dwell more on them in chapter 3.

The density of the sections in *Contributions* is uneven. By density I mean, for instance, very compact and complex sections like the one on time-space and abyss I just referred to that think "from within" an experience of a moment of decision and carefully and slowly seek the appropriate words. There are also less dense sections, such as those in which Heidegger criticizes metaphysical ways of thinking or works with the notions of machination and lived experience. The denser sections gather thought toward its most radical attempts at a saying of the event. There are, however, many other sections where Heidegger explores themes that are more accessible to the reader. Some of these sections sound more as if he were speaking to himself, working his thinking out in writing (as many sections from the "Prospect" do). Other sections seem to occur out of his preoccupation with blocking off misunderstandings or paving a way for others to find access to his thought, for instance, by reflecting on *Being and Time* or working with concepts from this earlier work.[39] I mentioned previously that later Heidegger would criticize *Contributions* for being "too doctrinal" and for adhering too much to the difference between guiding question (metaphysics) and grounding question. I see him having in mind, here, the less dense and more accessible sections of *Contributions*.

As I see it, a large part of the thinking of *Contributions* is devoted to the preparation of the transition to the other beginning. He sets up parameters through the sequence of junctures and places emphasis on the first two junctures (The resonating and The interplay). The leap also suggests a sense of break between preparatory reflections and preliminary experiences on the one hand, and the full immersion into the thinking of the event on the other hand. Heidegger himself "leaps" back and forth between different levels of engagement with a saying of the event. It makes sense, then, that in *Die Geschichte des Seyns* he would say: "'Contributions' are still frame, but not a conjunction" (GA 69: 5). It seems, though, that at least in 1938, Heidegger still had in mind a "work" that would replace the first attempt in *Being and Time*, maybe not a work in the traditional sense but certainly an articulation of the "basic position for the question of the truth of beyng" (GA 66: 424; my translation).[40] This is what "A Retrospective Look at the Pathway" (written in 1937–1938) in the appendix to *Besinnung* suggests. Here Heidegger also says that with *Contributions to Philosophy* "the form has not yet been reached, which I demand precisely here for a publication as a 'work;' for here the new style of thinking must first announce itself—the restraint in the truth of beyng; the saying of bearing silence—the making ripe for the essentiality of what is simple" (GA 66: 427).

Heidegger is, then, not satisfied with the "style" of thinking in *Contributions* in that he does not find it to be disposed by restraint in an adequate manner. What does he mean by this? Does not a certain attunement by restraint resonate quite clearly in his writing? I find restraint resonating especially through the frequent use of words like "withstanding," "enduring," "sustaining," "standing in . . . ," and "steadfastness." Consider the following passages (these are just a few examples): "Da-*sein* is humanly endured and sustained in the steadfastness that withstands the 'there' and belongs to the event" (GA 65: 31; C: 26). "The restraint of Da-*sein* first grounds care as the steadfastness that withstands the 'there'" (GA 65: 35; C: 29). "The necessity of philosophy as meditation consists in the fact that it may not do away with that plight but must instead withstand it, ground it, and make it the ground of the history of mankind" (GA 65: 45; C: 37). "The task of *questioning* (resoluteness for meditation and for withstanding the plight)" (GA 65: 60; C: 48). "Da-*sein*: withstanding the openness of self-concealing" (GA 65: 301; C: 238). "Hence the steadfast withstanding of the essential occurrence of the truth of beyng. This conflictual duality the riddle. Therefore Da-sein the 'between'— between *beyng and beings*" (GA 65: 342–343; C: 271). "What does it mean to 'stand' in the clearing of concealment and to withstand it? *The basic disposition of restraint. The extraordinarily historical non-repeatability of this steadfastness,* that here first, and here alone, a decision is made about "what is true." Which sort of *constancy* is involved in this steadfastness? Or, to ask the question in a different way: who is able to *be* Da-*sein*, and when and how?" (GA 65: 352–353; C: 278).

In the section "Beyng and Beings: Grounding and Sheltering" (see above), Heidegger spoke of restraint as the "will" that joins the shock that displaces thinking from everydayness and discloses the abandonment of beings by beyng, and I interpreted this "will" in relation to the withstanding Heidegger finds necessary.[41] There is, however, also another moment he mentions with respect to the basic disposition of inceptual thinking, namely, diffidence (*Scheu*), which is less marked by a tension and more by an attention, a gathering toward silence.

It is interesting that there are fewer passages in *Contributions* devoted to diffidence and silence than to withstanding and its cognates. Besides sections 37 and 38, in which Heidegger speaks more about the necessity of bearing-silence (*Erschweigen*), there are only a few passages in which he explicitly mentions silence. There is one section (31, "The Style of Inceptual Thinking") that I did not mention earlier and that is of interest because in it we also find an indication of what Heidegger means by "style":

> Style: the self-certainty of Dasein in its grounding *law-giving* and in its enduring of wrath. . . .
> Restraint is subservient to the gentle measure—enduring it through silence [*es erschweigend*]—and undergoes the bitter wrath; these both— belonging to each other—encounter each other in different ways out of the earth as well as from the world.

Style as a grown certainty is the law of the carrying out of truth in the sense of the sheltering in beings. (GA 65: 69; C: 55)[42]

Heidegger thinks restraint as a "style,"[43] and he relates style to certainty (we must assume that he is not speaking of certainty in the Cartesian sense) and law. In the above section "gentle measure" and "bearing silence" remain tied, however, to "the bitter wrath" and thus, again, to a sense of tension.

Heidegger associates style with grounding in the sense of sheltering truth in beings as it happens in the work of art. The sheltering of truth, however, is precisely that which *Contributions* cannot yet do (according to Heidegger). Thinking does not yet have the style, the certainty, and the firm measure. Nevertheless there are passages in *Contributions* where he affirms knowing (*Wissen*) and decidedness (*Entschiedenheit*) already in the transitional space of *Contributions*. For instance in section 237, "Belief and Truth," he writes:

> If the essence of truth is the clearing for the self-concealing of beyng, then knowing is an abiding in this clearing of concealment and is thus the basic relation to the self-concealing of beyng and to beyng itself.
>
> This knowing is then not deeming true just something or other that happens to be true or even something preeminently true; instead, it is originally an *abiding in the essence of truth*.
>
> This knowing, essential knowing, is then more original than any belief, for the latter is merely concerned with something true [i.e. with a being and not being itself]; therefore, if belief is ever to escape utter blindness, it must indeed necessarily know what it means to be true and to be a truth!
>
> Essential knowing is an *abiding* in the essence. What is supposed to be expressed thereby is the fact that such knowing is not a mere representation of an encounter; it is persistence within the bursting forth of a projection which, in the very opening up, comes to know the abyss that bears it. (GA 65: 369; C: 291)

Heidegger is here rethinking the notion of knowing outside the realm of representation. Knowing is not the immediate presence of an object of thought but the steadfast relation to what conceals itself (truth as unconcealing concealment). In section 26, Heidegger characterizes knowing as well as renunciation: "the highest knowing is the one that becomes strong enough to be the origin of a *renunciation*." This renunciation not only "holds fast" but also brings forth "through struggle and suffering" the "in-between," the time-space of decision for another beginning (GA 65: 62–63; C: 50).

What Heidegger retains of the more common understanding of knowing is—again—a sense of steadfastness, of abiding and being firm in the midst of struggle. Bearing-silence is characterized as well by this sense of knowing,[44] and questioning occurs within this knowing.[45]

Why this persistence of attunements and dispositions that emphasize a holding fast, withstanding, steadfastness, knowing, and so on? Heidegger gives us a clear answer: because of the plight of our age, because of the urgency in the face of the possibility of a complete abandonment of beings by being in the leveling down of all modes of being and disclosure of beings through the exclusive dominion of machination and lived experience.

Notes

1. Daniela Vallega-Neu, *Heidegger's* Contributions to Philosophy: *An Introduction* (Bloomington: Indiana University Press, 2003). I would also like to note that in this book I tried to stay close to the first translation of *Contributions to Philosophy* by P. Emad and K. Maly, and that I am now using (mostly) the new translation by Richard Rojcewicz and myself.

2. Friedrich-Wilhelm von Herrmann, "Von 'Sein und Zeit' zum 'Ereignis,'" in *Von Heidegger her (Meßkircher Vorträge 1989)*, ed. H.-H. Gander (Frankfurt am Main: Klostermann, 1991), 30–31.

3. See chapter 5, where I discuss Heidegger's own critique of *Contributions*.

4. See the "Afterword of the Editor," von Hermann (GA 65: 514; *Contributions*: 405–406).

5. Hereafter Heidegger's *Contributions to Philosophy (Of the Event)* will be cited as "C" following the German GA citation.

6. This is reconfirmed in a later section as well (GA 65: 81; C: 64).

7. Friedrich-Wilhelm von Herrmann, *Wege ins Ereignis: Zu Heideggers* Beiträgen zur Philosophie (Frankfurt am Main: Klostermann, 1994), 29.

8. Martin Heidegger, "The Origin of the Work of Art," in *Basic Writings*, ed. David Farrell Krell (San Francisco: Harper San Francisco, 1993), 139–212.

9. Martin Heidegger, *Nietzsche*, vols. 1 and 2: *The Will to Power as Art* and *The Eternal Recurrence of the Same*, trans. David Farrell Krell, and vols. 3 and 4: *The Will to Power as Knowledge and as Metaphysics* and *Nihilism*, ed. David Farrell Krell (San Francisco: Harper San Francisco, 1991); GA 45, *Basic Questions of Philosophy: Selected "Problems" of "Logic,"* trans. Richard Rojcewicz and André Schuwer (Bloomington: Indiana University Press, 1994).

10. The futurity of the future ones thus is meant in this sense of "coming toward" and should not be confused with the futurity of a time understood in a sequential way.

11. See the short part 7 of *Contributions* dedicated to the last god. His role in Heidegger's thinking can only be indicated here.

12. See especially Heidegger's *Basic Questions of Philosophy* but also Heidegger's reading of Nietzsche, in which he interprets Nietzsche more and more decidedly as the one who "completes" the first beginning.

13. See Krysztof Ziarek's discussion of *Einzigkeit* and *Einmaligkeit* in "Imageless Thinking: The Time-Space for the Imagination in Heidegger," *Hermeneutisches Jahrbuch* 14 (2015): 145–162.

14. That is, "Where beyng is conceived as event, essentiality is determined out of the originality and uniqueness of beyng itself. There the essence is not the general but is the essential occurrence [*Wesung*] precisely of what is unique in each case" (GA 65: 66; C: 53).

15. See Daniela Vallega-Neu, *The Bodily Dimension in Thinking* (Albany: State University of New York Press, 2005), ch. 5. It is true that Heidegger will always avoid speaking of the body but in an early black notebook, where Heidegger allows himself some looser remarks, he writes

about how in the throw, the lived body (*Leib*) is pulled into it. He then writes: "In the throw the lived body gains a completely new, transformed empowerment" (GA 94; Ü II, 118).

16. In his 1929/1930 lecture course titled *Basic Concepts of Metaphysics: World, Finitude, Solitude*, Heidegger considers the grounding attunement of "deep boredom." One can read the sequence of grounding attunements Heidegger discusses over the years (*Angst* in 1927, deep boredom in 1929/1930, and restraint in 1936) in conjunction with a deepening of his interpretation of being in terms of historical being. Attunements become implicitly historical. I worked this out in a paper titled "Attunement, Truth, and Errancy in Heidegger's Thinking," Proceedings of the 50th Annual Meeting of the Heidegger Circle (De Paul University, Chicago, September 2016).

17. This is why he sometimes speaks also of the fundamental attunement of "presentiment," a "sentiment" directed toward (disposed by) what is to come, what announces itself. (See section 6 of *Contributions*.)

18. See Vallega-Neu, *Heidegger's* Contributions to Philosophy, 47.

19. This is one of the few places where Heidegger uses "will" in a positive sense (notably in quotation marks), since he understands will in terms of philosophies based in subjectivity and takes a critical stance especially with respect to Nietzsche's notion of will and will to power. The appeal to "will" here also highlights the closeness between *restraint* and *resoluteness* in *Being and Time*.

20. In section 5, he refers intimation to shock and disposition together.

21. Heidegger writes: "'primordial temporality': the occurrence of the having-been/preserving and futural/anticipating transporting, i.e., the occurrence of the opening and grounding of the 'there' and thus of the essence of truth" (GA 65: 73; C: 59).

22. See John Sallis, "Grounders of the Abyss," in *Companion to Heidegger's* Contributions to Philosophy, ed. Charles Scott, Susan Schoenbohm, Daniela Vallega-Neu, and Alejandro Vallega (Bloomington: Indiana University Press, 2001), 181–197.

23. See Daniela Vallega-Neu, "Poietic Saying," in Scott et al., *Companion to Heidegger's* Contributions to Philosophy, 66–80.

24. See sections 37 and 38 of *Contributions*.

25. Martin Heidegger, "Das Wort," in *Unterwegs zur Sprache*, GA 12: 205–226. English translation by Joan Stambaugh: "Words," in *On the Way to Language*, trans. Peter D. Hertz (San Francisco: Harper, 1971), 139–156.

26. See Heidegger's *Basic Questions of Philosophy* and, above all, the 1930 "On the Essence of Truth," in which he traces how truth comes to be understood as correctness.

27. Heidegger tries to show this, for instance, in his lecture course of 1935, *Introduction to Metaphysics*, trans. Gregory Fried and Richard Polt (New Haven, CT: Yale University Press, 2000). Martin Heidegger, *Einführung in die Metaphysik*, GA 40, ed. Petra Jaeger (Frankfurt am Main: Klostermann, 1983). Heidegger thinks that φύσις was so overpowering that it forced humans to find a stance in it by holding on to what presented itself as present (beings).

28. In Martin Heidegger, "On the Essence of Truth," in *Basic Writings*, ed. David Farrell Krell (San Francisco: Harper, 2008), 111–138.

29. I believe that the reason Heidegger does not speak of nature is that (at his time) the Kantian conception of nature was current.

30. I am writing "what" in quotation marks because, strictly speaking, there is nothing already there before it is said.

31. See sections 190 and 191 of *Contributions*.

32. There remains a residue of foundational thinking in *Contributions* since Heidegger takes the decision of humans and god to precede (in terms of origin, not of time) the opening of the strife of earth and world. See GA 65: 390–391, 470; C: 308, 370.

33. See, for instance, section 8.

34. In "The Origin of the Work of Art," Heidegger thinks ahead toward how a work of art may shelter truth by opening up a world and setting it into the earth. In *The Bodily Dimension in Thinking*, I show how this *always* implies a sheltering of truth in the body.

35. He criticizes his earlier thinking in terms of the ontological difference, for instance, in sections 132, 137, 258, and 266.

36. For a more thorough discussion of the relation between *Being and Time* and *Contributions*, see Vallega-Neu, *Heidegger's* Contributions to Philosophy, part 1.

37. See sections 187 and 188.

38. If we follow Heidegger's thinking of Da-sein, however, to speak of an interior space does not make sense.

39. See, for instance, section 5, when Heidegger rethinks the notion of "care" in *Being and Time*, or section 122 in which he takes recourse to the notions of thrownness and projection from *Being and Time*.

40. The volume *Besinnung* (GA 66) has been translated as Martin Heidegger, *Mindfulness*, trans. Parvis Emad and Thomas Kalary (London: Continuum, 2006).

41. See in this context Bret Davis's insightful book, *Heidegger and the Will: On the Way to Gelassenheit* (Evanston, IL: Northwestern University Press, 2007). Davis traces Heidegger's thinking along the notion of the will.

42. See also section 13: "Restraint, as style: the self-certainty of the grounding measure and of the sustained wrath of Da-sein. It determines and disposes the style, because it is *the basic disposition*."

43. See, for instance, GA 65: 15.

44. Section 27 of *Contributions*: "that knowing which speaks by first keeping silent out of the steadfastness which withstands in Da-sein" (GA 65: 64; C: 52); and section 36: "the will and knowing of bearing silence" (GA 65: 79; C: 63).

45. See section 26 and section 226, where Heidegger speaks as well of a "knowing that questions."

3   Attunement and Grounding

A Critical Engagement with Heidegger's *Contributions to Philosophy (Of the Event) (GA 65)*

I ENDED CHAPTER 2 (my expository interpretation of Heidegger's *Contributions to Philosophy*) with remarks on the performative aspect of Heidegger's thinking. I could cite many passages to highlight the sense of tension and steadfastness that characterizes *Contributions*, a sense of tension that has disposed my own reading and interpretation of Heidegger. A number of issues have arisen for me in relation to his grounding attunement of restraint, all of which are related to some extent to the question of grounding and sheltering, which means implicitly to the relation between beyng and beings.

The first issue regards what Heidegger calls the "simultaneity" of beyng and beings in the thinking of *Contributions*. If it is true that the truth of beyng discloses always only in and as Da-sein and Da-sein requires its sheltering in a being, should we not understand his thinking to be already grounding?

This leads to the second issue, namely, the body and physicality. Grounding attunements bring with them affective dispositions that can be "physically" felt. Granted that we need to rethink what we mean by body in Heidegger's thinking— should we not still say that the body must play a distinctive role in sustaining the clearing of truth in *being*-there? How could we articulate this role?

Third, if there is a simultaneity of beyng and beings, how is it that a speaking of the event is held in a suspension in Heidegger's thinking, how is it that he understands his thinking only as opening up Da-sein but not yet as grounding? This is closely tied to the next issue.

Fourth, is there not an indecision in Heidegger's thinking of the historicality of beyng as a being-in-decision? Is the tension in his thinking a withstanding that precisely does not allow what his thinking at the same time strives for, namely, to articulate being as it occurs?

Fifth, how does the notion of the last god come into play in relation to the question of decision, grounding, and the uniqueness (*Einmaligkeit und Einzigkeit*) of being?

Sixth, how can Heidegger be sure, that is, speak of "knowing" in relation to what discloses for him in the attunement of restraint? Should he not hold in question precisely what discloses in grounding or dominant attunements? Is history not far more complex and fragmented than he appears to believe? Is it not constituted by lineages that do not all have larger historical dimensions? How can we be so sure about what attunes and disposes our thinking? Do we not inevitably have "blind spots" of some kind? Do more "local" events not dispose us as well? What about family lineages and "character"? What would it mean for our understanding of Heidegger if we kept these doors to "smaller" historical dimensions open? For instance, how does his relation to Nazi Germany transpire in his thinking? Is it justified to completely exclude the import of "personal" issues?

The Simultaneity of Being and Beings

In section 5, Heidegger writes: "beyng is not something 'earlier'—existing in itself, for itself. Instead, the event is the temporal-spatial simultaneity for beyng and beings" (GA 65: 13; C: 13). The leap into the in-between (Da-sein) transforms "into their simultaneity, both beyng and beings" (GA 65: 14; C: 14).

Heidegger does not use the word "simultaneity" (*Gleichzeitigkeit*) often, probably because it suggests that things happen "at the same time" and thus seems to presuppose a linear sense of time (which he conceives as arising from a more fundamental time, or rather, time-space). The notion of simultaneity is, however, helpful to remind us that beyng is not something one could represent as some "thing" existing "in itself" and that then would somehow infuse a being (a thing or event) with "being" (*Sein*). We could rephrase the notion of simultaneity of beyng and beings by saying (still with Heidegger) that the truth of beyng opens up, finds a site in Da-sein only if this opening is "sheltered" in a being (*Seiendes*). Thus truth would shine forth through beings in a world. "The Origin of the Work of Art" is an essay where Heidegger tries to work out how to think the sheltering or grounding of truth concretely. The artwork is a good example because we can experience how an artwork "speaks" or reveals something to us. This revealing is an occurrence of truth in the Heideggerian sense. Poetry has a similar power to unsettle us and reveal the "being" of "something" in the widest sense. What is primary for the one who sees a work of art or reads a poem and finds herself unsettled in some way is indeed not their "thing"-character (thing taken now as an objectively present entity) but rather the event-character of what is said or seen, the motion that seems to draw us out of ourselves and into ourselves at the same time.

Being eventuates only in or through beings, then. But has Heidegger's task not always been to think being precisely "in itself," that is, not on the basis of beings (things) but out of its (being's) temporality? Did he not precisely insist on the difference between being and beings, a difference that metaphysics leaps over and does not properly think through? And what should we make of the fact that, although in *Contributions* he speaks of the simultaneity of beyng and beings, he still speaks of their difference?

I have always had the tendency to emphasize that Heidegger's thinking in *Contributions*, although transitional, is already grounding, a sheltering of truth in words.[1] If his thinking is attuned by shock and restraint as he says and as it transpires in what he writes, if he has a sense of a leap or a being unsettled into the in-between that he calls Da-sein, does this not mean that truth opens up in some way? Does beyng not resonate as refusal in his thinking? And is this not a historical event, albeit one that occurs locally rather than for a whole people? Do I not find myself addressed and drawn by this thinking of beyng as refusal, as abyssal opening?

I would, then, differentiate between two ways in which grounding plays out in *Contributions*. In a larger sense, Heidegger's thinking would not properly be grounding because it could not initiate but only ground the *possibility* for another beginning for Western history. This is because machination cannot simply be done away with but manifestly only intensifies its dominion (the emphasis on production—not only of academic books and articles but also of "knowledgeable" students and administrative tasks—under greater and greater time constraints in universities is one of the ways in which I find myself affected by this almost daily). In a more limited or narrow sense, however, Heidegger's thinking would already be grounding, insofar as it makes visible the dominion of machination and opens up a different sense of truth, that is, other possibilities of being through Da-sein.

Heidegger's emphasis on the transitional character of *Contributions* does not quite go along with my emphasis on thinking in the sense of already being grounding. Furthermore, if we read carefully, we can see how he emphasizes and articulates a differencing between beyng and beings (although they always occur "at once"), how he seems to hold in suspense the very simultaneity he announces, and how he retains a quasi-foundational thinking in *Contributions*. Here, as in "The Origin of the Work of Art," Heidegger suggests that the truth of beyng in its originary occurrence as unconcealing concealment of beyng (in its refusal) is *more originary* than the strife of world and earth. The strife of world and earth is that through which things shelter truth. The work of art, "opens up a world and sets this world back again on earth, which itself only thus emerges as native ground" (GA 5: 28).[2] The strife of world and earth is the openness through which truth (the originary strife of unconcealing concealing) occurs. Let us just briefly remind ourselves (and only in an indicative way) what Heidegger means by earth and sky:

> The world is the self-opening openness of the broad paths of the simple and essential decisions in the destiny of a historical people. The earth is the spontaneous forthcoming of that which is continually self-secluding and to that extent sheltering and concealing. World and earth are essentially different from

one another and yet never separated. The world grounds itself on the earth, and the earth protrudes through the world. . . . The world, in resting upon the earth, strives to surmount it. As self-opening it cannot endure anything closed. The earth, however, as sheltering and concealing, tends always to draw the world into itself and keep it there. (GA 5: 35; BW: 174)

Heidegger addresses earth as arising and bearing the self-secluding aspect of the being of things. Earth is that into which the work of art is set.[3] With this notion he also rethinks the material aspect of things, yet in such a way that he thinks this material aspect out of the *how* of a thing's appearing or manifestation. He would speak, for instance, of the heaviness of the stone, of the shining of colors. Heaviness and shining manifest themselves (they arise) and through them the stone appears as stone but, at the same time, heaviness and shine cannot be penetrated.[4] Earth secludes and shelters the being of a thing (GA 5: 33; BW: 172). The world, on the other hand, is the opening up of historical relations. Through the openness of the world things have their time, their nearness and farness. The world bears in it as well the relation to the gods (GA 5: 31; BW: 170).

Truth thus does not immediately shine forth in a being but "mediatedly" through the strife of world and earth. This is what Heidegger thinks in section 244 of *Contributions* as well:

Whence does *sheltering* derive its urgency and necessity? From self-concealing. The sheltering of this *occurrence* is needed to preserve the self-concealing rather than do away with it. The occurrence is transformed and maintained (Why?) in the strife of *earth and world*. The playing out of the strife sets truth into work, into tool, and it experiences truth as a thing, consummates truth in deed and sacrifice.

Yet there must always be a preservation of self-concealment, for only thus does the history which is grounded through Dasein remain in appropriation and accordingly something belonging to beyng. (GA 65: 390–391; C: 308)

Much more would need to be said here, but my main interest is to show how world and earth "mediate," in Heidegger's thinking of them, the truth of beyng and beings. When we try to articulate a sense of disclosure in relation to things, we speak "at the level" of the disclosure of earth and sky. Heidegger seems to want to maintain that truth itself in its occurrence as unconcealing concealment (the primordial strife, the *Urstreit*), is "more originary" than what opens up in the appearing of things (the strife of world and earth).

He suggests something similar in section 267 from the part of *Contributions* titled "Beyng," which was written later (1938) than the rest of the book (1936–1937). Here he unfolds the appropriating event in terms of a multiplicity of appropriations. The sequence of these appropriations is telling. First he speaks of the plight of the gods who necessitate Da-sein in their need for beyng. This opens up the de-cision (*Ent-scheidung*) of gods and humans who emerge in their separateness (*Geschiedenheit*). The appropriation of this decision at the same time brings humans and gods to their encounter. Next, Heidegger writes: "4. The en-counter is the origin of the strife, and the strife essentially occurs by unsettling beings from their lostness in mere beingness. The *un-settling* [*Ent-setzung*] characterizes the appropriating event in its relation to beings as such. The ap-propriation of Da-sein allows Da-sein to become steadfast in what is unusual in relation to just any being" (GA 65: 470; C: 370).

The strife and relation to beings originates in the encounter of humans and gods. Again (or still) Heidegger thinks the decision of humans and gods as being "prior" to the strife of earth and world, prior to the relation of the event to beings; prior, of course, not in time (we can still assume that all this happens at once), but prior still in terms of origin and origination.

The decision that marks the transitional in-between of Heidegger's thinking in *Contributions* contains, then, a differencing of beyng (in its refusal) and beings. His thinking withstands this decision, withstands the abyss of beyng, the refusal of beyng, the lack he finds to be constitutive of our epoch. He withstands the lack of words for the self-concealing that he attempts to speak of at the same time.

And yet Heidegger speaks, yet he writes and articulates a lack in our relation to beings, a groundlessness of being. Is this not a grounding or sheltering of what is said? Could we not simply affirm the necessary limitedness of any sheltering? Why does he hold on to the idea that there could be a saying where this saying would be freely enjoined or appropriated by the conjuncture of the truth of beyng?[5] He could even hold on to the difference between on the one hand, particular modes of grounding that constitute a minority with respect to usual ways of living in the oblivion of beyng and, on the other hand, a historical grounding that would have vaster changes for a majority of people.

As I pursued these questions in my reading of Heidegger, I was led as well to the question of embodiment.

The Body in Da-sein

Heidegger does not speak much of the body although one can find openings to think the body especially in the horizon of *Being and Time*.[6] I believe that the body is always at play in his thinking, although he addresses it obliquely through his notion of attunements or dispositions (*Stimmungen*) as well as in his notion of earth. His attempt is to speak in or out of Da-sein in a nonrepresentational way, and it is hard to speak of the body without representing it. I see this as the main reason that he says so little about the body, but one should also take into account his resistance to life-philosophy and "biologism," an aversion he expresses at times in his poietic writings especially in reference to Nietzsche and also in the *Black Notebooks* in reference to Nazi ideology. In order to question the role of the body in Heidegger in such a way as to avoid its simple objectification, I prefer to speak of "bodily being."

To speak out of grounding attunements also means to utter or write words, which always involves the body. When I want to emphasize this bodily aspect it is indeed more helpful to translate the German word *Stimmung* as "disposition" rather than as "attunement." We are disposed bodily in certain ways before the hand or mouth moves such that a word gets written or spoken. Dispositions orient our actions. They could not do this if they were not "physical," "concrete." To think the body out of a sense of disposedness is also helpful for decentering the notion of body from subjectivity. Dispositions as Heidegger thinks and articulates them insightfully, arise out of the contextualized and historically determined being-in-the-world. If we pay attention to them we find that they reveal to us how our bodily being is open, exposed, and finite in the sense of being limited by our spatiotemporal context as well as limited by our mortality. Expressed in more common terms (leaving aside the way in which Heidegger speaks of disposedness), we do experience how the news we hear of the death of a friend disposes us in certain ways, how tensions during a professional meeting do so too. The warmth of the sun also plays into our disposedness and the noises on the street. There is also something like a disposition of an epoch in a specific culture. Despite the cultural mingling of people, being in France still "feels" different from being in Germany or in the United States, and one can sense something changing in one's disposition when events affect a whole country (as the attack on the Twin Towers). Everywhere the temporality and rhythm of language and events seem to bear certain characteristics that differentiate them.

In the earthly character of our body there is also an aspect of self-secluding and bearing. With Merleau-Ponty I might want to speak of "sedimentations" of incisive events and habitual bearings and actions in our body. I would say that these sedimentations also play a role in our dispositions. We bear these sedimentations with us as habits, "scars" (in a variety of senses), "psychological knots," "unconscious fears and desires," to use somewhat inadequate terms to indicate aspects of our bodily being that would need to be articulated differently in relation to Heidegger's notion of Da-sein. These aspects of our bodily being tend to escape us. We might say that this is the case because of the self-secluding character of the earth.

Granted that Heidegger would have found the way I just explained our bodily being out of its disposedness inadequate, since I made recourse to ways of speaking that easily make us represent relations between entities instead of making us think out of our being there—it is completely consistent with his thinking to say that in every creative sheltering involving humans, the body is at play as a site that holds open the temporal-spatial span of Da-sein.[7]

But what about those times when no Da-sein discloses truth and conceal-ment or beyng in its refusal? What about those people who never seem to experi-ence any abandonment? Do their bodies still bear an abandonment? In other words, is there simultaneity between beyng and beings only when we are un-settled into Da-sein, when lack and refusal as such open up for us? Does the aban-donment of beings by being mean their nonsimultaneity?

In the way he writes, Heidegger seems to suggest so. How else would the leap into Da-sein "transform" into the simultaneity of beyng and beings? Consider as well what he writes in section 225: "Only if self-concealing reigns throughout all realms of production, creation, action, and sacrifice by weaving them together in essential occurrence, and if self-concealing determines the clearing and thus at the same time essentially occurs by encountering what secludes itself within the clearing, only then does *world* arise and at the same time (out of the 'simultane-ity' of beyng and beings) the *earth* springs up. Now for a moment there is *history*" (GA 65: 349; C: 276).

That beyng has abandoned beings means for Heidegger that beyng does not occur in beings and that there is no proper world, no proper earth, no proper his-tory in terms of an originary history of beyng. Beyng refuses itself. It refuses itself, according to Heidegger, at the end of metaphysics, an end that may never end. Yet when thinking finds itself unsettled into this truth (the truth of beyng's refusal) thinking experiences precisely how beyng is occurring, unknown to most. That refusal is what characterizes how beings, things, events, appear to people in our epoch. Should we not say, then, that beings bear the mark of beyng's refusal. Should we, then, not say that bodies bear the mark, the trace of this refusal?

I believe so. Otherwise we would be turning "beyng" into this mysterious "event" that is not yet happening. We would not be thinking being in how we find ourselves in it. We would not be thinking out of being-there. If we take the no-tion of embodiment in a large sense in which it does not simply refer to the human body, we could say that being is always embodied, always physical; even when being holds sway as refusal, that refusal is embodied as a lack. The bodily being each of us is, disposed by events well beyond the physical delimitation of our skins, bearing in the earthly character of our flesh histories that escape our aware-ness,[8] this bodily being is a region of access or closure of world and earth.

Highlighting as I do the bodily aspect of being shifts a certain emphasis in thinking being in its historicality. It shifts the emphasis away from the projection of one large history of beyng to particular and manifold ways of being and of senses of refusal and lack permeating different lives. This shift relates to how the emphasis on bodily being makes us rethink truth as unconcealing-concealment. Let me indicate this briefly.

Already in "On the Essence of Truth," Heidegger distinguishes two modes of concealment of truth: one is the originary concealment (the "mystery") belonging to any unconcealment, to any disclosure. This concealment is reflected in human mortality as the possibility of not being at all, which is the limit from which possibilities open up. The second mode of concealment is errancy, that is, the concealment of the originary concealment through our relation to beings. This refers to the fact that when we relate to particular things and events we do not relate to others; it also indicates that things may always seem other than they are such that the originary concealment does not disclose "purely" for us. Heidegger thinks that errancy essentially (and not only occasionally) belongs to being.[9] This would mean that concealment is always double concealment.

If we now think our bodily being as the site through which unconcealment occurs, and if our bodily being is always also earthly and thus "a being" (*Seiendes*) with the tendency to seclude itself (as earth), this reinforces that truth is always a double concealing, that there can never be a sheer disclosure of originary truth without relation to beings. Our bodies, both exposed to and also sedimented with histories whose origins are not simply subjective, delimit, open up, hold open, and limit dispositions out of which we find ourselves to be oriented and related in being. (I am rethinking here dispositions in their "earthly" body-aspect, which will orient a series of questions below regarding the fundamental attunements of *Contributions*.)

Thus, being and beings occur not just "simultaneously" but co-originarily. I could see someone argue that Heidegger does think beyng and beings also co-originarily since with a disclosure of beyng a relation to beings occurs right away. But the way his thinking remains gathered especially toward the concealed dimension of beyng leads to a prioritizing of being over beings. It seems to me that to let go of that prioritizing would mean to pluralize the question of being. Heidegger would see this as falling back into metaphysical thinking that prioritizes beings. His thinking resists at its core such a dissemination of the question of being into a plurality. The grounding of the truth of beyng in Da-sein remains an announcement, a presentiment, something that can only be prepared. Thus his thinking restrains itself to hold open the "in-between" of beyng and beings as a space of decision. This is also tied to the grand narrative of the history of beyng and to his notion of the last god.

Withstanding in the History of Being: Heidegger's Being in Decision

Heidegger's resistance to letting go of the primacy of beyng over beings is reflected in the way he uses the word *Loslassung*, "letting loose," with an entirely negative connotation as the "letting loose" of beings into machination (GA 65: 416; C: 329; GA 66: 311, 382). (On the other hand, he does use terms like "letting be" and "letting hold sway"—always in relation to truth and being—in a positive sense.) Most fundamentally his resistance relates to a sense of plight and urgency out of an experience of loss that has to do with how he experiences the world around him.

It should also be telling that Heidegger is reading Nietzsche while he works on finding a different approach to the question of being. Nietzsche, who is so close to Heidegger in how he (Nietzsche) experiences and announces nihilism, Nietzsche with whom Heidegger shares a sense of liveliness in Greek thinking and culture, which got lost. Nietzsche becomes Heidegger's strongest opponent in relation to whom Heidegger works out his thinking of the utmost limit or end of metaphysics, the utmost abandonment of beings by being in the will to will. Heidegger's engagement with Nietzsche resonates throughout *Contributions*.[10]

We may not be able to say anything definite about the origin of Heidegger's resistance to letting go, but I believe that we can say something about its effects. The in-between in which Heidegger tries to hold his thinking, attuned by restraint, is what makes his creative thinking possible and at the same time (de-)limits it. Withstanding the lack that urges his thought, Heidegger rethinks the whole Western history of philosophy as one determined by that lack. It is as if the lack stretched out over Heidegger's reappropriation of Western history, infusing every reading of traditional texts. I believe that if there is a unity of the history of metaphysics, the center that structures this unity is the sense of withdrawal that animates Heidegger's thinking. As I will discuss in the next section, I see that unity of history also as tied to his notion of the last god. Should we say that he constructs this history? It certainly appears so, especially if we begin to turn toward cultures that clearly do not belong to Western history and to which in our day we are much more exposed than Heidegger was.

On the other hand, there is something appealing to Heidegger's thought that thinking is fundamentally responsive and develops with respect to what gives itself to thought. Thinking develops within and in relation to a tradition even when it departs from aspects of that tradition. The return to the Greeks was deeply infused in German intellectual culture in Heidegger's times. Furthermore, Hölderlin's poetry spoke to Heidegger in decisive ways. It seems clear as well that Heidegger was a German philosopher, indeed a nationalist philosopher (involving a nationalism that one cannot attribute in the same way to Hölderlin), although the German people he hoped for was not "yet" reality. One can make all these observations, however, without entering into a consideration of the performative dimension of Heidegger's thought. It is not enough, then, to point to "historical influences" (in a more common sense) in Heidegger's thinking. Something is lost when we reduce thinking to historico-social-political occurrences; what is lost is precisely the creative or originary dimension of thinking; that dimension where thinking exceeds what can be limited to a human subject, its histories and social-political circumstances. And still, the way Heidegger articulates the history of being in terms of the history of the first beginning (metaphysics) performs a delimitation and limitation that are somehow related to historico-social-political circumstances (circumstances he would see as being rooted precisely in the history of beyng he articulates).

Heidegger's reading of the history of philosophy is powerful and insightful. I believe that he is right when he traces a further and further differentiation of being and thinking stemming from the solidification of thinking in terms of subject and object in a dominant strain of Western philosophy. Furthermore, there is clearly a schism forged in Western societies by modern science with respect to human life, which is the consequence of an objectification of the world that alienates us from many aspects of life. Once all truth claims are supposed to be grounded in scientific methodology and assessment, all aspects of life that are not quantifiable and verifiable through experimentations get neglected and shrivel. Our educational system will suffer for a long time (maybe indefinitely) from the absurd attempt to ascertain all human events in scientific terms, to grasp "progress" in educating human sensibilities by means of numbers (assessment at higher institutions). Heidegger provides a compelling genealogy of what he calls machination, to which belongs the demand for makeability and calculability. Still, "his" construction of Western history as the history of the abandonment of beings by being initiated in Ancient Greece and his projection of another beginning of history do not hold, especially if one thinks outside traditional Western parameters and in an intercultural context. It makes little sense in our times, to speak of *the* history of being.[11] And not all that happens in Western capitalist societies is reducible to machination.

Let us speak of histories of being, then. Or should we let go of that too and speak only of histories of beings and events? What would histories of being address? What is at stake here, together with the differentiation of being and beings, is Heidegger's differentiation between *Geschichte* and *Historie*. *Historie* is the word Heidegger uses for what we traditionally understand to be history: facts that happened in the past situated on a chronological linear time line, facts we can represent. *Geschichte* is a word he reserves to the history of being. It addresses historical *being*, that is, the way the truth of beyng occurs such that it brings to presence and/or withdraws from beings, yielding different ways in which humans find themselves addressed and related to things and events. The truth of beyng predisposes, so to speak, how we relate to things. Machination is one modality of how the truth of beyng occurs, or rather, recedes behind the machinational deployment of beings and this occurs differently in antiquity, the Middle Ages, and modernity according to Heidegger, since, for instance only in modernity does human subjectivity (consciousness) become the center for our relation to the world and to things. Heidegger's history of beyng thus addresses different epochs that bear characteristic ways of relating to beings and understanding the being of beings. (I will address another, more restricted and originary sense of history below.) Thus, when he speaks of a history of being, he indicates that what constitutes history hitherto (in the West) is the withdrawal of beyng that releases and underlies those events we can objectify and observe.[12] History (*Geschichte*) thus addresses a temporal-spatial occurrence hidden to the eye.

Back to the question of histories of being, the question would be whether it would be possible to pluralize being without representing "being" as a thing. My own attempt, here, would be—following a radicalization of the simultaneity of being and beings such that I would understand them as co-originary—to think being as always embodied being and I would understand being as relational modes of temporalizing and spatializing of various things in the widest sense. Another way of entering a thought of histories of being would be through attunements that for Heidegger are disclosive of being. Focusing on embodied being and taking recourse to how being discloses for us in attunements, one could say that our relations to things are predisposed by senses of being (by attunements and dispositions) that are always manifold and complex and that arise through various and complex lineages sedimented in bodies, institutions, and habitual behavior. I find myself thinking in these terms especially when I consider Heidegger's own thinking in its "historical" context, that is, in relation, for instance, to Germany in World War II. (I will say more about this in chapter 5.)

Yet Heidegger had never thought of histories of being in his poietic writings. He found himself compelled (appropriated), disposed to hold on to the thought of *the* history of beyng as he continuously emphasized singularity, uniqueness, nonrepeatability. I believe that this is due largely to the fact that he attempted to not think representationally but rather *from within* a sense of being. He had to rescue the question of being *itself*, in its differentiation from beings. He found himself compelled to hold open the withdrawal of beyng, to hover in a time-space that he understood as the time-space of decision over history. He felt the necessity to hold on to a space of decision that is also one of indecision, of *not* letting go, of *not* disseminating, *not* pluralizing. There is, for Heidegger, *no Da-sein in plural*.

The reason that there cannot be Da-sein in plural becomes clear when we attempt to pluralize Da-sein while trying to think from within Da-sein, that is, out of *being* there in the disclosure of a sense of being. Thinking from within a moment remains bound to the temporality of that moment, to its temporal expanse. The attuned thinking that tries to remain in a fundamental disposition *concentrates*, *gathers* in a moment toward what calls to be said. Is seems that in order to think Da-sein in plural one has to take a more distanced view, one Heidegger would call *vorstellungshaft*, that is, representational. Da-sein would be turned into a mode of being that I represent—unless there could be a thinking that "slackens" the concentric force at play when we concentrate, a thinking that holds itself in the dispositional awareness of a multiplicity of occurrences. But this is not something Heidegger was looking for. Could part of the reason be a millennial old habit of thinking in terms of single origins?

Sometimes Heidegger speaks of history in an even more restricted sense than that referring to epochs of the history of beyng. In a more narrow and originary sense for him (in the context of *Contributions*) history would happen only when the truth of beyng is grounded in Da-sein. Only then would humans be truly historical. This history of beyng has not yet happened, however (GA 65: 492). I am not sure what to make of this history of beyng that has not yet happened, that event that would be marked by the passing by of the last god, where truth (and especially the concealment belonging to truth) would be sheltered in beings and determine a historical world. This truly singular history announces itself for Heidegger's thinking, gathered in reticence, out of the intimation that he comes to understand as the beckoning of the gods.

The Last God

Is the last god something like a single origin? There is no straight answer to this question, partly because of the difficulty of understanding what Heidegger means by the last god. In an earlier section, I mostly said what the last god is not: he is not a being, nor is he above being or a creator god, nor is he simply the same as beyng (and this is why I prefer not to write Beyng with a capital B). Heidegger writes that the last god is "wholly other than past ones and especially other than the Christian one" (GA 65: 403; C: 319). The last god is wholly other especially to the Christian one because the Christian creator god is tied to the notion of machination, that is, to an interpretation of being along the lines of producing and making, which is precisely what for Heidegger needs to be overcome in the other beginning.

I will try to give a more positive characterization of the last god. The way Heidegger speaks of the last god addresses him as an occurrence rather than an entity. He speaks of his (the last god's) "intimation" (*Wink*) and his passing by (*Vorbeigang*). Heidegger speaks of the "last" in order to indicate the most profound beginning (*der tiefste Anfang*) (GA 65: 405; C: 321). The word "last" points both ahead and back and thus fits well his understanding of the other beginning as occurring through a deeper appropriation of the first. The last god marks precisely the moment of decision over the other beginning of history. Thus, Heidegger asks: "Yet what if the last god must be so named, because the decision about the gods ultimately leads under and among them and so raises to the highest the essence of the uniqueness of the godhead?" I explained in previous sections how the other beginning of history requires the sheltering of the truth of beyng in beings through the grounding of Da-sein. Only in Da-sein does the truth of beyng find a site and this requires the sheltering of the site in a being. The passing by of the last god requires, then, sheltering; the god *"pervades* beyng *with divinity* always only in work and sacrifice, deed and thought" (GA 65: 262; C: 206). Yet, again, this other historical beginning, the passing by of the last god, is "only" a presentiment; it first needs to be prepared through the grounding of Da-sein. The last god is not beyng but needs beyng (and thus the grounding of Da-sein) in order to pass by: "For beyng is never a determination of the god as god; rather, beyng is that which the divinization of the god needs so as to remain nevertheless completely distinct from it" (GA 65: 240; C: 189).

In the transitional thinking of *Contributions* that holds itself in restraint in-between the first and the other beginning, the last god takes place as a hint or intimation (*Wink*) in the abyssal opening of Da-sein. The intimation of the last god befalls the future ones who endure the utmost abandonment of beings by being in restraint and reticence and thus come to experience that "refusal is the intimacy of an allocation. What is allocated in the trembling [*Erzitterung*] is the clearing of the abyssal 'there.' The 'there' is allocated as something to be grounded, as Da-sein" (GA 65: 240; C: 189).

The last god takes the form not only of a climax, the last juncture in the grand fugue of the truth of beyng, but is there, hidden, right from the beginning, in the plight of the lack of plight, in the utmost abandonment of beings by being when the abyssal "there" gapes open.[13] He is there, for those who withstand the plight, who face their own mortality, and become transitional grounders of the abyss, in an intimation. He is announced in a "trembling" of the abyssal opening of Da-sein in the undecidability of his passing by.

Even if we distinguish Heidegger's last god radically from the monotheistic creator God, it is difficult not to be reminded of a traditional idea of salvation by a god, not to hear a metaphysical hope in the intimation of the last god as well as will to ground the divine in beings. I wonder why Heidegger could not stay with the notion of the gods in plural, as we find it in Hölderlin, why there is this masculine god in the singular. According to David Farrell Krell, Heidegger gets the notion of the last god from Schelling and Nietzsche. As Krell points out, in the first draft of the *Ages of the World* "Schelling stresses the 'terrors' and 'monstrous births' suffered by the deity in its primal state; deity 'trembles,' *zittert*, in the face of its own nascent being."[14] But perhaps more central is Nietzsche's *Thus Spoke Zarathustra*, when Zarathustra invokes the last god in the section "On the Three Metamorphoses."[15] Heidegger's emphasis on the "stillness" of the passing by of the last god (GA 65: 17; C: 26, and many other places), on how the decision takes place in the stillest stillness (GA 65: 100; C: 79) is quite reminiscent of "The stillest hour" in *Zarathustra*.[16] But certainly in Heidegger the question of the last god takes a unique shape. I believe that it is constitutive of the grand narrative of the history of beyng in the 1930s, of the movement of gathering into the intimacy of beyng's withdrawal that holds thinking in the time-space of the no longer and not yet, the time-space of decision that resists dissemination and allows one to think of Da-sein only in the singular.

That Heidegger's notion of the last god is tied to a decisionism characteristic of his thinking in the context of *Contributions* is confirmed by the fact that when he begins to think in terms of releasement (*Gelassenheit*) in the 1940s, the notion of the last god begins to disappear. Heidegger's thinking of the fourfold has no more space for the last god but speaks of the gods (in plural). (One may wonder, though, whether the god of which he speaks in the famous 1976 *Spiegel* interview when he says, "Only a god can save us,"[17] still addresses the last god he introduces in *Contributions to Philosophy*.)

Thinking in the Co-originarity of Being and Beings

Whatever holds Heidegger in a space of decision, whatever makes him withstand a sense of lack, cherish and nurture it, is, I believe, not one single thing. The roots of the restraint disposing his thinking must be complex. And in some way he affirms the complexity of the grounding dispositions of his work when he gives many names to the basic attunement of *Contributions*.[18] I am wondering, though, how he could be so assured about what gives itself to thought in the fundamental dispositions underlying his question of being, what made him write about a "knowing" of being, especially in light of his deep insight into the errancy belonging to all truth.[19]

What gives itself to thought is being "itself," being in terms of the "to be," certainly, but being itself *is* only through beings, and (when it comes to thinking, I would say) always also through the body. Being itself is always determined, concrete, unique in its moment. Heidegger, however, always pushes toward understanding this determination, concreteness, and uniqueness *not* in relation to beings. He seems to put beings in service to the truth of beyng. For instance, in section 242 of *Contributions* he underlines that the emptiness that opens up in exposure to the abyss of the truth of beyng is a "determined emptiness" (*eine bestimmte Leere*; this relates to *stimmen* and *Stimmung*, i.e., to attunement or disposition) (GA 65: 381–382; C: 301–302), and he thinks this determination as arising from the event and not in relation to a being (things, words, concrete events, etc.).

Yet how do we get from an attunement to a conceptual determination? How do concepts and words accrue to attunements?

If we think beyng and beings as not only occurring simultaneously but also co-originarily, we would have to say that every moment is characterized and determined *as well* by beings. When we seek words, there is our body in its open configuration, embodying lineages and concrete spatial-temporal settings. As soon as we articulate something, there are beings, words in the "how" of their meaning something. This does not preclude that, in being, there is always something exceeding beings, the nonsaid, the silence, the withdrawals at the fringe of which one may search for something to say.

Thinking in such a way (a way of thinking that takes us closer to Merleau-Ponty) has consequences with respect to reading and interpreting Heidegger's texts. We would have to understand Heidegger's thinking as always being in some way "contaminated," "tainted," or—using more positive terms—"infused" or "colored" (we might even use the word "mediated") by his concrete settings and experiences. The words "contaminated" and "infused" arise when one thinks of Heidegger's attempt to speak "purely" of the event. The words "infused" and "colored" arise when one thinks of the richness of occurrences and things marking each moment of being.

Should we not say that even grounding attunements (*Grundstimmungen*) that overcome us and unsettle us arise not out of a "pure" being but always also in certain contexts, contexts that remain mostly hidden to our awareness? But what about the primal anxiety relating to our own death? Does it not come, as Heidegger says in *Being and Time*, from "nowhere"? Is it not precisely nonrelational as it unsettles us from our involvement with beings? Basic dispositions or grounding attunements are marked by interruption and unsettlement, but such interruption and unsettlement are also interruption and unsettlement *from* determined situations and *toward* them. Yet when it comes to the fear of death, one might argue that its primal character gives it a special status such that it occurs not in relation to any specific modes of being or ways of being related.

However, above I sketched how over the years, the grounding attunements Heidegger discusses (anxiety, deep boredom, restraint) acquire more and more historical determinations. Whereas in *Being and Time*, anxiety discloses the possibility of not being at all and with that being possible as such (it discloses finite temporality as the horizon of being prior to any historical determination), in *Contributions* restraint discloses historical beyng: beyng's self-withdrawal as marking an epoch and bearing the possibility of the other beginning. Yet this history of beyng occurs with things and events even if they fail to disclose being in a fuller sense. We always also remain in a relationship with beings. This is why Heidegger says that errancy (which arises from our relation to beings) is always part of truth.[20] Grounding attunements also remain related to beings, even if in the mode of removal and distancing from them.

But what about attunements that are more clearly related to beings, such as the fear about something or a hopeful expectation of something, or an aversion toward something? Although we may differentiate attunements related to specific things from grounding attunements conceptually, is it not the case that part of the complexity of attunements has to do with undecidability with respect to how and in relation to what they arise? How can Heidegger be so sure that the lack he experiences is exclusively the lack marking an epoch of being? Furthermore, does this sense of lack or deficiency not arise as a response to concrete events? When we realize that dispositions arise always *also* in relation to the way being occurs concretely, we open the door to considering singular occurrences and the way they play into our dispositions. I say "play into" and not "cause" because I believe that causal thinking would be far too reductive for the complexity of the multiple encroaching modes of being that play into the formation of dispositions. Awareness of this complexity opens, however, a space of questioning that never allows us to be sure of the sources of our attunements and dispositions. In relation to Heidegger's thinking this means that we should keep in question the sources of the dispositions directing his thinking of the historicality of being.

It seems to me that what Heidegger lived through concretely, events of larger and smaller import, had to have an effect on his thinking, notwithstanding his powerful creativity and capacity to think at the limit of being and in constant awareness of dimensions of being withdrawing from our grasp.

The fact that we cannot be sure about the sources of our dispositions, especially of more unsettling dispositions, carries with it another issue: We may be mislead by our dispositions, misinterpret what they disclose, maybe because we are overwhelmed and blinded by them. I believe that this is what led Heidegger to his big mistake in embracing actively (if even for a short time) the National Socialist movement in the belief that it opened up the possibility of an originary call to the German people.[21] One may very well say that he did clearly sense that a fundamental unsettling event was happening, that with Hitler's rise to power the destiny of the German people was being shaped. But how could he really know, in those early years, in which direction this shaping of the German people and of many other people around the world would go?

On the other hand, it is apparent that when Heidegger interprets, with the notions of machination and lived experience, the dominant ways of being in our "Western" world, the fundamental dispositions at work in his thinking did disclose pervasive modes of being that are there for us to experience. Heidegger began to see events in Germany on the way to World War II and during the war not as openings for the other beginning of Western history but as being determined by machination and lived experience. (The *Black Notebooks* are a clear testimony to this.) The symptoms of machination Heidegger describes in section 58 of *Contributions* (organization, speed, "massification") and his emphasis on the negative power of "lived experience," which does not leave room for questioning because one believes to be closest to life (one "feels" truth in one's "guts")—all this fits our image of Nazi Germany and it makes sense to assume that Heidegger was responding to his historical situation. His description and analysis of machination, however, fits as well dominant ways of life that continue to evolve today in the Western hemisphere.

We may say, then, in concluding, that Heidegger's rethinking of the history of being was fundamentally animated not only by "the event" and by the history of Western philosophy, but also by "events," by concrete (embodied) historical occurrences of his time, even if his interpretation of them often seems reductive since everything, all religious and educational institutions and all political standpoints, were for him a form of machination. (I will take a more critical look at this in chapter 4.) The way he experienced his times drove him to continuous meditations (*Besinnungen*) on the roots of the abandonment of beings by beyng he experienced. This may be part of the reason that Heidegger would title the next volume of his poietic writings *Besinnung*.

Notes

1. This was the primary impetus for my first book: Daniela Neu, *Die Notwendigkeit der Gründung im Zeitalter der Dekonstruktion: Zur Gründung in Heideggers "Beiträgen zur Philosophie"; unter Hinzuziehung der Derridaschen Dekonstruktion* (Berlin: Duncker & Humblot, 1997).

2. Martin Heidegger, "The Origin of the Work of Art," in *Basic Writings*, 2nd ed., ed. David Farrell Krell (San Francisco: Harper San Francisco, 1992), 168 (hereafter cited as BW); "Der Ursprung des Kunstwerks," in *Holzwege*, ed. F.-W. von Herrmann (Frankfurt am Main: Klostermann, 1977).

3. Michel Haar distinguishes four meanings of earth: (1) the earth as arising-sheltering in an ontological sense; (2) earth in the sense of φύσις; (3) earth as the "material" of the work of art; and (4) earth as the native ground. See Michel Haar, *Le Chant de la Terre: Heidegger et les assises de l'histoire de l'être* (Paris: Editions de l'Herne, 1985), 122–126. In English: *The Song of the Earth: Heidegger and the Grounds of the History of Being*, trans. Reginald Lilly (Bloomington: Indiana University Press, 1993).

4. We can certainly explain the manifestation of heaviness and colors scientifically, but Heidegger is interested in the question of how we experience the being of a thing in its "earthly" quality.

5. *Contributions*, section 1.

6. See Kevin Aho, *Heidegger's Neglect of the Body* (Albany: State University of New York Press, 2009).

7. I worked this out in Daniela Vallega-Neu, *The Bodily Dimension in Thinking* (Albany: State University of New York Press, 2005), ch. 5.

8. This relates to the notion of "immemorial time" that, for instance, Ted Toadvine has developed in relation to Merleau-Ponty: Ted Toadvine, "Natural Time and Immemorial Nature," *Philosophy Today*, SPEP supplement (2009): 214–221.

9. "Errancy belongs to the inner constitution of Da-sein" (BW: 133). In "The Origin of the Work of Art" Heidegger speaks of the double concealment of truth as well. See GA 5: 40–41; BW: 178–179.

10. Babette Babich is right to highlight as well the strong influence of Nietzsche in Heidegger's *Black Notebooks*. See Babette Babich, "Heidegger's Black Night: The Nachlass and Its Wirkungsgeschichte," in *Reading Heidegger's* Black Notebooks 1931–1941, ed. Ingo Farin and Jeff Malpas (Cambridge, MA: MIT Press, 2016), 60, 63.

11. See in this context the work of Alejandro Vallega on ana-chronic simultaneous temporalities. Alejandro A. Vallega, *Latin American Philosophy from Identity to Radical Exteriority* (Bloomington: Indiana University Press, 2014), esp. 115–116.

12. See *Contributions*, section 87.

13. This is why Heidegger can rethink the event in section 267 starting with the indigence of the gods. Let me note as well that Heidegger will not speak of "the last god" in the last part of *Contributions* with the title "Beyng." This part was written later than the rest and shows a different emphasis in Heidegger's thinking of god and gods. In this part, he speaks mostly of the "indigence of the gods" or "indigence of the god" (*Notschaft der Götter*), thus stressing an approach to the gods out of the refusal of beyng.

14. See Friedrich Schellega, *Die Weltalter Fragmente in den Urfassungen von 1811 und 1813*, ed. Manfred Schröter (Munich: Biedersteing und Leibniz Verlag, 1946), 40–41. The quotation is part of a book by David Farrell Krell, *Ecstasy, Catastrophe: Heidegger from* Being and Time *to the* Black Notebooks (Albany: State University of New York Press, 2015), 167.

15. Friedrich Nietzsche, *Also Sprach Zarathustra*, in *Sämtliche Werke: Kritische Studienausgabe* (hereafter cited as KSA), vol. 1, ed. Giorgio Colli and Mazzino Montinari (Munich: DTV de Gruyter, 1980), 30. Cited in Krell, *Ecstasy, Catastrophe*, 167, 180–181.

16. KSA 4:187–189.

17. Richard Wolin, ed., *The Heidegger Controversy: A Critical Reader* (Cambridge, MA: MIT Press, 1993), 107.

18. See sections 5 and 6 of *Contributions*.

19. I will return to this question as well in the second part of chapter 4.

20. I discuss Heidegger's notion of errancy in chapter 4, "The Clearing of Beings and Errancy," and chapter 5, "Heidegger's Silence: Exposedness and Impotence."

21. See Heidegger, "The Rectorate 1933/34: Facts and Thoughts," in *Martin Heidegger and National Socialism: Questions and Answers*, trans. Lisa Harries, ed. Günther Neske and Emil Kettering (New York: Paragon House, 1990), 29.

4 *Besinnung* (*Mindfulness*) (GA 66)

The Composition of *Besinnung*

Besinnung was written in 1938–1939, right after *Contributions to Philosophy* and—although it thinks within the domains of questioning opened up by *Contributions*—it has a distinctly different character from the earlier volume. From the appendix to *Besinnung*, which contains reflections by Heidegger (written in 1936–1938) on his philosophical path so far, we can gather that since 1932 Heidegger was seeking "the basic position (*Grundstellung*) for the question concerning the truth of beyng" and that *Contributions*, which he refers to as *Of the Event* (*Vom Ereignis*), constitutes the first "shaping" or "form" (*Gestalt*) of the sought-after basic position (GA 66: 424).[1] In this first shaping of a new basic position, the task was not to unfold single issues but to open up the broad paths of questioning. Furthermore, Heidegger writes, "even here [in *Contributions*] *that* form has not yet been attained, which, precisely at this point, I demand for a publication as a 'work'" (GA 66: 427).

Besinnung is not a second attempt at drafting the new basic position Heidegger was seeking. The volume does not so much sketch out paths and domains of inquiry (as *Contributions* does) but contains many longer sections that indeed have the character of *Besinnungen*, of "meditations" on a variety of topics that were opened up in *Contributions*.[2] As an introduction to this volume we find a number of thoughts in verse that look like poems but that, Heidegger explicitly states, are not to be understood as poems or poetry but as "*a binding of the thinking word in the moment of gathered meditation [Besinnung]*."[3] The German word *Besinnung* would usually be translated as "mindfulness." It commonly connotes inwardness and stillness, a moment of gathering where one lets go of the hustle and bustle of everyday affairs and takes the time to reflect. It is also used in the context of someone who went astray and finally comes to her senses ("Sinn" means "sense" in the double sense of the word). While "mindfulness" captures much of what resonates in the word *Besinnung*, one might prefer to speak of "meditation" in order to avoid a sense of subjective inwardness. For Heidegger, his meditations are historical; they pertain to and address the historicality of beyng beyond (or prior to) any presupposed subjectivity. Like *Contributions*, *Besinnung* is an attempt to speak out of a disposition or attunement arising from historical beyng. Indeed, I would say that the tone of this volume is probably the only thing that holds it together, since there is no recognizable structural development in it. Heidegger does not move along the six junctures of *Contributions*, although one could say that he moves within them in various ways. He sometimes uses the word *Anklang* (resonating); he does not use the word *Zuspiel* (interplay) in the sense he gave it in *Contributions*.[4] He emphasizes the *leap*, and sometimes he speaks of the future ones and of the last god.

The attunement that prominently marks *Besinnung* is very much what resonates in that very word. We might address this as a certain gathering that occurs when we are mindful of something; Heidegger takes his time to reflect on many topics he had sketched out in *Contributions*. With respect to this peculiar tone of *Besinnung*, we can make sense of what he writes in the first section to *Die Geschichte des Seyns* (*The History of Beyng*, written in 1938/1940): " 'Contributions' are still frame but not a conjuncture; "Mindfulness" is a center, but not source" (GA 69: 5).[5]

Just as *Contributions*, *Besinnung* situates itself within the task of preparing the decision between the ultimate entrenchment of machination and the other beginning. It contains extensive meditations on the history of being, on machination, and power, and in that respect is close to both *Die Geschichte des Seyns* (to which I will refer in this chapter as well) and the *Black Notebooks* from that time. In 1938/1939 Heidegger is still lecturing on Nietzsche, and Heidegger's confrontation with Nietzsche's will to power reaches an extreme that emerges strongly from the text. One can also intimate that war was in the air, since Heidegger begins to speak of war and peace in relation to his notion of conflict (*Kampf*). The twenty-eight parts, into which the volume is divided, often contain only a few sections/meditations (thirteen of them contain only one section/meditation). The divisions have titles addressing beyng, philosophy, truth and knowing, beyng and humans, anthropomorphism, history and technology, power, the thinking of beyng, the forgetfulness of beyng, the gods, metaphysics, being as reality, being and time, and meditation. I will be able to address only a few concepts and am focusing on the ones I find most striking in this volume as I keep in mind Heidegger's path of thinking and the historical situation in which he writes. Given that the title of the volume is *Besinnung*, I will begin by looking at some passages in which he addresses this concept; then I will proceed to discuss the notions of power and what is without power (*das Machtlose*) and relate both to his Nietzsche lectures and to references he gives with respect to his current political situation. Next I will discuss how he now thinks the event as the carrying out (*Austragen*) of the encounter of gods and humans and the strife of world and earth. This will be followed by considerations of how he addresses truth in the notions of clearing and errancy. I will end my exposition of major themes in *Besinnung* with one of my main guiding threads in reading Heidegger's poietic writings: the relation between beyng and beings.

Besinnung and *Die Geschichte des Seyns* are perhaps the poietic writings that in their character are closest to the *Black Notebooks*. For this reason, I will dedicate a longer section to these notebooks in chapter 5, prior to continuing with *Über den Anfang* from 1941.

Besinnung (Meditation/Mindfulness) in Preparation of the Decision over History

The notion of "meditation" already appears in *Contributions* in the same contexts in which it appears in *Besinnung*. Heidegger speaks especially of (1) "historical meditation" (*geschichtliche Besinnung*), that is, of the necessity to meditate on the history of being. But he also addresses meditation in a second context, that of (2) philosophy meditating on itself (*Selbstbesinnung der Philosophie*).[6]

1. Heidegger repeatedly and emphatically places meditation in the context of *the* decision over history. Section 8 is titled "Zur Besinnung,"[7] which could mean either "concerning meditation" or "for meditation," and begins with a dramatic tone. It highlights the preparation of the grounding of "the *one decision*": "Whether the machination of beings would overpower humans and unleash them to the unshackled essence of power, or whether beyng would gift the grounding of its truth as the plight out of which the *encounter* of the god and humans crosses the *strife* of earth and world. Such a crossing is the conflict of all conflicts: the appropriating event, in which beings first are consigned to their belongingness to beyng" (GA 66: 15).

The following three sentences all highlight the world "conflict" (*Kampf*) that Heidegger contrasts to "mere" war and peace (which are dominated by machination).[8] The notion of *Kampf* is prevalent in all of his writings of the 1930s and in a variety of contexts. Some remarks in the *Black Notebooks* give me the impression that Heraclitus's *polemos* inspired Heidegger's predilection for this term (GA 94: 113, 217; Ü III: 7; Ü IV: 10).[9] In the passage from section 8 just quoted, conflict names the appropriating event that has the character of carrying out: *Aus-trag*. (I will consider this concept more closely later.) The crossing of gods, humans, earth and world in the appropriating event would mark the moment of history (the decision) that Heidegger can only prepare, and this preparation requires a historical meditation on the truth of beyng. In the following section 9, he highlights especially the meditation on the essence of his age, an age that (in another sense) this meditation has already left since beyng historical thinking is already determined by the other beginning it seeks to prepare (GA 66: 25).[10] In other words, the preparation for the decision over history, for the conflict, is already wedded to the truth of beyng in its inceptuality and requires the leap ahead into Da-sein and thus into another, more inceptive realm of history. From here Heidegger meditates on the history of metaphysics especially in its completion (modernity) that he thinks predominantly in relation to Nietzsche's notion of will to power. Using the fugue structure of *Contributions*, one might say that historical meditation addresses the resonating and the interplay, but out of the leap ahead into the truth of beyng. That thinking is already decided here (for or rather by the other beginning) is important for Heidegger: "The preparation for that unique decision can be enacted only by leaping ahead into an appropriate decidedness that—reckoned 'historically' [*historisch*]—is not yet 'actual,' discernible or effective, and has nonetheless taken over the history of the other beginning as the history of the essential occurrence of the truth of beyng" (GA 66: 23).[11]

2. The second way the notion of meditation figures prominently (besides its necessity in order to prepare the other beginning of history) is in the context of philosophy's meditation on itself. Since philosophy as the thinking "of" the truth of beyng is (or tries to be) appropriated by the event, philosophy's meditation on itself amounts to meditating on how thinking belongs to the truth of beyng. Insofar as philosophy stands in the clearing of the truth of beyng and thus preserves this clearing, it has the character of an "essential knowing" (GA 66: 50).[12] And yet, such knowing is always in danger of losing its essence, says Heidegger, and he mentions as dangers philosophy's losing itself either to "science" or to poetry (from which philosophy remains distinguished in "the cold audacity of the question of being") (GA 66: 51), or in world views. Part of philosophy's meditation on itself concerns, then, its differentiation from science, poetry, and worldviews, in order to find a way back to philosophy's proper essence. Philosophy has to meditate on the unique way in which it belongs to beyng such that it leaps ahead into the truth of beyng and "*is* inception [*Anfang*]" (GA 66: 53). Only if philosophy occurs as inception, says Heidegger, "is the power of beings and their pursuits broken and with these reckoning with aims" (GA 66: 53). Philosophy has to continuously find its way back to beyng (out of which it is granted) in order not to be lost in the pursuit of beings and the reckoning with them.

The path of beyng, though, is a lonely one. In section 14 Heidegger will continue, then, to meditate on thoughtful saying of the event (in distinction to the word of the poet), on the "strangeness," "loneliness," and "exposedness" of this saying. Philosophy's saying has this character and must occur as meditation because beyng itself is *unabwägbar*, it cannot be weighed or measured, and *is* as "lonesomeness" (*Vereinsamung*). Beyng cannot be compared or contrasted to beings or nothingness. Beyng is not a concept Heidegger can hold on to, but the groundless happening of all that is. Thus, inceptive philosophy is without shelter and always remains exposed to the danger of losing its essence as it prepares the possibility of the event in its historical happening, a happening that would be marked by the encounter of gods and humans, and the strife of world and earth.[13]

The few moments of section 14 (titled "Philosophy in the Meditation on Itself") I am highlighting let resonate certain attunements permeating this text and indicate the intimate connection between the questioning of philosophy (thought as inceptive thinking) and the questioning of beyng itself in its (possible) occurrence as historical event. Later in the volume we find a whole subdivision with sixteen sections in it, titled "A Gathering of Meditation" (*Eine Sammlung des Besinnens*) that bespeaks as well the more intimate dimension of the historicality of beyng, in which Heidegger thinks ahead into the possibility of the other beginning.

* * *

Before discussing the themes in *Besinnung* that in some way move along the two contexts of the notion of "meditation" as I just introduced it, I would like to make an anticipatory remark regarding the performative dimension of Heidegger's writing. In my reading of *Contributions*, I highlighted a certain tension in his style of speaking, a tension tied to the notion of decision, withstanding, and steadfast knowing. *Besinnung* has a similar character in that this volume still emphasizes decision and steadfast knowing; the clear allusions to present times give this emphasis an even more urgent character. At the same time, it is noteworthy that Heidegger hardly speaks of restraint (*Verhaltenheit*), which is the predominant name for the grounding attunement in *Contributions*, and let me also recall that *Verhaltenheit*, has the word "halten," "holding," in it and contributes much to a sense of tension in the earlier volume. In *Besinnung*, however, at the same time that he presents more forcefully his critique of power and machination in his current age, a different tone starts to emerge and with this tone a different comportment. This different tone is tied to the notion of "what is without power" that comes up later in *Besinnung* and contrasts with the will to power that Heidegger sees at work in his present age.

Power and Nietzsche's Will to Power

Heidegger addresses power and what is without power especially in sections 9 ("Machination [Violence, Power, Dominion]") and 65 ("Beyng and Power"). We saw in chapter 2 how in *Contributions to Philosophy*, he speaks of machination in a wider and a narrower sense. In the wider sense, machination names the approach to being through the way thinking relates to beings, namely, representationally along a sense of "makeability" in the widest sense. In this sense, machination finds its roots in the Ancient Greek notions of τέχνη and ποίησις and comes to the fore in the medieval notion of the creator god and the *ens creatum* (created beings). In the narrower sense, machination addresses the final stage of metaphysics where beings are unleashed into machination such that the ultimate dominion of machination threatens to undermine the very possibility of questioning being and with it the possibility of transforming our basic relation to things. (Let me recall here that machination is not in the power of humans but rather that humans are in the power of machination; we find ourselves compelled to think and act in terms of machination.) It is the more narrow sense of machination that Heidegger has in mind in section 9 of *Besinnung*, where he relates machination to violence (*Gewalt*) and power. He writes: "Now, however, machination disposes beings as such into the playing field of continuous *annihilation*, a playing field that constantly plays into machination. The essence of machination that already by threatening annihilation always annihilates and unfolds itself, is violence. This violence develops into the securing of power; a capacity that immediately breaks out and becomes less and less capable of transformation, a self-surpassing and spreading capacity for subjugation without discretion" (GA 66: 16).

What Heidegger addresses here as annihilation does not refer to the destruction of things or killing of people but relates more fundamentally (if we think here with Heidegger) to the annihilation of the very being of beings, to a degree of abandonment of beings by being as a whole that threatens to sever the possibility that beings may ever become again "more being," that is, that they may ever again harbor truth and thus participate in providing a site for the encounter of humans and gods and the strife of earth and world. Heidegger thinks ahead into this possibility of a definite loss of the possibility of essential history in his interpretation of Nietzsche's will to power (as will to will) and the eternal return. Clarifying this connection warrants a look at Heidegger's Nietzsche interpretation.

* * *

Heidegger's Nietzsche lectures span from 1936 to 1940 and place Nietzsche more and more decidedly in the position of the one who completes metaphysics. One may only wonder if this interpretation of Nietzsche was influenced by Heidegger's change of mind with respect to the National Socialist movement such that his criticism of his times brought him to read Nietzsche with "more narrow" eyes. In order to sketch out Heidegger's later interpretation of Nietzsche, I will refer to a text titled "Nietzsche's Metaphysics,"[14] originally composed in 1940. It provides something like a summary of Heidegger's interpretations of basic concepts of Nietzsche's philosophy in the previous lecture courses he gave and reflects the sharpest stance Heidegger took with respect to Nietzsche in his later lecture courses.

Heidegger interprets the "will to power" as the basic character of beings as such (N: 193). It is the basic character of "life," which Heidegger interprets as another name for being (understood as beingness). The will to power is a will to master. It is, however, not the will to master something else; rather the will commands such that the one who commands obeys the disposition over possibilities of action, which means that commanding aims at a self-mastering in the form of a self-overcoming (N: 195). Thus, the notion of "power" in "will to power" does not address something outside the willing; rather power is intrinsic to the willing. Now "power empowers solely by becoming master over every stage of the power reached" (N: 195). Given that power is intrinsic to the willing (power as a becoming master of oneself is a form of willing), and power strives for continuous enhancement, Heidegger can say that the will to power is a will to will. Self-overcoming and the enhancement of power also requires preservation since every stage of power must be established and secured in order then to be overcome. Heidegger interprets preservation and enhancement as conditions of power, which Nietzsche thinks as values. These values in turn are viewpoints. Thus Heidegger can say that every being, insofar as it occurs as will to power, is "perspectival" and "will to power is in its innermost essence a perspectival reckoning with the conditions of its possibility, conditions that it itself posits as such" (N: 199).

The movement of life as the will to power that wills itself in the continuous establishing and overcoming of established values, is intrinsically tied to nihilism and the eternal return of the same. Nihilism is the event that the highest values devalue themselves. This means that the movement of being or the movement of life (as a movement of will to power) has no value outside itself determining it; no final goal; it is valueless and meaningless (N: 209). It is here that the will to power connects with the "eternal return of the same." Since there is no final goal, no final "good" in which the movement of the will to power would come to rest, it can go nowhere else but back to the same. While the will to power names being in terms of *what* it is (the will to will), the eternal return names being in terms of *how* it is (N: 211–212).

For Heidegger, Nietzsche's experience of nihilism was genuine, although Nietzsche could not see how nihilism is ultimately rooted in the withdrawal of beyng that unleashes beings into machination (reckoning with values is a guise of machination). Nietzsche could not think the truth of being but remained bound to representational thinking and to thinking truth in terms of correspondence. Thinking with Heidegger, one might say that, thought to the extreme, the will to power is the movement of being insofar as it finds no more hold in beings because beings are groundless, abandoned by beyng. The representational comportment toward beings that for Heidegger marks metaphysics loses its *Gegenstand*, it loses what stands (*-stand*) over against (*Gegen-*) subjectivity.[15] All that remains now is the self-overpowering movement of subjective "life." Beings are, in a certain sense, annihilated; they are uprooted from the truth of beyng and absorbed into the self-overpowering movement of "life" that can stay alive only if it seeks ever-new "goals" and "values" by overcoming (and annihilating) previously set values.

The movement of the will to power and the eternal return of the same is a form of machination that completes itself, says Heidegger, in *Erlebnis*, in lived experience that in *Contributions* he describes in the following way: "To relate beings as the represented *to oneself* as the relational center and thus to incorporate them into 'life'" (GA 65: 129; C: 102). Beings are drawn into the self-relational movement of life. They are no longer objects for the perceiving subject but means of life enhancement.

In Heidegger's interpretation, Nietzsche's doctrine of the affirmation of the eternal return is the ultimate affirmation of nihilism, of the groundlessness of being. If we look at Heidegger's powerful interpretation of the eternal return in the lecture course of summer semester 1937, *The Eternal Recurrence of the Same*, we can see that the issue is not that the same things return but rather whether one can *will* that *everything* return, everything without ground or meaning, without reason or final goal. The ability to affirm life to such an extent requires the overman (*Übermensch*), the overman Zarathustra could only announce. The overman alone can—in *amor fati* (love of fate)—give himself to the movement of the will to power in the eternal return such that he wills and incorporates this movement. The eternal return and the will to power belong together in that the self-overpowering power occurs in the eternal return of the same. There is no measure outside this movement of groundless and always anew goal-setting-and-destroying movement of life.

* * *

If we now go back to the quotation from section 9 of *Besinnung*, we can recognize in Heidegger's descriptions of machination the movement of the will to power as he thinks it in connection with the eternal return. Machination addresses the make-ability, the setting and reckoning with new goals that overcomes previous goals. Machination disposes things into annihilation insofar as it holds sway as violence in the securing of power by continuously subjugating everything anew for the sake of a constant increase and securing of power. The notion of overpowering power reappears in many other passages in the same section:

> As the essence of beings, as the way how beings as such *are* through and through, machination compels the complete unleashing of all forces capable of power and of transforming power into the self-overpowering of power. (GA 66: 17–18)

> The self-overpowering distinctive of all power does indeed leave behind each level and range of power that was gained (the annihilation belonging to power as the preliminary form of the devastation that is essential for the unconditionality of power). And yet, this self-surrendering with respect to each phase of power contains and carries on the self-addiction [*Selbstsucht*] of the unconditioned self-entrenchment. (GA 66: 20)

For Heidegger this self-entrenched self-overpowering of power relates to the way people insist on what is "right." Furthermore he interprets the seeking for ever-new and appropriate opponents as being rooted in the deployment of power, given that power needs opposition for its movement of self-overcoming. One can see, thus, a clear connection Heidegger makes between his interpretation of Nietzsche and events he concretely observed around him. When Heidegger found people seeking power or exhibiting self-righteousness, he saw this as being rooted in an event that "transcends" single individuals. Strictly speaking, the overpowering of power is not dependent on any single individual; rather individuals are caught up in this movement.

Heidegger is explicit about this earlier when (still in section 9) he links machination to technology and the participating subject. To machination belongs a reckoning with things such that in advance things are required to be available for being installed or arranged. He then writes: "Out of this essential and at the same time concealed requirement springs modern technology. The latter frees humans into the drive to arrange its masses such that through this arrangement [*Gliederung*] any human particularization is overpowered, because any particularization—in [the] form of the participating [*mitmachende*] subject that only *seemingly* still drives and guides—must insert itself into what can be made" (GA 66: 17).[16]

The insight Heidegger has here is close to what Hannah Arendt termed "the banality of evil" after observing the trials of Eichmann.[17] She found in Eichmann an ordinary man following orders without any sense of responsibility. The evil lies in the system governing in advance the actions of individuals. Foucault has a similar insight when he thinks of the Panopticon as representing the play of power beyond individual subjects. Power effects (creates) submissive subjects and is in the hands of no one.

*   *   *

I noted above how Heidegger understands the essence of machination, insofar as it unfolds into annihilation such that power is secured through continuous submission, as violence (*Gewalt*). To violence he contrasts *Herrschaft* and *Entscheidung*, sovereignty and decision (GA 66: 16–17), a contrast that might seem odd given that one can easily associate violence with sovereignty and decision, and that the notions of sovereignty and decision bear a certain force with them. Heidegger, however, thinks sovereignty *without* violence out of and in relation to beyng. Just as violence, sovereignty is not an attribute of a human being but rather something determining human being in an originary way. "Sovereignty springs from the grounding capacity of decision" (GA 66: 16), Heidegger writes. It belongs to beyng itself and has "dignity" (*Würde*). Violence, on the other hand, precludes any kind of essential decision, closes off the essential realm of beyng. "Everything that has the nature of power or despotism . . . inherently avoids such decisions" (GA 66: 19). There is decidedness (*Entschiedenheit*) in the commanding of power but this decidedness does not derive from an essential decision that harbors, let us say a more "genuine" or originary relation to the truth of beyng.

The notion of sovereignty in relation to the truth of beyng in its concealed inceptuality was already very much present in *Contributions*. "Herrschaft" has the word *Herr* (lord) in it but is often used in the verbal form *herrschen* in terms of "reigning"—such as when a certain tone reigns in a speech or a sovereign reigns over his people. Heidegger will always hold on to this sense of sovereignty with respect to beyng in its originary occurring. And yet, all the while, beyng refuses itself and lets machination "reign." The inceptual reigning of beyng, though, is more intimate, more concealed, and all-preserving; whereas the dominion of machination is loud, public, and all-consuming.

And yet, insofar as—or rather if—it occurs as decision (something that Heidegger's meditations can only prepare), beyng occurs in a thrust that severs (*scheidet*) from the abyss of beyng "the machination of beings and the human as the historical animal" such that the latter "are left to their own lack of origin" (GA 66: 24).

What Is without Power (*das Machtlose*)

Such a forceful appeal to the thrust (could we say "power"?) of beyng as Heidegger thinks it with respect to the historical decision concerning the other beginning stands in stark contrast to the notion of "what is without power" (*das Machtlose* is to be distinguished from *Das Ohnmächtige*, "the powerless") that emerges later in *Besinnung*. The texts in this volume were written 1938–1939 and if the order of the texts is chronological, one might infer that some change happens in 1939, the year World War II broke out.

The first occurrence of the notion of what is without power (and Heidegger highlights this word) occurs in section 49: "As the event of refusal, beyng guards its singularity in the uniqueness of its clearing, through which what is essentially *without power* becomes alienating with respect to beings in how they 'usually' are (the effective [*Wirkendes*]) and yet it [what is without power] disseminates them in their hidden groundlessness and ensconces for the gods the time-space of a nearness and remoteness" (GA 66: 130).

When beyng's refusal clears up, it becomes manifest as occurring without power and in strangeness with respect to beings and their effectiveness. This creates a spacing, a time-space for a realm that seems removed from what happens with beings. "The unusualness of beyng . . . has the whole of beings against it" (GA 66: 130), writes Heidegger. Thus, the notion of what is without power is tied to the differencing of beings and beyng (that I will look at more closely later).

In section 51, being without power appears in a slightly different context, namely, in the context of human steadfastness in the truth of beyng: "Beyng-historically, this steadfastness [*Inständigkeit*] . . . is without power the domination over machination. The power of machination only collapses when it reaches the empowerment of its overpowering such that it can no longer eschew what uniquely withholds itself from its violence: the groundlessness of the truth *of* being that itself is in a machinational way" (GA 66: 135).

Here human indwelling in the abyssal truth of beyng is said to be without power, such that it "dominates" (*beherrscht*) machination. "What is without power" (*das Machtlose*) is *outside* of power and powerlessness (*Unmacht*). The power-less (*das Ohn-mächtige*), on the other hand, still relates to power in that it lacks it (GA 66: 187–188). That the human being is outside of the power play of machination is what constitutes its "dominion" over machination; such dominion has the sense of being removed from machinationally deployed beings to such an extent that one is no longer touched by machination. Indeed, we find this interesting sentence later in *Besinnung*: "What is without power can not be disempowered" and this is a consequence of its "nobility" (*Adel*) (GA 66: 191).

What begins to appear here, in the notion of "what is without power," is a sentiment or disposition (Heidegger, of course, would not want to speak of "sentiment" because of its subjective connotation) that will become increasingly dominant in Heidegger's thinking of the 1940s and that will be tied to notions such as poverty, nobility, and dignity. This new disposition arises at the same time that he thinks a most extreme development of machination. He thinks of machination as escalating into the empowerment of its overpowering to such a point that it removes itself from its hidden origin that now clears itself, removed from the self-encircling raging of machinational being. One is reminded here of the beginning lines of Hölderlin's *Patmos*: "Where there is danger, there rescue grows too."[18] In the most extreme abandonment of beings by beyng lies the possibility of a clearing of beyng in its withdrawal, that is, the clearing of the truth of beyng.

Section 65, "Beyng and Power," is where Heidegger speaks of what is without power most pronouncedly. The word appears in the context of his critique of an understanding of beings as being real or actual and efficacious. The German words I am translating with these adjectives are *das Wirkliche* and *Wirklichkeit*. *Wirklich* means "real" or "actual" and *Wirklichkeit* means "reality" or "actuality." The words are closely related to *Wirken*, "to effect," and Heidegger plays with these different interwoven notions. That beings are seen in terms of their "effective actuality" is linked to their being objects for a productive comportment, a productive comportment that in the final stage of machination takes the form of will to power. The effectual capable of effecting (*das Wirkunsfähige Wirkende*) is "will as power" (GA 66: 187).

It is because beyng remains outside the domain of power that it remains sheltered from machination. Yet on the other hand, machination, that is, the abandonment of beings by being, has its roots in the truth of beyng (roots from which, at the completion of metaphysics, it begins to uproot itself in the self-encircling will to will). Again and again, Heidegger rethinks this event of the first beginning, the beginning of the abandonment of beings by beyng, in which being arises in its determination as presence. In the accounts he gives, at the beginning, being occurs as presencing of beings (φύσις) so powerfully that the truth of being (the unconcealing-concealing of beyng) remains unthought and ungrounded. What is interesting, here, is that Heidegger attributes to inceptive φύσις power in a "positive" sense.

In *Contributions*, Heidegger thinks the first beginning in which the truth of beyng remains ungrounded, in terms of the "Entmachtung der φύσις," that is, the disempowerment of φύσις, and in connection with the collapse (*Einsturz*) of ἀλήθεια. Φύσις loses its power with respect to τέχνη in that through τέχνη humans gain a stance (indeed, find themselves compelled to take a stance) in the midst of the overwhelming power of being (φύσις). Heidegger already worked these relations out in the lecture course *Introduction to Metaphysics* (SS 1935).[19] In *Basic Questions of Philosophy*[20] (a lecture course he held at the same time he was writing *Contributions* in WS 1937/1938), he describes the relation of τέχνη to φύσις roughly in the following way. Originally, τέχνη is a know-how, a form of knowledge through which beings are grasped as they emerge, that is, as they appear and are seen (*eidos*) in unconcealment. Τέχνη is literally a productive knowledge, a knowledge that brings forth and holds present what presences. "Τέχνη is a mode of proceeding *against* φύσις, though not yet in order to overpower it or to exploit it . . . but on the contrary, to retain the holding sway of φύσις in unconcealedness" (GA 45: 179–180; BQP: 155). Yet, as a consequence, thinking unfolds as a stance toward beings, in a "constant assimilation to them" (GA 45: 181; BQP: 156). Thus truth begins to have the character of correspondence between things and intellect and the original essence of truth as unconcealment (ἀλήθεια) remains unthought. At the same time, φύσις is disempowered (*entmachtet*). Yet in Heidegger's reading, with the earliest Greek thinkers, τέχνη does not overpower φύσις; this happens only later when the stance of thinking against beings develops in such a way that the *eidos* or ἰδέα is taken as the essence of being itself. The presencing (φύσις in its arising) recedes for the sake of what is constantly present (beings in their *eidos*).

The phrase Heidegger uses to describe the beginning demise of Western history: "disempowerment of φύσις" betrays an affirmation of the notion of power as something "positive." If we look at his notebooks from 1932, we can see that he speaks of a necessity of empowering being (*Seinsermächtigung*) (GA 94; Ü II, 46, 48, 54, 57, 74–75, 83, 238, 243) and in *Contributions to Philosophy*, he also speaks of power in affirming ways.[21] In *Besinnung*, however, he begins to question even his phrase "disempowerment of φύσις": "Earlier considerations ("Contributions") speak of the disempowerment of φύσις. Thus inceptively and properly 'power'— in what sense?" (GA 66: 188). At the same time, he still seems to want to justify or make sense of it: "The power of φύσις . . . is its being without power" (GA 66: 188).

A generous reading of Heidegger would require that we distinguish different meanings of power, that we distinguish the power of beings from the "power" of being that in the first beginning is so "powerful" that it compels a stance against it. Thus, being as φύσις will lead to machination and is the source of machination, a source, however, that somehow disengages itself from what it gives rise to. Indeed, Heidegger goes so far as to say: "In leaving beingness to beings beyng . . . refuses itself and preserves itself for the unique gifting—without trace and without power" (GA 66: 200).

I already pointed out that although beyng is without power, for Heidegger, it nevertheless has "sovereignty." I also announced that this notion is tied to the notions of poverty and dignity. In section 65a, he writes: "Sovereignty in the inceptive sense does not need power; it reigns out of the dignity, that simple superiority of essential poverty that, in order to be, does not need something below or against itself" (GA 66: 193). As far as I know, this is the first passage in which he speaks of poverty. In *Geschichte des Seyns* (*History of Beyng*), which gathers texts from 1938 to 1940, the notion of poverty appears increasingly together with that of dignity,[22] and both will remain basic words for Heidegger in the 1940s along with the notion of *Gelassenheit* (releasement). The same is true for the word *Langmut* (forbearance, patience, literally "long-animity"),[23] and other words ending in -mut (courage or mood).[24] In *Besinnung*, he pairs *Langmut* with *Starkmut* ("strength of spirit"). He writes: "The decision remains whether the human being can experience the plight that is prepared in advance by such need, whether he knows that strength of spirit [*Starkmut*] and forbearance [*Langmut*] that essentially surpasses all power, violence, and entrenchment" (GA 66: 85).[25]

All these new words that I have been emphasizing bear attunements that begin to emerge in *Besinnung* and will take more and more space in Heidegger's poietic writings. In *Langmut* resonates a sense of time that is not pressured by outside events; in dignity and magnanimity resonates—in the context of poverty—a noble-mindedness that, again, is not disturbed by the hustle and bustle of common life; there is no need, no plight in the poverty and dignity of beyng. This is a different attitude from the emphasis on the acknowledgment of the lack of plight characterizing *Contributions*, as well as from the predominance of restraint (*Verhaltenheit*), which suggest tension, sustaining, and enduring a lack.

It is noteworthy that in *Besinnung*, the new attunements appear at the same time that Heidegger pushes his reading of Nietzsche to the extreme. He combines his interpretation of the will to power as a will to will with accounts of the unfolding of machination into violence and with critiques of current events. It appears that his thinking finds a refuge from the escalations of machination in the poverty and dignity of beyng.

A look at *The History of Beyng* (GA 69) might be helpful to see how the word clusters I have been looking at develop. The notion of "what is without power" is not as prominent. But Heidegger will speak more often of poverty (*Armut*). Indeed two sections (99 and 100) bear it as a title (GA 69: 105–107, 110, 111, 116, 117, 119, 123, 217, 219). Here as well as in other text passages, he speaks of poverty not in the sense of neediness but rather in terms of a process (*Verarmung*, becoming poor) out of which a gifting occurs. Thus poverty comes to designate the essence of beyng as appropriation (GA 69: 110). As to the notion of dignity, it appears in *The History of Beyng* (just as in *Besinnung*) in contrast to power (GA 69: 74; section 58). The notion of *Langmut*, "forbearance," is now mentioned together with *Zuversicht*, "confidence."[26] In section 91 this confidence gains a new tonality, that of joy: "The essence of joy, this confidence is what disposes in the grounding attunement of serene magnanimity and intimate forbearance. This confidence strong enough in its essence in order to take on *shock* and *unsettlement*" [sic] (GA 69: 105–106).[27]

My emphasis on these new attunements should not lead erroneously into thinking that the decisional tone disappears in Heidegger's writings of 1938–1940. Heidegger continues his meditations on machination, devastation, and power, and more often in clear reference to current events. But a shift begins to occur in the grounding attunements, a shift that appears to coincide with the beginning of the war and I will reflect more on this in chapter 5. First, however, I will continue my exposition of major themes in *Besinnung*. I will now turn to the notion of "the event," marking some shifts in how Heidegger thinks it compared to *Contributions*.

The Event: The Carrying Out (*Austrag*) of the Encounter (*Entgegnung*) between Gods and Humans and the Strife (*Streit*) of World and Earth

The first striking change with respect to *Contributions* is that in *Besinnung* as well as in *Geschichte des Seyns*, Heidegger drops the notion of *Kehre*, the "turning" in the event. (It does not appear once in either of these volumes but it will play a major role again in *The Event*.) In *Contributions*, the notion of the turning is central for Heidegger and I believe that the reason we find this notion in *Contributions* but not in the subsequent two volumes is due to the way Heidegger introduces the event in departure from *Being and Time*. I noted in chapter 1 how Heidegger found the language of *Being and Time* to be inadequate for addressing the question of being as such and that whereas in this earlier work he approached being in its temporality (the truth of being) through Dasein's transcendence *into* the temporal horizon of being, in *Contributions* he ventures to think and speak *out of* the horizon of being. This has led Heidegger scholars to speak of a *Kehre*, a turning in his thinking. As Heidegger explained in his famous letter to Richardson, however, what is at stake in the turning is not simply a change of viewpoint; rather we ought to situate the turning in the very way the truth of being itself occurs.[28]

In *Contributions* Heidegger speaks of the turning in the event in different ways. He most often speaks of it as the turning between call and belonging (*Zugehörigkeit* contains the word *hören*, "hearing") of Da-sein (and with Da-sein of humans) to beyng;[29] or he speaks of the turning relation between the throw of beyng and the thrown-projection of Da-sein.[30] In any case, the emphasis is on the relation between the event and human being. Heidegger himself noted this with respect to section 255 of *Contributions*: "Here the event is viewed with respect to the human being, who is determined as Dasein on the basis of the event" (GA 65: 407; C: 322). I suspect that the emphasis on the relation to the human in the notion of the turning in *Contributions* (which we find especially when he speaks of call and listening-belonging) may be a main reason why he will (temporarily) drop the notion of turning in *Besinnung* and *Die Geschichte des Seyns*. Instead, in *Besinnung* the essential occurrence of the truth of beyng (*Wesung der Wahrheit des Seyns*) is articulated repeatedly as the carrying out (*Austrag*) of the encounter of gods and humans and the strife of earth and world.[31] The shift away from articulating the event primarily in terms of the relation between the throw or call of the event and the response or thrownness of humans, is consistent with a growing effort to think beyng not primarily in relation to humans, that is, *neither on the basis of human beings relating to being nor on the basis of the relation of beyng toward humans.*[32] That shift occurs in many places in *Contributions to Philosophy*, but not consistently.[33] I would like to note, however, that in the last part of the *Contributions to Philosophy*, which was written later than the rest (1938), Heidegger already does not think the event along the notion of turning (*Kehre*) and begins to articulate the event out of the relation between gods and humans. Sections 267 and 277 both say how out of the encounter between gods and humans arises the strife between world and earth and out of this strife beings arise into the clearing. But only in *Besinnung* will he speak of the *Austrag*, the carrying out of the strife between earth and world and the encounter between humans and gods, and this without the sequential unfolding of the event suggested in sections 267 and 277 of *Contributions*.[34]

In section 16 of *Besinnung* Heidegger writes:

> Appropriating event—that mutually assigns into the carrying out [*zum Aus-trag*] the encounter and the ones that en-counter, the strife and the ones that stand in the strife, and that—as the appropriation of this appropriating assignment— clears the abyssal ground [*Ab-grund*] such that in the clearing itself their essence—and this means the most inceptive truth—grounds itself.

> Beyng—nothing divine, nothing human, nothing worldly, nothing earthly—and still for all in one the in-between—unexplainable, without effect, outside of power and powerlessness beyng essentially occurs. (GA 66: 83)

Here we can see how Heidegger introduces the notions of the event and of beyng not in the dual structure beyng–human (call–belonging), nor out of the primary encounter between gods and humans, but rather as the eventuating of a fourfold opening or clearing. (This may be what he alludes to when in the first section of *Die Geschichte des Seyns* he writes that *Besinnung* is a center but not yet origin. That it is not yet origin will become clear once we look at the later poietic writings *On Inception* and *The Event*.) The four in the fourfold clearing are paired differently; gods and humans en-counter each other, world and earth stand in strife. In the appropriating event they are carried out such that the event occurs as this carrying out. *Aus-trag* highlights both the "aus-," which means "out" and the "-trag," which means "to carry." In this carrying out (we may hear this as well literally), a clearing of abyssal truth happens, that is, Da-sein, the "there-being" of the four. Or perhaps one should say instead: in the carrying out, a clearing would happen if the appropriating event occurred (since this is still to be historically decided).

A little later in section 13 of *Besinnung*, Heidegger will highlight that such carrying out needs to be "fought out" or decided. He will speak again of the event as conflict (*Kampf*) (that is to be distinguished from war and peace) between encounter and strife. He writes of the encounter as a decision concerning the essential occurrence between gods and humans and how in the strife the essence of world and earth are assigned (GA 66: 84).

Thinking needs to situate itself in this conflict and needs to think out of it. The task of thoughtful questioning is to think beyng as event "from the 'world' and from the 'earth,' from the human and from the god—but at the same time always out of the strife and their encounter and above all out of their conflict" (GA 66: 84). Such thinking is itself appropriated by beyng and can be carried out only in steadfastness or indwelling (*Inständigkeit*) in *being* there (Da-*sein*). This requires the projecting leaping into the clearing itself such that humans do not think beyng (as directed) toward themselves but rather think "ahead of *themselves* into beyng and its clearing" (the grammar of the German sentence is quite unusual: *der Mensch denkt . . . sich im Wesen in das Seyn und seine Lichtung zuvor*, which suggests that Heidegger placed great heed in articulating the movement of thinking even against standard grammatical rules) (GA 66: 85). The movement of thinking that he suggests here again seems closer to the movement of projective ek-stasis (standing out) as we find it in *Being and Time*, but Heidegger's unusual phrasing tries to convey the "always already" being ahead of oneself more radically. We find the same movement in the fifth thinking "poem," titled "The Knowing," from the introduction to *Besinnung*:

Indeed we never *are* ones who know,
yet in knowing we *are* [beings]
questioning beyond ourselves,
the clearing of beyng. (GA 66: 7)

The Clearing

The emphasis in the way that Heidegger thinks the event shifts, then, in *Besinnung* away from the perhaps more preparatory call-response structure to the thinking ahead (in a leaping ahead and into the clearing of beyng) into the carrying out of the event in the encounter of gods and humans and the strife of world and earth.[35] With the notion of "carrying out" also comes a slightly different sense and more pronounced emphasis on the notion of clearing (*Lichtung*),[36] such that Heidegger emphasizes not only the opening up of encounter and strife but also more pronouncedly light (*Licht* means light) all the while maintaining the abyssal character of the clearing.

In section 36 of *Besinnung*, titled "The Clearing," Heidegger speaks of a "double essential occurrence of clearing: *as dark glow* (*Glut*) of the attuning attunement out of the abyss of beyng and *as simple clarity* (*Helle* means the state of being brightly lit) of the knowing comprehension (*Inbegriff*) for steadfastness in the in-between.[37] Both are not yet gained in their originary unity. Both necessitate the transformation of the essence of human beings into Da-sein" (GA 66: 108). The word "glow" appears several times both in *Contributions* and in *Besinnung*. *Glut* is also the name for embers that can yield another fire. They bespeak the clearing of the abyss, of what is most concealed and "what" (there is not really a "what" here but only a middle voice occurrence of clearing) disposes or attunes inceptual thinking and saying. In section 109 Heidegger makes this context apparent as well: "Light and what has the quality of light is at the same time the still glow. Understood beyng-historically, clearing therefore always and also says the coming to glow [*Erglühung*] of the open span, pervasive attunement. The saying of the clearing is attuned" (GA 66: 109).

As for the *simple clarity* in section 36, this bespeaks the clearing in which humans are (-sein) steadfast in the "there" (Da-), that is, in the clearing of encounter and strife. It seems to address especially thoughtful grasping in attuned being-there. This can be backed up as well with what Heidegger says about inventive thinking (*Erdenken*) later in the volume, namely, that it is "what brings to shine [*zum Leuchten*] the clearing out of the most proximate [*nächste*] glow" (GA 66: 246).

Although the clearing addresses the opening up of the abyssal truth of beyng both in *Contributions* and in *Besinnung*, if we pay attention to the way in which Heidegger speaks of the clearing in *Besinnung*, we can notice further differences.

In *Contributions to Philosophy*, Heidegger speaks of the clearing almost exclusively in three phrasings: he most often speaks of "the clearing for self-concealment," but he also speaks of "the clearing of concealment," and "the clearing of the 'there'" (Da). The three phrasings all address the opening of truth, although with slightly different emphases. That he emphasizes the clearing for self-concealment (*die Lichtung für das Sichverbergen*) makes sense in relation to the fact that the truth of beyng first resonates as withdrawal and that the foremost task in transition to the other beginning is to withstand the withdrawal and thus to *be* (-sein) steadfast (*inständig*) in the clearing (Da-) of self-concealment.

In *Besinnung* and *Geschichte des Seyns*, Heidegger speaks of clearing in a variety of contexts and phrasings, including the one emphasized in *Contributions*. Most often, however, he speaks of the clearing of beyng (*Lichtung des Seyns*).[38] The relation to concealment and the abyss remains essential (in several passages, Heidegger speaks of the clearing of the abyss),[39] but we saw above how he now thinks beyng more pronouncedly as the carrying out of encounter and strife. Section 87 shows this context clearly: "*Truth* is the clearing that belongs to beyng as appropriating event. Clearing: carrying out the encounter and the strife into the openness of their crossing. Clearing is: Clearing 'of' the carrying out" (GA 66: 314).

Heidegger then specifies what he means by the clearing "of" the carrying out: "the transporting [*Entrückung*] and making room [*Einräumung*] of what is untied [*des Entbundenen*] into differentiation as what is assigned to each other." Transporting and making room "are appropriated in the appropriation and carried toward each other in the carrying out. Clearing essentially occurs out of the carrying out and is proper to the latter" (GA 66: 314).

Transporting and making room are the temporalizing and spatializing that is the clearing of encounter and strife. Such clearing comes to be in that it occurs out of the carrying out. This carrying out is not just empty but, says Heidegger, it is always determined and attuned (*bestimmt* means both). What he writes here is reminiscent of the analysis in section 242 of *Contributions* of the time-space as which the abyss occurs: a clearing without ground that carries attunement and determination prior to any specific being (thing) (GA 66: 314).

The Clearing of Beings and Errancy

The determination of the clearing of beyng does not arise from specific beings that show themselves in the clearing but from the appropriation of the encounter of gods and humans and the strife of world and earth. Beings first come to appear in the clearing. Heidegger pays attention to emphasizing this:

> And only very far out there [*sehr weit draußen*] where the "world" is at strife with innerworldly beings, does the essence of the clearing occur as the *self-showing* of beings; the self-showing claims [*beansprucht*] the inceptive essence of the clearing.
> Starting from the self-showing, the essence of truth can never be questioned. (GA 66: 314)

We see, then, how there is still a differencing of beyng and beings at play such that the clearing of being somehow precedes beings. And yet, history (the history of the other beginning as well) requires the coming to appear of beings that Heidegger already addressed in *Contributions* as a "standing into the clearing" (*Hereinstand in die Lichtung*). The standing into the clearing of beings occurs in (and the following phrasing is new) a "differentiation of beyng toward beings" (*Unterscheidung des Seyns zum Seienden*) (GA 66: 68).[40]

Here, too, we find a decisive difference between *Besinnung* and *Contributions*. In *Contributions* Heidegger always emphasized how the clearing needs to be sheltered (*geborgen*) in beings. Only through beings does the clearing of truth find a concrete site. In *Besinnung* he entirely drops this phrase of the "sheltering of truth in beings" and emphasizes the difference between beyng and beings in a variety of ways.

In section 21, for instance, he writes: "Beyng does not give its essential occurrence away to beings, but fulfills this essential occurrence as itself and thus clears itself as the abyssal ground in which rise up and decline and remain at a level *that* which humans then call beings" (GA 66: 92).[41]

The essential occurrence of beyng appears to occur independently from beings at the same time that beyng in its happening clears itself and thus allows for the rising up and decline of beings. The difference between beyng and beings is strongly emphasized as well in section 66a: "In beings, however, beyng never leaves a trace. Beyng is that which is without trace, never a being and never to be found amongst them, at most in its initial appearance [*Schein*]—in being as being-ness" (GA 66: 202).[42]

That beyng in its withdrawal leaves no trace in beings suggests a relation to beings where these are completely "hollowed out," or indeed where beings are not.

In *Contributions* we find Heidegger saying: "Beyng occurs essentially; beings are."[43] In the last part of *Contributions*, however, the one he wrote later, which is closer to *Besinnung*, he finds what he conceives to be a more originary naming that says: "only beyng *is*" and beings are *not* (GA 65: 472). It is because beings are not, because they are abandoned by beyng and beyng is forgotten, that metaphysical thinking assigns to them beingness ("being") as their most general characteristic. Thus beings are left with the "claim" to being and yet, truly speaking (according to Heidegger) they are not.

And still, in the other beginning of history, beings come into the clearing. There would be no history if this did not happen. Heidegger sometimes even writes of the clearing of beings, only that the "of" means something different here from its meaning in the phrase "the clearing of beyng." In the latter case, the clearing belongs to beyng; in the former case, beings are that which is cleared (GA 66: 217, 219). How can we grasp the standing of beings into the clearing (their self-showing) and at the same time their not being?

Perhaps section 68 can get us closer to some understanding of this. Here Heidegger speaks of the clearing of beings in the context of the forgottenness of beyng. Let me quote a longer passage from this section:

> Humans can never get rid of the forgottenness of being; even if they honor what is most question-worthy in the question of truth and precisely then do they confirm that they must be appropriated by an appropriation; refusal remains and the turning toward *beings* and steadfastness in them is required and with this again a forgetting of being that is not diminished through the questioning of beyng but only made manifest in its uncanniness. In being-historical thinking only the surface [*Oberflächlichkeit*] of the forgottenness of being is broken through; never, however, is the *forgetting* itself overcome but it is "only" opened up in its abyssal dimension. This forgottenness belongs to the steadfastness in the *clearing* of beings. To *be* the *there* into which beings protrude, at the same time means to be away from being itself and its truth within the clearing of the there. This being away belongs into Da-sein [being-there]. . . . Being away from the concealed refusal holds humans *away* [*ab*] from the ground of their essence that therefore is in itself the abyssal ground [*Ab-grund*] that forgottenness holds open. (GA 66: 219–220)

There is no passage in *Contributions* where Heidegger emphasizes in the way he does above (in *Besinnung*) that the forgottenness of beyng cannot be removed and that it is constitutive of the very experience of the abyssal character of truth. In *Contributions*, he writes how the forgottenness of being entrenches (*verfestigt*) the abandonment of beings by being and how the abandonment is the ground of the forgottenness (GA 65: 107, 114). This would let one presume (and maybe he did think so) that once one acknowledges the forgottenness and is dislodged into the clearing of abyssal truth such that the abandonment of being is experienced as such, that in this moment one no longer stands in the forgottenness of beyng. Yet in *Besinnung* Heidegger clearly thinks otherwise. One finds oneself turning toward beings because beyng continues to refuse itself even when this refusal is experienced and acknowledged. Beyng withdraws without a trace and steadfast being-there in the clearing of the abyssal ground remains in the midst of beings that *are* not.

Errancy is essentially constitutive of the truth of beyng, an insight Heidegger already had in *Being and Time* and that he developed in his essay "The Essence of Truth" in 1930. In *Besinnung* this insight appears with renewed emphasis. Let us recall that there is a double concealment occurring in the clearing of truth. The originary concealment (mirrored in being toward death) is the concealment belonging to the withdrawal of beyng. Errancy is the concealment of this withdrawal in the appearing of beings. In *Contributions* he does not highlight errancy (*Irre*) although he does speak of *Weg-sein* (being-away) in the twofold sense corresponding to the double concealment of truth.[44] In *Besinnung*, there are three sections in which Heidegger emphasizes errancy; the first appears at the end of the introduction (section 7). The section translates and interprets "freely" a passage from Pindar that begins: "Truth (clearing) of beyng is the beyng of errancy" (GA 66: 11).[45] We find the same phrasing in sections 38 and 72. In all these sections Heidegger also stresses that errancy needs to be sharply distinguished from falsity, a notion that presupposes truth as correctness. In section 38 he writes that errancy is grounded in the "dignity" of the clearing, that it is "nothing 'human' but essentially occurs in the in-between of god and human as the playing field of time-space of the strife of earth and world" (GA 66: 112).

Although Heidegger embraces errancy as part of what occurs in the clearing and as part of what the thought of beyng must be with and cannot escape, in section 7 of *Besinnung* he distinguishes errancy from distortion (*Verkehrung*) that is rooted in errancy and that addresses a falling for beings and their exclusive predominance. This suggests that although beyng-historical thinking is prone to be turned toward beings, it can hold at bay their prevailing power. Such power manifests itself in a reckoning with causes such as "drives, inclinations, pleasures, and delectations [*Triebe und Neigungen, Lüste und Vergnügen*]." Against such powers one can prevail, Heidegger suggests, in the final paragraph of section 7: "What is true occurs [*ereignet sich*] only in the truth: that we belong to its essential occurrence, that we know the danger of distortion as being rooted in it and that we do not let enter what is distorted in its unfettered power and don't fear it, steadfast in the venture of beyng, belonging to the unique service of the not yet appeared but announced god" (GA 66: 12).

This passage suggests that beyng-historical thinking experiences errancy, the turn toward beings, their ambiguity between standing in the clearing and concealing the clearing (GA 66: 259), but that because it knows about errancy, it can keep distortion at bay, provided it occurs in steadfast *being*-there. The clearing of the truth of beyng as a clearing of errancy thus occurs as a space of decision that decides between truth (with its errancy) and distortion through beings. In relation to the human being, this requires that beyng-historical thinking keeps at bay a reckoning with things according to drives, inclinations, pleasures, and delectations. The German word that I translated as "pleasure" is *Lüste* (as in lust) and has a strong bodily, sexual, "animal-like" connotation. There are many passages in *Besinnung* in which Heidegger admonishes that the human be dislodged from animality.

Human Indwelling in the Clearing against "Human Animality"

The clearing of beyng comes to stand against "human animality." In section 74 Heidegger is quite explicit about this. Only in questioning what is most questionworthy, he writes, "is the clearing in beings, is beyng itself guarded against being ripped away into the dullness and blindness of the mere animal; only that—with the remaining residual and robbery of that clearing and mindfulness—humans can avow 'consciously' the blindness of a drive and definitively thrust the dignity of their essence into misrecognition" (GA 66: 269–270).

Heidegger does not simply say that humans become animals. He will always maintain an essential difference between the human and the animal and that difference lies in the clearing of being that he thinks is not granted to animals. This is why even when humans seek their "animality," there remains a "residual" of the clearing. And yet in his confrontation with Nietzsche (and one might surmise also in relation to contemporary events), Heidegger is thinking the danger of an entrenchment of the distortion of human being into a kind of animality. This is how he reads Nietzsche's *Übermensch*, the "overman." Thus he writes, in a text pertaining to one of his lecture courses in 1939, "Overman is extreme *rationalitas* in the empowering of *animalitas*; he is the *animal rationale* that is fulfilled in *brutalitas*" (N: 177). Heidegger's critical reflections on the "human animal" also arise in confrontation with Oswald Spengler's notion of the human as the "predator" and Ernst Jünger's book *The Worker*. Heidegger refers to them in section 10 of *Besinnung* (GA 66: 27), and more references to Jünger can be found in *Die Geschichte des Seyns*.[46] Jünger profoundly influenced Heidegger's thought concerning machination and according to David Farrell Krell, "Heidegger's opposition to Jünger's notions of will and power translates eventually into a resistance— quite strong by 1939—to Nietzsche's notion of will to power."[47] Jünger played an important role in how Heidegger came to view his current political situation and this played a role in the decisive stance Heidegger takes toward Nietzsche as he reflects on human animality.[48] This can be backed up with what Heidegger writes, for instance, in section 10 of *Besinnung* (titled "The Consummation of Modernity"): "The thinking in terms of world war out of the highest will to power of the predator [*Raubtier*—this is a reference to Spengler] and out of the unconditional armament [this is a reference to Jünger] are in each case a sign for the consummation of the metaphysical age" (GA 66: 28). References to humans as animals ("the historical animal," "the thinking animal," "the human predator") are much more present in *Besinnung*[49] than in *Contributions*,[50] which testifies to an intensified critical confrontation with the epoch that Heidegger identifies as the consummation of metaphysics. That human beings understand themselves as rational animals is grounded, for Heidegger, in machination. Along with an approach to being through a representation of beings occurs the determination of the human as animal rationale, as a (representable) being (*Seiendes*) endowed with reason, which goes along with a distinction between body and spirit. With modernity, subjectivity determines the being of beings in such a way that—thought in the extreme—beings are entirely determined by reason (Hegel) and then the body (Nietzsche). In *Besinnung* Heidegger sees this as a consequence of the "botched humanizing" of the human, *die Vermenschung des Menschen*.[51] In this botched humanizing, humans are pressed down to a "present at hand animal-being" that occurs along with other things (GA 66: 161). What is required in order to reach a more essential understanding of human being is, for Heidegger, a "dehumanizing"

(*Entmenschung*). Human essence needs to be dislodged from animality (GA 66: 113) into the clearing of beyng.

In the clearing of beyng (in the Da- of Da-sein) human being stands in errancy such that thinking can remain vigilant against the turn toward beings, vigilant against the power of beings over being, and against a reckoning with things according to drives, inclinations, pleasures, and delectations.

This brings my discussion of *Besinnung* back to the question of decision and the historical context of this volume, with which I began my exposition of the texts it contains. I close this expository chapter of *Besinnung* with three possibilities of history that Heidegger contemplates in section 70. These decisions also concern the difference between beyng and beings that came to the fore in various contexts above as well.

The Decision between Beyng and Beings and Three Possibilities of the History of Beyng

In chapter 2, I laid out how in *Contributions to Philosophy* Heidegger attempts to overcome the ontological difference and the transcendental framing of the question of being in *Being and Time* by thinking in the simultaneity of being and beings and from *out of* what he previously conceived as the temporal horizon of being and what he now calls the truth of being. We saw, however, that thinking in the simultaneity of being and beings does not abolish their difference since Heidegger thinks in transition from the first to the other beginning of history in preparation of Da-sein, the historical site of the other beginning. Da-sein occurs transitionally as a time-space of decision regarding the history of beyng, that is, words and other things do not yet "shelter" the truth of beyng; beings are still abandoned by beyng. At the same time, in this transition, a saying of beyng is ventured that attempts to stay steadfast in the clearing of the truth of beyng. Such saying occurs in words, that is, through beings, and continuously needs to hold at bay a drifting into a representational approach to beings. Thus, in the transitional thinking of *Contributions*, Da-sein occurs as an in-between that both differentiates (beyng from beings) and brings together (in the thinking word) being and beings. In chapter 3, I noted as well that Heidegger distances beyng from beings in how he differentiates the originary strife of the truth of beyng from the strife of earth and world and furthermore situates the encounter of gods and humans "prior" to the strife of earth and world. In *Besinnung* there is no evidence for a priority of the encounter of gods and humans over the strife of world and earth; encounter and strife are always mentioned together; furthermore Heidegger thinks the event right away as the carrying out of encounter and strife that occurs as a clearing into which beings come to stand. This suggests that in some way Heidegger radicalizes the overcoming of the ontological difference, that is, he thinks more radically in the simultaneity of beyng and beings.

And yet Heidegger often articulates a differencing of beyng from beings in a number of ways. In the discussion of errancy above, we saw how thinking in the clearing of beyng, if it is steadfast in this clearing, holds at bay a turning toward beings such that these become dominant and distort the clearing of being. Furthermore, a differentiation from beings also emerges in Heidegger's discussion of beyng as what is without power. In this context, he speaks of an estrangement or alienation of beyng with respect to beings and their "effectiveness." Compared to *Contributions*, in *Besinnung* a different mood prevails with respect to beyng. Outside of power and powerlessness, beyng is held in a strange emptiness that is different from the draw of beyng's withdrawal that thinking withstands in *Contributions* (in acknowledgment of the plight of the abandonment of beings by beyng). That same emptiness resonates in *Besinnung* when, in the context of the forgottenness of beyng, Heidegger speaks of beyng as differentiating itself from beings and withdrawing without leaving a trace in beings, insisting at the same time that even being-historical thinking cannot overcome this forgottenness. Only beyng is, Heidegger says, whereas beings are not.

In each of these cases in which Heidegger emphasizes the difference between beyng and beings, history is at play. The question of the simultaneity and difference of beyng and beings is, then, intrinsically tied to the question of the history of beyng. History as he thinks it, addresses precisely our transformation in relation to what is; it marks a moment of crisis, a revolution that literally turns over and around the way things and events are disclosed in our daily lives.[52] In 1933 he believed there to be an opening toward such transformation. By the time he writes *Contributions*, he limits himself to thinking of the possibility or, more precisely, of holding open the possibility of a revolution in our basic dispositions and worldly relations. But he also continuously keeps in sight the possibility that no grounding of truth will happen. In section 70 of *Besinnung*, Heidegger speaks of three possibilities of history "through which in different ways the differentiation of beings and beyng is held open as *the* decision" (GA 66: 229). This section addresses, then, precisely the question of the decision of history in relation to the difference between beyng and being. The order in which he presents the three possibilities of history is, as he emphasizes, of no importance:

1. One possibility is that the revolution of beyng occurs and that Da-sein and through it beings are inceptively grounded. Through the grounding of Da-sein "beyng and truth, divinity and humanity, history and art first find in poetry and thought the origin of their essence" (GA 66: 230).

2. Another possibility is that beings remain stuck in the "shackles" and "common paths" of beingness and "compel a complete lack of decision" (GA 66: 230). It would be the endless continuation of the dominion of machination and lived experience.

3. The remaining possibility is a hybrid situation. The grounding of Da-sein does not happen but "in the unknowable concealedness, the history of beyng . . . begins in the successive conflicts of the lonely ones, and beyng enters in the most proper and estranging history whose jubilations and mourning, victories and falls carry over into the region of the heart [*Herzensraum*] only of the most rare ones" (GA 66: 230).

Heidegger speaks of these possibilities in a section titled "Gods. The Essential Knowing." We saw how for Heidegger essential knowing (*wesentliches Wissen*) names more a disposition than a cognitive grasp of something.[53] To use his language, what he calls essential knowing addresses an alert thoughtful steadfastness in Da-sein, in being-there unsettled from the everyday relation to beings, dis-lodged into clearing of beyng. In this essential knowing his questioning unfolds, a questioning that "honors" (*verehrt*) what is most question-worthy. Especially when it comes to meditating on the gods, he says, thinking must occur in relation to the first possibility, that of the grounding of the truth of beyng. Yet even here the other two possibilities are known as well since questioning in the first possibility cannot claim to begin the history of beyng in a decisive way. This originary questioning is, Heidegger stresses here, unsettled or dislodged (*entsetzt*) from beings, from the precedence (*Vorrang*) of beings in the forgetfulness of being; this unsettlement must be "withstood [*ausgestanden*] . . . without ever falling into discontentment of the indignation over superficial conditions" (GA 66: 232). He continues: "Essential knowing in its honoring questioning already is too close to the distant proximity of beyng to tolerate a perturbation by what only is a being." When Heidegger says here "essential knowing does not tolerate a perturbation of what only is a being," he is accentuating again a distancing from beings toward beyng. So, when thinking questions farthest toward the gods and the possibility of the occurrence of the event, the distancing from what are "only beings" is most pronounced.

At the same time that Heidegger questions into the possibility of a historical grounding, this questioning must remain open to the second possibility, that of no grounding, and he ends up giving this second possibility much more space in his reflections (in *Besinnung*) than the other possibilities. He writes that this second possibility is hardest to sustain while carrying out inceptive questioning in the stance of essential knowing. Historiographical viewpoints keep sliding in (*die historische Blickstellung schiebt sich dazwischen*), he writes (GA 66: 233).

I would say that here Heidegger's thinking is always in danger of remaining determined by what it seeks to overcome. Precisely when he thinks about machination and lived experience he writes in the mode of warding off metaphysical thought, of differentiating himself from it. Yet in this way he remains tied to what he differentiates himself from, and this includes beings in their actual machinational occurrence.

Let us recall what Heidegger writes before he speaks of the three possibilities of history. He says that through them "the differentiation of beings and beyng is held open as *the* decision" (GA 66: 229). Yet how is it held open?

The differentiation is opened up through the unsettlement or dislodging from the general way beings "are" or rather "are not" truly in our epoch. Within this unsettlement that opens the differencing of beings and beyng, the disposition of thinking might be turned either more toward the "positive" possibility of grounding beings or toward the "negative" possibility that they may stay ungrounded endlessly, or toward some hybrid situation where in terms of the general way the Western world unfolds, beings remain ungrounded but where in an untimely hidden realm the history of being takes its course only with a few individuals.

One could read Heidegger's poietic writings by orienting oneself in relation to which of these possibilities of history weighs in more. It seems to me that Heidegger emphasizes the second possibility (that the history of being ends in the total domination of machination) extensively in *Contributions* as well as in *Besinnung* and *Die Geschichte des Seyns*, and I also believe that at that time he believes this to be important in order to keep open the first possibility, the one of epochal grounding. The possibility of the closing down of the other possibilities of being and thus of essential history, resonates in his language that emphasizes resistance, standing, withstanding, steadfastness, decision, and knowing. I believe that this emphasis is intrinsically tied to the first possibility in that the necessity to think toward the possibility of a historical grounding of a people comes out of a resistance to the domination of machination.

Heidegger's stance will begin to shift in the later poietic volumes, *Über den Anfang* and *The Event* and I will suggest that this is connected to the fact that his thinking will move more into the third possibility, the hybrid one where the history of beyng occurs in concealment, hidden to most, without any revolutionary grounding of the truth of beyng in *Da-sein* for a people. This goes along with a shift in mood or disposition that begins to announce itself already in *Besinnung* in the notions of the *Machtlose*, that is, "what is without power," coupled with the notions of poverty and dignity, as well as in the notion of beyng's withdrawal that leaves no trace in beings.

Notes

1. All translations are mine. Since the translation by Parvis Emad and Thomas Kalary has the German pagination in brackets, readers can find the passages I quote in the published English translation as well.

2. They definitely were not intended for publication. In his afterword to this volume the editor (von Herrmann) points out that when Heidegger's brother typed Heidegger's handwritten

pages on a typewriter, this was done not in view of a publication but rather for allowing Heidegger a more expedient access to his manuscript (as was the case for other manuscripts as well).

3. The quotation from Heidegger can be found in the editor's afterword: "Kein 'Gedicht' und nicht Dichtung—nur eine Bindung des denkenden Wortes im Augenblick gesammelter Besinnung" (GA 66: 435).

4. Only in the appendix do we find it in the context of a reference to *Contributions* when Heidegger says that his lectures belong in the domain of what he calls in *Contributions* the *interplay* (GA 66: 421).

5. All translations from GA 69 are mine.

6. See GA 65, section 16; GA 66, sections 13 and 14.

7. Section 8 is the first section of the second subdivision of the volume, a section that begins Heidegger's meditations after the preceding thoughts in verses, that is, after the "introduction" that is the first subdivision.

8. Emad and Kalary translate *Kampf* as "struggle," which seems to me a little too "mild." Whether Heidegger was inspired not only by the Heraclitean *polemos* but also by Hitler's use of this word in his autobiography *Mein Kampf* (published in 1925–1926) may be conjectured but I have not seen any textual evidence for it.

9. All translations from the *Black Notebooks* are mine. Since each of the volumes of Heidegger's *Gesamtausgabe* that contain Heidegger's *Black Notebooks* also contain the more specific titles and page numbers of the various notebooks collected in them, I am adding references to these more specific titles and paginations as well (e.g., *Überlegungen* X: 1 or *Anmerkungen* I: 1, which are abbreviated as Ü X or A I, followed by the page number).

10. Heidegger says this again on page 46.

11. Heidegger will bring together the notions of decision and meditation on modernity in section 13 as well.

12. I discussed this notion of "knowing" at the end of chapter 2.

13. It may be noteworthy to mention that, compared to *Contributions*, in *Besinnung*, Heidegger speaks more of the four (god and humans, world and earth) and less of the last god.

14. In Martin Heidegger, *Nietzsche*, vols. 3 and 4: *The Will to Power as Knowledge and as Metaphysics* and *Nihilism*, ed. David F. Krell (San Francisco: Harper and Row, 1991) (hereafter cited as N).

15. Compare section 115 of *Besinnung*, in which Heidegger indicates how metaphysics begins with the differentiation of being and beings that is on the one hand preserved, but on the other hand effaced in the completion of metaphysics in Hegel and Nietzsche. The differentiation between being and beings goes along with the development of a representational thinking that is placed more and more over against the object it thinks.

16. "Mitmachen" has the connotation of going along with a group or a crowd.

17. Hannah Arendt, *Eichmann in Jerusalem: A Report on the Banality of Evil* (London: Penguin Classics, 2006).

18. Friedrich Hölderlin, *Sämtliche Werke*, Historisch-kritische Ausgabe, 2nd ed. (Berlin: Propyläen, 1923), 4:2, 227. Heidegger will quote these lines in his Bremen lecture of 1949, "The Turning" (*Die Kehre*). See GA 79: 72.

19. In this lecture course, see Heidegger's interpretation of the chorus of Antigone in Sophocles's *Antigone*, where Heidegger thinks through the emerging of the differentiation of being and thinking (GA 40, sections 52–56).

20. GA 45, section 38. English translation, Martin Heidegger, *Basic Questions of Philosophy: Selected "Problems" of "Logic,"* trans. Richard Rojcewicz and André Schuwer (Bloomington: Indiana University Press, 1994) (hereafter cited as BQP).

21. Heidegger speaks, for instance, of dispositional power (GA 65: 21–22; C: 19). See also section 18, in which he reflects on power and powerlessness.

22. Heidegger speaks of *Armut* (poverty) in GA 66: 105–107, 110, 111, 116, 117, 119, 123, 217, 219, and of *Würde*, 74, 135, 141, 171, 180, 211.

23. Because -mut has the sense of "mood," *Langmut* literally means "long mood" and *Großmut* "great mood," and *Starkmut* "strong mood." By itself the word *Mut* means courage. The word *Langmut* appears three times in *Besinnung* (GA 66: 85, 244, 375) and seven times in *Geschichte des Seyns* (GA 69: 31, 105, 109, 212), often together with *Großmut* (magnanimity).

24. *Mut* relates to *Gemüt* and the latter can mean mind, soul, disposition, feeling, and nature as when we say that someone has a good nature.

25. See also other uses of *Langmut* (GA 66: 244, 375).

26. "Renunciation—magnanimity and forbearance—renunciation, not desperate turning away but waiting confidence out of the knowing of beyng" (GA 69: 31).

27. Heidegger writes something similar in "Koinon" (GA 69: 212).

28. See the preface to William J. Richardson, *Heidegger: Through Phenomenology to Thought* (New York: Fordham University Press, 1993).

29. GA 65: 56, 64–65, 67, 236, 247, 262, 311, 342, 372, 380, 407.

30. See sections 122 and 123 of *Contributions*.

31. I found one instance in *Contributions* (section 10 from the introduction) in which Heidegger addresses the turning in relation to the "carrying out of the strife [of earth and world] and of the encounter [of humans and gods]" (GA 65: 30; C: 25). This is the only place in *Contributions* where Heidegger uses the word *Austrag* (carrying out) in the way he will later use it in *Besinnung*, which makes me wonder whether he made some later changes to this section.

32. For instance, Heidegger writes: "Since it is appropriated by *beyng* as the carrying out [*Aus-trag*] Dasein is never related to the *human* as its ground" (GA 66: 329).

33. For instance, in section 191 of *Contributions*, Heidegger first speaks of Da-sein as "the self-opening center of the counter-play between call and belonging" and then emphasizes how Da-sein is the *between* between humans and gods (GA 65: 311; C: 246–247).

34. GA 66: 64, 83, 88, 92–93, 108, 307–308, 311, 314, 339, 350.

35. The notion of a leap of thinking is very much present in *Besinnung*. See GA 66: 4–5, 7, 23, 41, 85, 93, 99, 116, 123, 143, 147, 210, 212–213, 348–349, 269, 352, 404, 406.

36. "*Carrying out* does not mean 'getting done with' and removing but opening up, *clearing of the clearing—appropriating event* as carrying out—*carrying out essential for the abyss*" (GA 66: 84).

37. The word *Inbegriff* is difficult to translate. It is composed of "in" and "Begriff." The latter usually means concept. It contains the word "greifen," "to grasp."

38. GA 65: 7, 11–12, 31, 37, 42, 50, 93, 113–114, 116, 118, 121, 147, 154, 168, 311, 363, 380. Similar examples can be found in *Die Geschichte des Seyns*.

39. GA 66: 52, 83, 91, 94, 145.

40. Regarding the relation between history and the clearing of beings, see section 166 of *Die Geschichte des Seyns* (GA 69: 162).

41. Compare GA 69: 168: "Refusal, however, grants clearing in which beings can come and go, be revealed and concealed as such."

42. See also GA 66: 203.

43. "Das Seyn west; das Seiende ist" (GA 65: 260).

44. GA 65, sections 177, 201, and 202.

45. In GA 66 there is referenced the following source: Pindari Carmina cum Fragmentis Selectis. Iterum edidit O. Schroeder. In aedibus B.G. Teubneri Lipsiae 1914.

46. GA 69: 62–63 and 223. For Heidegger's reading of Jünger, see Martin Heidegger, *Zu Ernst Jünger*, GA 90, ed. Peter Trawny (Frankfurt am Main: Klostermann, 2004), 67–69.

47. David Farrell Krell, introduction to the paperback edition of Martin Heidegger, *Nietzsche*, vols. 1 and 2: *The Will to Power as Art* and *The Eternal Recurrence of the Same*, trans. David Farrell Krell (San Francisco: Harper and Row, 1991), xix.

48. Heidegger himself highlights the importance of Jünger for understanding contemporary history. He read Jünger's essay "Total Mobilisation" in 1930 and *The Worker* in 1932 and discussed these writings in a small group "and attempted to show how in them an essential comprehension of Nietzsche's metaphysics is expressed, insofar as the history and the contemporary situation of the West is seen and foreseen in the horizon of metaphyscis" (quoted from Richard Wolin, ed., *The Heidegger Controversy: A Critical Reader* [Cambridge, MA: MIT Press, 1993], 121. German version in Martin Heidegger, *Die Selbstbehauptung der deutschen Universität/Das Rektorat 1933–34* [Frankfurt am Main: Klostermann, 1985], 24).

49. GA 66: 17, 24, 27–28, 30, 103, 113, 123, 137, 138, 140–142, 154, 161–162, 181–182, 210, 230, 250–251, 270.

50. GA 65: 275, 491.

51. GA 66: 137, 153–154, 161, 230. David Farrell Krell suggested this translation of *Vermenschung* (botched humanizing).

52. Heidegger uses the term "revolution" (*Revolution*) in his 1937/1938 lecture course *Basic Questions of Philosophy*, 39; GA 45: 41.

53. See the end of chapter 2.

5 Heidegger and History

A Critical Engagement with Heidegger's *Besinnung* (GA 66), *Die Geschichte des Seyns* (GA 67), and the *Black Notebooks*

Heidegger's Poietic Writings and the *Black Notebooks*

Besinnung and *Die Geschichte des Seyns* stand in closer proximity to Heidegger's *Black Notebooks* than the other poietic writings.[1] The years 1938–1939 are indeed the years Heidegger wrote the most in his notebooks. Not only are there several references to the *Black Notebooks* (he referred to them as *Überlegungen*) in the poietic writings of that time, but also the themes and style of writing are often quite similar.[2] Just as in *Besinnung*, he reflects on the history of beyng and on philosophy as well as on the task of thinking. Generally speaking, however, he gives more space in the *Black Notebooks* to "political" deliberations sparked by contemporary events. His conceptuality is looser and the tone often far more polemical than in the poietic writings. On the one hand, it seems clear that if one is interested in Heidegger's "philosophy" of the event, what one should read first are (besides his published writings) the poietic writings and not the *Black Notebooks*. On the other hand, because since the 1930s Heidegger understands being historically (in terms of beyng), and because he understands the *Black Notebooks* as belonging to his beyng-historical thinking, taking them into account becomes necessary. The proximity between his poietic writings and the *Black Notebooks* is deeply troublesome as it leads us to question the delicate and porous boundaries between the "personal" and the "philosophical" dimensions of his thought and opens up wounds of history (especially when it comes to his anti-Semitism) that for many of us may never heal.

In Heidegger's own understanding his deliberations in the *Black Notebooks* are "inconspicuous outposts—and rearguard positions in the totality of an attempt at a meditation that as yet is unsayable on the way to conquering a *way* for an anew inceptual thinking that is called . . . *beyng-historical* thinking" (GA 95: 274; Ü X: a).

Outposts (*Vorposten*) and rearguard (*Nachhut*) connote positions of troops in order to secure the army in relation to enemies or conquests lying ahead or in the back. With respect to Heidegger's thinking, this might mean something like demarcating and defending certain limits of beyng-historical thinking. One might conjecture that his many polemics against the state of the university, historiographical thinking, religious and cultural institutions, and political organizations, for instance, help to secure the space for a more "inceptive" thinking by holding current sociopolitical organizations and events at bay.[3] At the same time, Heidegger gives himself leeway to reflect on states of affairs that are closer to him (the university, the national socialist party, for instance). Sometimes he even speaks in the first person,[4] although he is far away from being "personal" in any more common sense of the word.

In an earlier notebook he writes that the issue in the *Black Notebooks* is not to criticize states of affairs or see everything negatively, but to point to what is "most proximate" in order to "*think ahead* into beyng itself and its simple and basic movement" (GA 95: 24; Ü VII: 33).

There is some "thinking ahead" into beyng in the *Black Notebooks* (for instance, passages in which Heidegger reflects on the clearing of beyng),[5] but not much. Mostly there are critical reflections and condemnations of what is most proximate. The way this plays out is that when Heidegger makes reference to contemporary occurrences he clearly dislikes, he interprets them in terms of machination (*Machenschaft*), that is, along the lines of his interpretation of the history of beyng. He does not leave space for exceptions. The *Black Notebooks* testify that he had to interpret everything that happened beyng-historically (or perhaps there were events he did not interpret beyng-historically, but they had no room in his notebooks).[6] One might say that this is because he was a thinker to his bones. His steadfast knowing of beyng, the greatness of the task he believed to be responding to left no space for self-doubt, no room for an incident to be just that incident. With the exception of some very few places, where Heidegger speaks of himself, he does so in view of himself as a thinker, one to whom is assigned a destiny (GA 95: 290; Ü X: 22–23). But one might rightly question whether the lack of self-doubt he displays in the *Black Notebooks* testifies to him as a thinker.

I wrote in conjunction with *Contributions* that I see in Heidegger's disposition of restraint a resistance against dissemination and pluralization and that this leads him to read the whole Western history in terms of one history of beyng. I believe that the same attitude also determined his interpretation of what happened around him. But what does it mean to interpret concrete events beyng-historically? Is that even possible if we take seriously what Heidegger means by inceptual thinking?

Inceptual thinking (when it succeeds) is for Heidegger a thinking appropriated by the event, a thinking that responds to a "call of beyng" and that tries to bring forth beyng or disclose a sense of beyng in the saying. This is sharply differentiated from representational thinking, which is directed at beings. But are the university, the national socialist party, and the various other institutions Heidegger criticizes not beings? And what about a people or nations Heidegger thinks about in the *Black Notebooks* (he speaks of Americanism, Judaism, Christianity, Socialism, Bolshevism, and of the Germans and English and other people)? What about the war itself? The war is a being (*Seiendes*) too. What makes Heidegger's thinking of them beyng-historical? That he interprets them as being determined by will to power or machination (calculation and lived experience)?

What is decisive for beyng-historical thinking is that a grounding attunement needs to be sustained. For Heidegger, grounding attunements arise from beyng and not from beings. And yet, beyng is experienced as withdrawal precisely through the abandonment *of beings* by being, perhaps through something like a sense of hollowness or emptiness resonating in or behind things and events.

How should we understand the relation between grounding attunements and beings? For Heidegger, grounding attunements unsettle us from our relation to beings. They are nothing personal, not related to this or that event, but overcome us from the depths of historical beyng. But just as there is no purity in truth, for Heidegger, that is, just as there is no truth without errancy, is it not the case that there is no purity in grounding attunements either? I believe that what we might call Heidegger's errancies have their seat in the way attunements dispose his thinking and relation to things and in a blindness that prevents him from acknowledging that part of the complexity of attunements has to do with the complexity of what influences and shapes our lives. To acknowledge this complexity would require that one take into account not only grounding attunements but also attunements or affective dispositions relating to specific things and events. It is noteworthy that whereas in *Being and Time* and *Basic Concepts of Metaphysics*, Heidegger considers attunements that are not grounding, such as fear (of something) or boredom related to a specific situation, in his poietic writings he limits himself to speaking of grounding attunements.[7] He reflects on attunements insofar as they unsettle us from our relation to things but pays little heed to attunements through which we are related to more specific things and events. His thinking gaze is directed toward the great task of the thinker and not toward the intricacies of "everyday" dispositions toward things and events.

Acknowledging the complexity of attunements would require as well, in my view, that one take into account the lived body (*Leib*) and the way it is permeated and shaped through lineages and experiences that mostly escape our awareness.[8] Apart from some sparse indications that Heidegger did see a relation between attunements and the lived body, in his poietic writings he has little to say about this relation and more specifically about the body. But should we not see bodies just as much as words as beings that "shelter" and conceal truth and possibilities of being?[9] Do bodies not bear attunements and dispositions that delimit, make possible, and give directions to how and what we think and say?

This leads me to another aspect of Heidegger's errancies that one ought to question, namely, that delicate threshold between attunements and determinations arising from them, that is, between senses of being and what comes to thought and word.

The Strangeness of the War

Interesting in this respect is the text titled "Koinon: Out of the History of Beyng" from the years 1939 and 1940. In this text, we can see a slippage happening, from an attunement arising in relation to war, and the interpretation issuing from it.

Heidegger begins the text by writing: "Today everybody experiences and notes assiduously the 'strangeness' [*das Seltsame*] of this Second World War" (GA 69: 179). This strangeness manifests itself, he continues, in how "everything is incorporated into the war that apparently is not yet present [*noch gar nicht vorhanden*]" (GA 69: 180). I believe that the strangeness Heidegger speaks of is very much akin to a strangeness we can experience ourselves. Troops are sent overseas, there are wars that at the same time are not present. Pictures in a local supermarket fleetingly remind us of soldiers that were sent to battle, soldiers from a town we live in. Images of bombings we see on television in the comfort of our homes open a space of uneasy displacement before we turn our backs to the screen again and engage in an everyday activity.

Heidegger notes something particular about "world wars." This designation, "world war" indicates, according to him, that the world itself becomes bellicose. The distinction between war and peace disappears because "Freedom is now the overpowering control over all possibilities of war as well as the securing of the means for carrying out war" (GA 69: 181). This sentence, too, is one I could affirm to be true for our times. What is behind all this, according to Heidegger, is "the thrusting forth of power in the determining role of the world-game, i.e. the way in which beings are ordered and the mode of their rest determined. Power thus the name for the being of beings" (GA 69: 182). Characteristic of this predominance of power is that "in advance it allows as beings only beings that can be made" (GA 69: 185). Will to power thus is a form of machination—its final form. Humans become material for deploying power, everything is taken in advance as something that can be made, that is subject to calculation and organization for the sake of expanding power. Thus "machination is the ground of that unusual occurrence into which all beings are compelled" (GA 69: 187). Even to this point of Heidegger's text, I might feel inclined to affirm what he writes, although I feel uneasy with respect to the global picture that begins to form in my mind. The uneasiness is strengthened as I follow him further in the text. The next move he makes is to say that all forms of political organization, democracy and authoritarian states, are the same; they are the same forms of political deployment of power. That the people are in power in democratic states is only an appearance (*Schein*). The uniformity that takes place in the empowerment of power in all forms of states is *common* to everything and everybody. Heidegger calls this "communism" (which is obviously different from the usual notion of communism) (GA 69: 191).

At this point, I cannot simply follow Heidegger anymore. Not because I do not see something true in his analysis of the prevalence of power (Foucault analyzes this in another way), not because I do not see a certain pervasiveness of machination in all kinds of political institutions (including unions and wildlife organizations, which I generally tend to support), but because at this point he loses all sense of differentiation. Certainly, to become more differentiated at this point, one needs to bring into play more strongly representational thinking, something Heidegger clearly did not nurture in any particular way.

I find that a slippage happens in the movement of Heidegger's thinking here: first, there is an attunement or disposition (the feeling of strangeness) in relation to what *is*, then this attunement is nurtured, its resonances yield farther and farther . . . and almost imperceptively, the slippage happens, the singular has no more space except for the singularity of a sense of being.

Heidegger, Germany, and the Foreign

Perhaps it is because Heidegger has opened so many important venues for thinking, because he encouraged us to rethink what it means to be and taught us how to think with and through experiences and attunements, that we remain baffled and speechless when he writes things in his *Black Notebooks* that appear to us now as shortsighted, provincial, embarrassing, tasteless, outrageous, or unacceptable. His nationalism belongs to those things, even if he writes that the Germans, the people of thinkers and poets, clearly have not found their true essence yet. See, for instance, the following deliberations from around 1939:

> *Where did the Germans end up*? Or did they only still remain where they always already were and where Hölderlin found them last and Nietzsche still found them. . . . But perhaps *is* this the essence of the Germans—and perhaps what they are "capable" of comes to light only through the "Americanism" they carry out even more thoroughly and through the even "more restlessly" carried out "Romanism"—that they are called the "people" of thinkers and poets only because as a "people" they do *not* want this thinking and poetizing, that is, that they are not ready to seek their ground in such danger—but more and more ignorantly—glorify and imitate "the foreign"—but who wants to say then, that a *"people"* should and could be what prepares for beyng the site of its truth? (GA 95: 339; Ü X: 101–102)

Surely, one should differentiate Heidegger's utopic nationalism from the nationalism of the national socialist party, but the privileging of the Germans in Heidegger's narrative of the history of beyng (although anchored in the lineage of great philosophers such as Nietzsche, Schelling, and Hegel and Heidegger's favorite poet) betrays a total blindness toward the many other lineages and histories there are. Perhaps in some corner of his mind, Heidegger was aware that the notion of the "Germans" should not be placed too much in the forefront of his thinking of the history of beyng. It is indeed striking how little he mentions the Germans in his poietic writings compared to the *Black Notebooks*.[10] But troublesome remains what almost sounds like xenophobia in the passage quoted above: that the Germans are not finding a way to their essence and instead imitate the foreign (Americanism and Romanism).

Most difficult if not impossible to swallow for many of us are Heidegger's pronouncements in the *Black Notebooks* regarding world Judaism that he interprets—once again—as a form of machination. For him, Judaism clearly is far removed from the not yet found essence of the German people. He brings into play anti-Semitic clichés like the Jews' talent in reckoning (GA 96: 46; Ü XII: 67) and—although in terms of quantity, criticism against Christianity prevails—he ultimately sees Judaism as the source of Christianity and at some point (around 1942) even writes of the Judaic as "the principle of destruction" (GA 97: 20).[11]

What pushes Heidegger to such remarks? Grounding attunements? Or rather attunements and dispositions that are rooted in lineages and circumstances he cannot see, blinded by the all-consuming task of preparing the other beginning of Western history?

Although Heidegger's beyng-historical thinking clearly infiltrates in disturbing ways his interpretation of people, political occurrences, and institutions in the *Black Notebooks*, I do not see his anti-Semitism infiltrating his poietic writings in any explicit or implicit way. Still, his famous silence toward the Holocaust, his apparent lack of compassion and unwillingness to make any public pronouncement to that matter, haunt every serious reader of Heidegger. The man and the thinker. Somehow, it is hard to simply keep them apart.

Heidegger's Silence: Exposedness and Impotence

I often ask myself what I would have felt, thought, and done had I lived in Germany during the time of the Nazi regime. This is always accompanied by a strong sense of unease and almost disgust. I get that same feeling when I read Heidegger's speeches during the time he was rector at the university, how he refused to take on new Jewish students; or when I think that he went to visit Karl Löwith and his wife in Italy in 1936 (after his disillusionment with the Nazi movement as it had evolved) and did not have the good sense to remove the party insignia from his jacket; or, when I see official letters he wrote in 1942 ending with the salute "Heil Hilter!" Would I have signed official letters that way? Would you? Then there is the famous silence after the Holocaust.

Condemning Heidegger does not help. Perhaps I feel guilt by association; perhaps it is my memory of moments in my life when I let myself be guided by feelings and judgments of people that led to harm others whom I did not wish to harm. Perhaps it is because I know that I am not immune to the pressure of opinions from people and that I am prone to errancy. And yet there are moments in life where one needs to take a political stance (in the widest sense) and act. I decide and act but I am never certain of what I do. I know others feel the same way. I remember endless discussions with German friends with whom I studied in Freiburg, many of them with a deep anger against fascism; some of them had renounced their parents because they had complied with the Nazi movement. Open wounds transmitted to the children of those who were involved. Things seem to be easier for the generation following ours.

Heidegger knew about errancy: that it can never be removed. How is it, then, that he insists on a "knowing" (*Wissen*) and steadfastness (*Inständigkeit*) in the clearing of beyng that would allow one not to fall for errancy (albeit one remains exposed to it) and to be decided for the "other beginning"? If we look at what he means by knowing in *Contributions* and *Besinnung*, we can readily see that this has not shifted essentially from what he said at the beginning of 1934 in an address given at Freiburg University to six hundred beneficiaries of the National Socialist "labor service program":

> Knowing means: in our decisions and actions *to be up to* the task that is assigned to us, whether this task be to till the soil or to fell a tree or to dig a ditch or to inquire into the laws of Nature or to illumine the fate-like force of History.
> Knowing means: to be *master* of the situation into which we are placed.[12]

What if errancy took place precisely there, in this "knowing," in this more visceral feeling of resoluteness toward what one identifies as being essential or true? Are not many of Heidegger's pronouncements in the *Black Notebooks* bearing testimony to such errancy? What if errancy was not about being blinded by beings, that is, by things and events? Is it not the case that, prior to all concrete relations to things, attunements or dispositions dispose us toward thinking and acting in ways that may turn out to be destructive or distorting? Is this not precisely what Nietzsche taught us, and what drove him to perform a genealogy of morals and to engage in the revaluation of all values? Nietzsche, whom Heidegger so vehemently pushes away, whom he so ever more decidedly places at the end of metaphysics?

Perhaps pushing Nietzsche away was necessary for Heidegger to hold on to "knowing" of the truth of beyng, to keep safe and nurture that seed of truth he hopes one day will grow roots and sprout. On the other hand, do most of us not have a "seed of truth" we hold on to in various occasions? How else could we have "true friends" or dedicate ourselves to a task or idea? How else could we have a sense of honesty and deceit even if we cannot firmly decide between them in particular cases? To be able to question our "values" and ourselves appears to be decisive if we do not want to slide into some blind fundamentalism.[13] Was Heidegger able to keep his most cherished values in question? Should he have? Who can be juror and judge of these things?

Thinking in terms of values is, of course, something Heidegger criticizes as an outgrowth of machination and subjectivity. (Perhaps another way to keep "his" truth of beyng safe?) His thinking responds to a call that is not his but that is rooted in the historicality of beyng itself, he tells us. He is the custodian of the seed, not its maker. But speaking of a "seed" here seems somewhat inadequate; a seed is a far too material, too substantial, too sensible a metaphor for what Heidegger describes as the possibility or intimation of an event without ground, or rather of *the* event.

The singular is decisive for Heidegger because otherwise we would end up representing events and not thinking out of Da-sein. But it seems to me that there is more to his thinking in the singular than an attempt not to speak in relation to beings. In the context of *Contributions* I addressed this singularity in relation to staying in the draw of being's withdrawal. I interpreted this as a concentric force giving unity to Heidegger's thought of beyng. In 1939, however, a shift begins to happen such that he will begin not to think in the draw of beyng's withdrawal. Beyng, we hear him saying, withdraws without a trace. Thinking now stands in nonbeing, in the oblivion of beyng. And yet: the emphasis on the singular remains. What structures this singularity when it is no longer the draw of beyng's withdrawal? Let me now reflect more on the notions that begin to address this change in the fundamental disposition of Heidegger's thinking; the notions are "what is without power" (*das Machtlose*) and beyng insofar as it leaves no trace in beings such that beings "are not."

It appears to me that with these thoughts, Heidegger begins to shift away from what Krell addresses as Heidegger's "desire to *overcome* nihilism" that exhibits "a craving for *results* in history."[14] This shift, however, does not mean resignation although it is a form of acceptance of what is, yet in such a way that Heidegger's thinking does not succumb to what happens. He will continue to conceive of thinking as a highest form of action.[15] As we have seen, he finds a dignity in the "poverty" of what is without power. Somehow he begins to find a transformed time-space, a "clearing." He describes this not exactly as a sheltered space, since it is abyssal and has no preset measures. What gives unity to this unique experience of beyng? Perhaps nothing else but the continuous tending to this clearing in steadfast meditation. Perhaps also the way this clearing is delimited with respect to machination and the warding off of falling prey to beings. Probably both.

One is also tempted to look at the date when the first signs of a shift in the mood of thinking begin to emerge in Heidegger's meditations. By 1938–1939, Nazi organizations have already "settled" and structured social and political life. Nazi spies were sitting in Heidegger's Nietzsche classes to make sure he complied with directives. The big enthusiasm for the movement in 1933 is no longer alive. One can imagine a sense of powerlessness or futility with respect to efforts of contrasting the established system. But above all, in 1939, right around when the notion of "what is without power" appears, the war breaks out. Is it perhaps tied to "the strangeness of war" that Heidegger speaks of in "Koinon"? Was it the openness of this strangeness that provided him with a space to move into a different disposition toward historical beyng and even farther away from the public domain?

When I was talking with a friend (a Chilean poet) about Heidegger's withdrawal from the public domain, my friend looked at me and asked: "And how is this different from our current situation? What can we do? Will we try to do something when there is nothing we can do? Or do we stay home and write?" We looked at each other and found nothing more to say.

So "we" go on; we find meaning in teaching, writing, friendship, and we nurture our seeds of truth. I put "we" in quotations marks because of course there are many more who get active in organizations, many who perhaps still manage to believe that humanity will find some solution to the progress of ecological disaster, to human, animal, and vegetative exploitation. Then there are many who simply do not care.

World war, concentration camps, economic and ecological exploitation are consequences of machination, Heidegger tells us. They are not the evil but only symptoms. As long as the fundamental mode of being is determined by calculation, productivity, and lived experience, no change is in sight. And whether this change occurs is not primarily up to us. What appears to be an utterly passive stance that Heidegger takes outrages many, and they vindicate the human agency he fails to address. What if that outrage testified to impotence? What if, when we look at Heidegger, we find ourselves facing—and even ourselves experiencing something very like—that impotence; that impotence that fills us with discomfort and disgust, that impotence we wish to push away and expel from our bodies? Heidegger gives us no solution; he never apologized publicly for his involvement with the Nazi movement, he never publicly joined the outrage over the extermination of Jews. He leaves us hanging there.

Heidegger's Critique of the Human Animal and Dehumanization

Should we not say that Heidegger, too, was prone to the urge of expelling from his "body" what disturbed him most intimately? (Note that I do not mean to imply this to be a bad thing but one would hope that a thinker be aware of such expelling.) I am thinking here of his turn away from beings, of his growing aversion to Jünger, and of that passage in *Besinnung*, in which he speaks of trying to keep at bay a reckoning with drives, inclinations, pleasures, and delectations.

One may bring in, here, the Derridean move to show how Heidegger is still "infected" by the metaphysical tradition that keeps something like "spirit" safe from being contaminated by the body.[16] One should note, however, that even philosophers who affirm excess take care to differentiate what one may tentatively call "salutary excess" and philosophical passion from excesses and unbridled emotions that are considered nefarious. I am thinking, for instance, of Nietzsche, who in *The Birth of Tragedy* distinguishes the Dionysian festivals of the Greeks (that always included the Apolline element) from "that repulsive mixture of sensuality and cruelty which has always struck [him] as the true 'witches' brew'" (in reference to barbarian Dionysian festivals).[17] How do we find that fine, invisible line, that almost impalpable, abyssal measure that separates the nefarious from the salutary, decay from catharsis?

Destructive and cathartic passions cannot be separated categorically; they belong to the same family. Their distinction is more something that needs to be performed as one undergoes the passions. "We" (to think in terms of subjectivity does not quite fit here) perform separations and repel what threatens us on a dispositional level constantly or perhaps we should say that "we" become who we are in the separation and repulsion. I am thinking, for instance, of that family member who is the "bad apple" the rest of the family tries to stay away from, the one who strayed from the path and who, you "know," could drag you down with her.

It requires force to hold at bay and repel the threats that pervade one's being. Heidegger's emphasis on decision and his critique of machination testify to that force. Worse than machination is lived experience, he tells us in *Contributions*, since it closes off even more the possibility of questioning machination (GA 65: 127; C: 129). And the worst form of lived experience is its organized form: "The *organization* [*Veranstaltung*] of lived experience is the highest lived experience in which people find themselves together. Beings are merely an occasion for this organizing, and what place is beyng then supposed to occupy?" (GA 65: 450; C: 354). In lived experience, there is a dissolution of the character of beings or things as *Gegen-stand*, as what stands against us (recall that *Gegenstand* is commonly translated as object). Things are incorporated into the movement of "life." This brings lived experience quite close to a fundamental historical attunement in which, as Heidegger envisions it, we as a people are unsettled from our relation to beings and beyng as such discloses. How do we draw that fine abyssal line between a lived experience (especially in its communitarian form) and disclosive transformative attunements?

One of Heidegger's answers is: "dehumanize." "Dehumanization" (*Entmenschung*) is a fundamental word in *Besinnung*. The attempt to move away from the centrality of the humans is characteristic of his whole path of thinking. It is mirrored in the way Da-sein comes to designate less and less the human and more and more the clearing of beyng in which humans participate as "custodians" and as "the creative ones" who take the direction for their creating precisely not from anything human. Lived experience is anthropocentric, it centers especially on the human animal and highlights desires and drives, Heidegger would say. Fundamental attunements expose us to the nonhuman "mystery" of beyng, to what exceeds human grasp, to silence, to the gods. We need to empty ourselves out, repetitively, constantly, until our bodies are no longer drawn by what goes on around us, until there is nothing left in our being, nothing there we need to expel.

Heidegger's thinking will find more and more a dwelling place for his thinking in the time-space of being where beings are deprived of beyng, in the "poverty" and "dignity" of what is without power. And strangely, this is made possible by the ultimate entrenchments of machination. The dawn of the new era of machination and globalization has no more room for romantic longing of times past and hopes for fundamental revolutions. Thinking can find a rest in nonbeing. It is then that Heidegger can begin his ultimate descent into "the inception."

Notes

1. All translations from the *Black Notebooks* are mine. Hereafter I also will use the italicized and capitalized *Black Notebooks* to refer to the published notebooks and will use "notebooks" for the actual notebooks Heidegger wrote in or in order to refer to particular notebooks. For a more thorough and broader discussion of the relation between Heidegger's poietic writings and the *Black Notebooks*, see Daniela Vallega-Neu, "The Black Notebooks and Heidegger's Writings of the Event (1936–1944)," in *Reading Heidegger's* Black Notebooks, ed. Ingo Farin and Jeff Malpas (Cambridge, MA: MIT Press, 2016), 127–142.

2. Heidegger even inserted passages from the *Black Notebooks* into the volume *Geschichte des Seyns*: "Entwurf zu Koinon: Zur Geschichte des Seyns"—"Projection for Koinon: Regarding the History of Beyng" (GA 69: 199–214).

3. This is how Heidegger likes to see it: "What therefore at first looks like a rejection and 'critique' of the era, is indeed only the takeoff for a meditation on that which is older than the covered up and yet still essentially occurring ground" (GA 95: 221; Ü IX: 63).

4. "For a long time I have rejected the dawning insight, coming from my questioning the question of beyng, that technology and history are in a metaphysical sense the same" (GA 95: 235; Ü IX: 86–87). This is a passage Heidegger cross-references in *Besinnung* (GA 66: 183).

5. GA 95: 306–307, 328–329 (Ü X: 50, 84); GA 96: 59, 79 (Ü XII: 87; XIII: 1–2); and other passages.

6. It is in this sense that Peter Trawny speaks of Heidegger's anti-Semitism as a "beyng-historical anti-Semitism" (*seinsgeschichtlicher Antisemitismus*). Peter Trawny, *Heidegger und der Mythos der jüdischen Weltverschwörung* (Frankfurt am Main: Klostermann, 2014), 31–33.

7. In *Contributions* he also speaks of guiding attunements (*Leitstimmungen*) with respect to specific junctions of the truth of beyng, but this is different from attunements relating to specific things or events.

8. *Leib* indicates the body as we experience it and is contrasted in phenomenology with the objectified body (*Körper*).

9. I worked this question out in Daniela Vallega-Neu, *The Bodily Dimension in Thinking* (Albany: State University of New York Press, 2005), ch. 5.

10. In *Contributions* Heidegger speaks once of the German people (GA 65: 42) and once of the German will (GA 65: 54). In *Besinnung* he speaks of Germany only once when he mentions the future ones who will save the Germans into the plight of their essence (GA 66: 61). *Die Geschichte des Seyns* has more pronouncements that could have come from the *Black Notebooks*. Heidegger mentions the Germans three times (GA 69: 86, 108, 119) and in one instance writes, "The history of the world is allotted to the mindfulness of the Germans" (GA 69: 108). In *The Event* (hereafter cited as E) he mentions the Germans twice, once when speaking of how it is a danger for the West that the Germans are succumbing to the modern spirit (E: 78) and another time when he says that inceptual thinking is grounded by Germans (E: 251).

11. For further discussions of Heidegger's anti-Semitism, see, besides the book by Peter Trawny I referred to earlier, Donatella di Cesare, *Heidegger e gli Ebbrei: I "Quaderni Neri"* (Torino: Bollati Boringhieri, 2014); Jean-Luc Nancy, *Banalité de Heidegger* (Paris: Galilée, 2015); David Farrell Krell, *Ecstasy, Catastrophe: Heidegger from Being and Time to the Black Notebooks* (Albany: State University of New York Press, 2015) and, by the same author, "Troubled Brows," *Research in Phenomenology* 46, no. 2 (2016): 309–335; Ingo Farin and Jeff Malpas, eds., *Reading Heidegger's Black Notebooks 1931–1941* (Cambridge, MA: MIT Press, 2016).

12. Richard Wolin, *The Heidegger Controversy: A Critical Reader* (Cambridge, MA: MIT Press 1993), 58.

13. This is what animates the core of Charles Scott's work that keeps coming to my mind: to keep ethics in question is for him our most important ethical task.

14. David Farrell Krell, introduction to the paperback edition of Martin Heidegger, *Nietzsche*, vols. 1 and 2: *The Will to Power as Art* and *The Eternal Recurrence of the Same*, trans. David Farrell Krell (San Francisco: Harper San Francisco, 1991), xviii. See in this context David Farrell Krell, *Intimations of Mortality* (University Park: Pennsylvania State University Press, 1986), 138–140.

15. Das Erdenken des Seyns ist "ein *Handeln*" (GA 66: 70).

16. Jacques Derrida, *De L'Esprit: Heidegger et la question* (Paris: Editions Galilée, 1987). In English: *Of Spirit: Heidegger and the Question*, trans. Geoffrey Bennington and Rachel Bowlby (Chicago: University of Chicago Press, 1991).

17. Friedrich Nietzsche, *The Birth of Tragedy*, trans. Ronald Speirs (Cambridge: Cambridge University Press, 1999), 20 (German edition: Friedrich Nietzsche, *Sämtliche Werke: Kritische Studienausgabe*, vol. 1, ed. Giorgio Colli and Mazzino Montinari [Munich: DTV de Gruyter, 1980], 32).

6   Über den Anfang
(On Inception) (GA 70)

Content and Composition of *On Inception* (*Über den Anfang*)

With *On Inception* Heidegger indeed makes a new beginning (in 1941) in the thinking of the event.[1] The volume (that precedes *The Event*) is distinctly different from *Besinnung* and *Die Geschichte des Seyns* in that the often confrontational meditations on machination and will to power (or will to will) in the earlier volumes almost disappear and give way to a thinking of the event in its most inceptive occurring. Heidegger's thinking goes under into a domain of being and thinking removed from the machinational deployment of beings, withdrawn from both the power and powerlessness infusing the lives of people in the middle of World War II. One is almost reminded of the situation in which Descartes conceived his *Meditations*, except that the site of thinking for Heidegger is not consciousness, not the "I think," but the event in its most extreme inception that touches a limit not only beyond subjectivity but even beyond beyng.

I suggested earlier (see the end of chapter 4) that in terms of the history of beyng, Heidegger moves into a hybrid situation in which the grounding of Da-sein does not happen in the open for a people but rather in concealedness for the few who can listen to the call of beyng or in who's "heart-space" (*Herzensraum*) (GA 66: 230)—perhaps one could render this with "heart-mind"—reverberates a more inceptive history of beyng. But as we will see, the question of the history of beyng becomes anew a question when thinking ventures even beyond beyng and thus even beyond history.

Über den Anfang begins with the following foreword:

> The attempting word of inception can always only remain in the semblance of an exposition and, against its determination [*Bestimmung*], often sounds like a report.
> This is why for such an attempt the appropriate title is the heading: *On Inception*.

What Heidegger writes here already indicates the way in which *On Inception* differs from the following volume *The Event*. In *On Inception*, he introduces new basic concepts in an almost explanatory fashion, concepts to which he will take recourse in *The Event* without much explanation. In many ways, *On Inception* prepares the reader to engage the more difficult volume *The Event*.

On Inception has six parts that do not have any apparent order, although part I, "The Incipience of Inception" (*Die Anfängnis des Anfangs*), begins right at the heart of the theme and develops Heidegger's renewed thinking of the event as inception "from" inception. Part II, "Inception and Inceptive Thinking," has some sections meditating on the task of thinking and some sections that outline the history of beyng in relation to how Heidegger thinks it. Part III, "Event and Da-sein," can be seen as developing out of (and yet staying within) what the first part opened up. In the remaining sections he moves to exploring further related themes: part IV is titled "Explication [*die Auslegung*] and the Poet," part V is titled "The History of Beyng," and the very short part VI is titled "Being and Time and Inceptive Thinking as History of Beyng."[2]

Compared with *Contributions to Philosophy*, the "organization" of *On Inception* differs in that it does not indicate the transition from the first to the other beginning but rather begins, as I will show, "hither" the differentiation into first and other, which means that it begins already in (has already leaped into or entered) the other beginning and from here rethinks also the first beginning. The structure of this volume thus does not suggest something like a sequence in the movement of thinking.

My exposition of *On Inception* will largely follow the themes announced in the title of the various parts and subsections of the volume. The concepts I will focus on are "inception," "difference," and "differentiation" (of being and beings), "carrying out," "the nothingless" and "the beingless," "dignity," "poverty" and "mood" (*Gemüt*), "Da-sein," the relation between being and humans, and "exposition" (*Auslegung*) especially in the context of Heidegger's reading of Hölderlin (in 1941–1942 Heidegger holds two Hölderlin lecture courses), and the "history of beyng."

In chapter 7, I will reflect especially on the notion of inception or beginning, as well as on the difficult notion of the beingless that brings into play the nonbeing of beings as something prior to being and thus suggests a more radical "simultaneity" of being and beings at the same time that they are held most radically apart.

"What Does 'Inception' Mean?"

In the first section of *On Inception* (with the heading "What does 'inception' mean?") Heidegger gives indications as to what he means by inception (*Anfang*).[3] "Inception" names the truth of beyng and its occurrence as event. The reason he now explores the event in terms of inception has to do with a more radical attempt at articulating the event not primarily out of the turning relation between beyng and thinking (although he does discuss the relation between thinking and beyng in the second part of the volume) but out of the unfolding of the truth of beyng (the unconcealing concealment of beyng) itself. He thus introduces the notion of inception without any reference to thinking and articulates the occurrence of *Anfang* "from itself": "Thus *'Anfang'* is not the inception of an other; rather this word here thinks the taking-on-to-itself [*An-sich-nehmen*] and catching [*Auffangen*] of what is appropriated [*er-eignet*] in the reaching out that takes on-to-itself [*an-sich-nehmendes Aus-langen*]." What reaches out and takes on-to-itself is not thinking but "the clearing of the openness, the unconcealing. The taking on-to-itself is at once unconcealing and concealing" (GA 70: 10).

The word *An-fang* has the root meaning "fangen," to catch; "in-ception" has the same Latin root meaning (-ception comes from "capere," to catch) and this is why it makes sense to translate *Über den Anfang* with *On Inception*. "What" catches, here, in "the catching of what is appropriated" is not a human, not thinking, not even in the guise of Da-sein. (This is different, for instance, from section 122 of *Contributions* where Heidegger writes that thinking catches what is thrown to "it.") When he rethinks the event as inception he thinks it more radically in the middle-voice (i.e., neither active nor passive but rather as when we say "it rains"). In the occurrence of inception, there is, strictly speaking, nothing and nobody that catches. Instead, a "catching-itself" occurs of "what" is appropriated, which is not properly a "what" but an event that finds a site only in this occurrence of inception. The "catching-itself" is the occurrence of truth: unconcealing concealing happens; truth happens. What is decisive for Heidegger is that in the catching, "what" is unconcealed (the event) remains bound to concealment.

The movement of thinking here (which Heidegger does not explicitly address at this point) is not one of withstanding the abyss but rather one of departure. *Abschied*, departure, is a new essential word for Heidegger:

> In-ception is the taking on-to-itself of the departure into the abyss.
> This taking on-to-itself is the inceptual seizing [*Aneignung*] and therefore ap-propriation [*Er-eignung*] of the incipience [*Anfängnis*].
> In-ception is inceptively and this means in an abyssal way, the appropriating event. (GA 70: 11)

The German word for what I translate as "seizing" has the root meaning "eignung" just as appropriation ("Ereignung"), which is a cognate of *Ereignis*, event. In-ception is thus thought as a seizing of what is appropriated. Another new basic word we find in the context of thinking the event as in-ception (*Anfang*) is *Anfängnis*, "incipience."[4] This is a neologism Heidegger coins by making a noun out of the occurrence of inception. He speaks of the incipience of the inception, die *Anfängnis des Anfangs*, thus emphasizing the actual occurrence of in-ception he is thinking.

It is not an accident, I believe, that Heidegger introduces the notion of inception not only without explicit reference to thinking but also without specifying "other inception" (other beginning), since he thinks inception at a limit where the first and other beginning of history are not yet differentiated or where first and other both belong to inception. This is why he writes, for instance, in section 42: " 'Inception' is the word for being that has the capacity to name the first and the other 'beginning' " (GA 70: 55). Before proceeding to think further the differentiation between first and other beginning, however, in section 1 of *On Inception*, Heidegger gives a fuller articulation of the movement of inception (the catching of what is appropriated in the event of truth) by bringing into play beings: "The essence of unconcealment—in which is concealment [*Verbergung*] as sheltering [*Bergung*] and veiling—has its distinction in the fact that it lets beings rise up to themselves and thus takes in [*aufnimmt*] beings as such; and as what takes in [beings] it is ground in the sense in which we speak 'spatially' of fore-, middle-, and background" (GA 70: 10).

Truth (unconcealing-concealing) is the ground or grounding of beings and yet is quite different from a solid ground or fundament. Ground has more the sense of "element" of an "in which" beings become beings that is not defined by any borders but rather takes place in an abyssal way. Heidegger emphasizes this abyssal dimension a little later in the section when he writes: "This grounding that takes in and shelters [*bewahrt*],[5] however, essentially occurs only in such a way that the ground itself is no longer ground and essentially and always turns itself away [*ab-*] from what has the character of ground and thus remains abyssal ground [*Ab-grund*]. The concealment in which unconcealment essentially occurs is egress [*Entgängnis*] into the abyssal ground" (GA 70: 11).

In inception, beings rise into being without ground, without why, and when inception occurs inceptively, they remain bound to concealment. Heidegger now thinks the event (as inception) more radically than in *Contributions* in relation to beings such that the event and beings occur as the rising into being (or truth) of the "formerly" nothingless and beingless: "The inceptive appropriating event, however, has its full essence only in the fact that, by occurring as appropriating event and thus as a carrying out [*als Er-eignung austragend*], it clears the inceptive clearing and thus appropriates the openness. Such an appropriating is the coming-in-between [*Dazwischenkunft*] of the clearing as time-space. The appropriating appropriates the in-between (as in-the-midst and meanwhile) to that which—until the time span [*Frist*] that occurs essentially out of the appropriating—[is] the nothingless [*das Nichtslose*] which then arises as a being" (GA 70: 11).

The inceptive appropriating event clears an openness, with which Heidegger rethinks what he calls in *Contributions* the "there" of being-there, the open site (or time-space) for the truth of beyng. It is striking that now (in the first section of *On Inception*) he thinks this openness right away in relation to the "becoming being" (*seiend werden*) of beings out of the nothingless, which is ("is" needs to be crossed out here) precisely a being before it becomes a being, before it is differentiated into becoming a being. He writes that the in-between is appropriated to the nothingless (later he will speak of the "beingless") that in this appropriation becomes a being. He calls this event (here comes another basic word) *Dazwischen-kunft*, the "coming in-between" in both a spatial and a temporal sense.

In *Contributions* the relation between the event as the occurrence of truth of beyng on the one hand and beings on the other hand was held at a distance by thinking first the necessity to prepare Da-sein such that then a sheltering of truth in beings may occur; but now Heidegger brings beings into play right away. They are brought into play, however, in a most radical way, namely, as that which cannot be named because it is not yet something, so little, that not even nothingness can be applied to it, given that we think nothing in relation to something. Beings before they are, the nothing-less.

But how can we even think such a thought? How can we think what is not?

This difficulty is complicated even further by the fact that Heidegger thinks that even when beings arise into being, they are not (!):

> Beyng as inception and event uniquely has that essence that allows to say: "Beyng is." All beings only arise into being; beings never are; but always only "are" beings.
>
> A being is not, in so far as it is to have its circumstances [*Bewenden*], i.e. here the inception, in the "is." A being only is as a being; and this means: a being reaches being only at times, but a being is not itself being.
>
> A being remains so decisively differentiated against, through, and from beyng, that a being has as its own not even nothingness [*das Nichts*]; because only beyng has the essential occurrence of nothingness. Beings are the nothingless. (GA 70: 11–12)

Only being—not a being—*is* and has the essential occurrence of nothingness. How should we think this? Perhaps we may think this nothingness of being out of the draft of being's withdrawal or out of the horizon of death that determines our being. Beings do not have that dimension. They are not in the draft of being's withdrawal as we are when we face mortality or experience departure. As beings rise into being they only or simply "are" ("are" needs to be crossed out) *beings*.

What does Heidegger mean by this? He seems to say that trees, rocks, birds, words (can we include radios, cups, and chairs too? and what about "a people," "a nation," "history," a "god" or "gods"?—as someone suggested I add to the list) are not but at times rise into being, presumably at those times when the event appropriates the in-between. But even then they *are* not, if we take the "are" in the strong sense that includes nothingness. Even when beings rise into being, they are precisely differentiated from being. This seems to be the case both in the first and the other beginning.

Beings simply "are," but they *are* not in the sense in which being or beyng occurs as both withdrawal and appropriating event. Beings are not the event of withdrawal and coming to be, but rather are what arises *in* this happening.

Before exploring more the differentiation between being and beings that Heidegger now addresses as *die Unterscheidung* (the differentiation—I will get back to this further below), I will take a look at the last part of section 1 of "On Inception" where he begins to address the difference between first and other beginning, which are not two beginnings but rather seem to be differentiations relative to the directionality of inceptive thinking. Heidegger writes: "We have a presentiment of [*wir ahnen*] inception in the commemorating to the truth of beyng [*in der Erinnerung zur Wahrheit des Seyns*] and call the thus remembered inception the 'first beginning.' We have a presentiment of the incipience of inception and according to it think ahead into the inceptiveness of inception and thus have a presentiment of the 'other beginning'" (GA 70: 12).[6]

In section 2 Heidegger differentiates first and other beginning further but still thought out of inception as the "catching of what is appropriated":

> (f.b.) The in-ception—the catching itself over the own abyssal ground into the arrival of the arising disposing [*das Sichfangen über dem eigenen Ab-grund in die Ankunft der aufgehenden Verfügung*].[7]
> (o.b.) The inception—the catching itself over the own abyssal ground into the downgoing into departure.
> (f.b.) The catching itself as the taking in and catching of unconcealment.
> (o.b.) The catching itself as the taking in of the abandonment of being into the appropriation. (GA 70: 13)

In the first beginning, then, the abyssal movement of inception is one of arising and unconcealment; in the other beginning, it is a downgoing into departure, and this by virtue of taking in—in the appropriation—the abandonment of being. (I will develop this latter point further down.) Heidegger thinks not only the other but also the first beginning in its inceptiveness, that is, before the abandonment of beings by beyng that initiates metaphysics such that the truth of beyng remains concealed. Thinking the first beginning in its inceptiveness is, of course, only possible in the other inception.

In order to develop further the differentiation into first and other beginning I will recast again the event as inception in light of the notions of difference and differentiation, which lie at the heart of the distinction between first and other beginning.

The Difference (*Unterschied*) and the Differentiation (*Unterscheidung*)

In section 57 of *Über den Anfang*, Heidegger refers to the differentiation (*die Unterscheidung*) of being and beings as the first in the order of rank. This differentiation is thought more inceptively not only than the metaphysical difference of being and beings but also more inceptively than the ontological difference in *Being and Time* that remains tied to the transcendence of Dasein. (The reader of *On Inception* should be aware, however, that with the differentiation of being and beings Heidegger sometimes addresses not the inceptive differentiation but the differentiation characteristic of metaphysics.)

In the more originary sense, the differentiation "means the basic trait of beyng itself that as appropriating event inceptively arises from separatedness [*Geschiedenheit*] and seclusion [*Abgeschiedenheit*] into incipience [*Anfängnis*]" (GA 70: 68).

Heidegger addresses here the arising into being of beings as which beyng occurs but now in respect to the movement of beyng itself in its most radical inceptiveness that includes the notion of seclusion. Seclusion (*Abgeschiedenheit*) is akin and closely tied to the notion of departure (*Abschied*). In section 3 he indicates that seclusion addresses the "staying" of inception as "departure into concealment" and he relates it to the refusal of the word. In this section he grapples with this most concealed "moment" of inception as "being" (being needs to be crossed out here) something "timeless" given that one cannot really speak of a time before being (see GA 70: 15).

I find the passages in which Heidegger attempts to think the seclusion of inception among the most difficult to interpret and suspect that we ought to understand what he tries to think here as a precursor to the notion of *Enteignis* (that can be translated as "expropriation" or "dis-propriation") that emerges more fully in *The Event*. If we stay with the passage quoted above, we can say that the movement of beyng—as the clearing of an in-between—occurs in difference to the seclusion that itself is a movement of departure (*Abschied*) in the clearing of being. Heidegger addresses this movement of departure as *Unterschied*, "difference" and distinguishes it from "the differentiation" (*Unterscheidung*) of being and beings that occurs when beings arise into being in the clearing: "The essence of difference is not the differentiation; rather the essence of differentiation is difference as departure" (GA 70: 73).

The relation between difference and differentiation emerges more fully at the end of section 59: "In the event as the difference (the departure-like) beings arise into the standing [*Erständnis*] according to their own and through this standing—and according to the throw [*Zufall*] of beyng into beings—beings move from the difference into the possibility of being differentiated from being and thereby into the possibility of differentiation" (GA 70: 75).

Difference precedes (but not in the sense of linear time) and/or encompasses the differentiation of beyng and beings.

* * *

Up to now I have referred to passages that could address inception in the first and in the other beginning. In both cases in the movement of difference, a differentiation of being and beings occurs. Now I will consider how the first and other beginning come to be distinguished.

* * *

In section 9 of *Über den Anfang*, which is titled *Anfang und Aufstand*, "inception and uprising," Heidegger traces the inception of metaphysics as follows.

> As the coming-in-between of the in-between [*als Dazwischenkunft des Inzwischen*], the appropriating event is the calling forth of the nothingless [*des Nichtslosen*] into being, in order to be as a being. Beings thus rise up to themselves. By being appropriated to being [*übereignet*], beings seize [*aneignen*] being in such a way that from now on beings give themselves as that which carries and brings forth being in themselves, such that beings also must become the measure and foundation for the determination of being, which [being] thus has already enjoined itself to beingness. Beings thus rise up against being (as appropriating event). This uprising occurs out of the inception and belongs to it such that the inception incurs the danger that out of this uprising the covering over of the truth of beyng installs itself. This danger has its urgency in the fact that it disguises itself in the semblance that only now being is brought into its dignity. Metaphysics carries out this semblance. (GA 70: 27)

Heidegger describes here the movement of how in rising into being, beings may seize being (being with an "i") for themselves,[8] such that being becomes beingness (*Seiendheit*) and beings end up covering over the truth of being. If we think this differentiation from the vantage point of beyng (inceptively and beyng-historically thought being), it is the event of the withdrawal of beyng such that beings remain abandoned by being. Beyng differentiates itself and withdraws, leaving beings to themselves, groundless, without being. In the first beginning this is the event of the "unleashing of beings into being 'only' beings," as Heidegger says in section 44. He speaks of it also in terms of *Fortgang*, of "leaving" (which stands in opposition to the downgoing and departure into the abyss) (GA 70: 98, 102, 176).

But when the event appropriates, the rising of beings into being does not necessarily end up in the unleashing of beings. In section 97 of *Über den Anfang*, titled "The Event and Beings," Heidegger thinks the event when beings rise into the openness of being without covering over this event. Then, beings "come into the saying and into the word. But saying and word are not expression and grasp [*Fassung*]; rather they are the essential occurrence of being [*Wesung des Seins*]" (GA 70: 117).

Saying and word are the essential occurrence of being such that the formerly nothingless comes into being. Beings only rise into being in the saying and the word. Heidegger continues: "The rose blooms in the poem of the poet and only there, but this 'blooming' is not simply what is said afterwards about a so-called real thing, a being, instead it alone [the blooming] is the being [*das Seiende*]. That is why according to the uniqueness and rareness of being [*Sein*], inventive poetizing [*Er-dichtung*] happens rarely" (GA 70: 117). The blooming of the rose here addresses the being we call rose. There is not first a thing, the (nameless) rose-thing that then is brought into being. The being, the rose in the how of its being, that is, in the blooming, rises into its being in the saying or in the word. Beyng, thought as the event of appropriation, is the rising into being of beings.

We can think this in the context of the abandonment of beings by being such that in the abandonment, beings "are" nonbeings. Indeed, Heidegger writes a little later in the same section: "Being as ap-propriation is the consignment of nonbeings [*das Sein ist als Er-eignung die Übereignung des Unseienden*]—or of beings that are abandoned by being—into being [*in das Sein*]. This entails that beings themselves become what emerges [*das Aufgehende*] and that in emerging (now φύσις is thought more inceptively) they come to stand [*Erstehen*] into a permanence [*Verweilung*]" (GA 70: 118).[9]

Being is the consignment of nonbeings into being and beings come to stand into being. Being and beings thus occur always together at the same time that they always remain differentiated.

The rising up of nonbeings into be-ing is always unique, says Heidegger, and "is always different depending on beings being propriated to being as stone, tree, animal, human, god. . . . Rising is not representedness and not mere appearing; rising is emerging [*Aufgehen*] and yet at the same time staying back in the beingless [*zurückbleiben im Seinlosen*]" (GA 70: 119).

What Heidegger says here in the end—that beings, at the same time that they arise stay back in the beingless—is crucial, since only thus is the relation to being preserved. Again, what is preserved is not nothingness but the beingless. Perhaps we can think this beinglessness in terms of emptiness or utter nondetermination rather than as a sense of withdrawal or passing or lack.

The thought of the beingless, the *Seinlose* marks the most extreme thought and most inceptive moment in *Über den Anfang* and *The Event*. I will now try to follow Heidegger in how he thinks beinglessness (or the nothingless) as the most inceptive moment (which is not really a moment or anything at all) in thinking the event of appropriation as incipience of the inception.

The Last Downgoing; The Beingless

As I understand it, with the beingless, Heidegger thinks a more inceptive letting be of "not yet or no longer be-ing beings," which occurs in the most extreme downgoing into the abyss. I also believe that it is related to a new historical disposition in Heidegger's thinking, that of letting the abandonment of beings by being, that is, the historical unfolding and installment of machination at the end of the first beginning, *pass by*, rather than resisting it. His thinking thus enters into what I called the hybrid situation at the beginning of this chapter, the in-between the never-ending epoch of machination and the estranged realm where being is appropriated for the few. (This happens in 1941.)

The notion of beinglessness is, if I may say so, a positive notion for Heidegger, a most inceptive (indeed a preinceptive) notion, and it needs to be sharply differentiated from the abandonment of beings by being.[10] Together with beinglessness, Heidegger thinks also a positive notion of *Enteignis*, of "dispropriation," where dispropriation is again, not the movement of withdrawal of beyng that unleashes beings into machination, but points to the most inceptive moment in the downgoing into the abyss of inception in which the relation to the abyss is preserved.

What is most surprising in the notion of the beingless is that it implies the notion that beings somehow are "prior" to being: "Since, however, being comes in-between into the beingless [*Weil aber das Sein in das Seinlose dazwischen ankommt*] and begins as the inception of beings, therefore beings—namely as the subsequently be-ing beingless [*als das nachmalige seiende Seinlose*]—are in a certain sense 'prior' and older than being [*sic*]. Beings are the 'a priori' to being, if here confusion does not occur because of the use of metaphysical titles for being and being beings [*Sein und seiende Seiende*] outside of all metaphysics" (GA 70: 121).

As what was ("was" needs to be crossed out here) formerly beingless, beings "are in a certain sense 'prior' and older than being." (It is not clear that Heidegger would write that the beingless is older than beyng since with beyng he thinks also the departure "beyond beyng.") As we read this, we should keep in mind that Heidegger is not saying that beings are things in themselves before we think them and that in thinking them we attribute being to them. But he also does not want to say that beings arise from being, such that being somehow would generate beings. This is why he writes: "Although beinglessness is still conceived coming from being, it does not originate from being" (GA 70: 121). Perhaps this is also related to the fact that he first spoke of the not yet being beings as the nothingless. Beings before they rise into being are not even nothing. "Neither can be said, the beingless is, nor that it is not" (GA 70: 121). Furthermore, as mentioned above, the beingless is precisely not the abandonment of beings by being: "In the abandonment of beings by being (i.e. in the machination of beings) beings are completely outside of beinglessness" (GA 70: 121). Beinglessness is preserved only in the event of appropriation such that this event inceptively occurs as dispropriation.

The beingless are ("are" needs to be crossed out here) beings before and after they rise into being, that is, before a clearing of being is appropriated; before Da-sein! We should wonder how Heidegger or anyone could come up with such a thought. Is not his thinking in *Contributions* and the following writings precisely an attempt at thinking of being, that is, out of a basic attunement that already is a being in the "there," that is, in Da-sein? How can he think "prior to" Da-sein? He cannot. So in some way, in Da-sein is announced or indicated for thinking a seclusion (beinglessness) from and in relation to which in the other beginning the clearing of Da-sein is differentiated.

Still in section 98 he writes:

> But in beinglessness can be conceived something most extreme belonging to the essence of being (inception—downgoing—departure).
> Here—in the "beinglessness" and in the "beingless"—lies a challenge [*eine Zumutung*] in the face of which no metaphysics finds a way. (GA 70: 121)[11]

Heidegger here does not say anything about the beingless as being experienced in restraint or withstood in Da-sein. The beingless is thought in a movement of departure (*Abschied*) and allows him to conceive something most extreme belonging to the essence of being. This is not the concealment belonging to truth that is held in hesitation; it is not the nothing that we experience in the draft of being's withdrawal or in the face of our mortality. It is the not-yet and no-longer begun inception of being as event.[12]

It may be helpful here to consider at what point he thinks this thought of the "unsayable" (*das Unsägliche*), as he calls it (GA 65: 85). He thinks this most extreme thought in "the last downgoing":

> This [the last downgoing] determines an inceptive time in-between [*Zwischenzeit*], in which history does not necessarily continue in the same manifestness [*Offenbarkeit*]. . . .
> When the inception of beyng is and beyng essentially occurs only inceptively, then beyng itself (as event) must once bring forth the "time" (temporal-spatial-playing field) in which and with which it [beyng] essentially attains [*erwest*] its downgoing.
> "Then" every possibility of a "then" has disappeared; then—spoken still again and only out of the *transitional leaving* [*aus der übergänglichen Überlassung gesprochen*]—there also are no "beings." Non-beings, which—said transitionally—continue, are neither nothingness nor not nothingness. They "are" (but thought only in a *more inceptive* sense) the μηδέν Parmenides thought (but *differently*) in the first beginning.[13] (GA 70: 51)

Heidegger here qualifies the last downgoing of his thought as a transitional *überlassen*, which in current German has the sense of leaving something to someone. We may think of this as a letting go that leaves beings to machination where beings are nonbeings.

Although nonbeings (beings abandoned by being) are not the same as the beingless, they are intimately connected: "Downgoing leaves beings to beinglessness. This beinglessness is the last thing that can still be said out of inception. The beingless is the name for the unsayable" (GA 70: 85). In leaving beings to machination, Heidegger's thinking leaves beings to (inceptive) beinglessness.

This most inceptive move in Heidegger's inceptual thinking—its downgoing, in which occurs a *Verwindung*,[14] a twisting out of metaphysics and machination—marks a time outside of time. It is a time-space without "when," a suspension of history in an in-between. I already pointed out above that this new disposition of Heidegger's thinking (first announced in the notion of "what is without power" in 1939) is tied to the notions of poverty and dignity that he continues to refer to in *On Inception*.

Dignity

The way Heidegger speaks of dignity (*Würde*) is strange if we think of dignity primarily in the sense of someone's attitude or characteristic. For Heidegger, dignity is neither a character of humans, nor is it proper to thinking, but rather to beyng (with a "y," i.e., historically happening beyng) itself. The following quotations are taken from section 21 of *On Inception*, titled "Inception is the dignity of beyng":

> Dignity is not proper to beyng by means of an honor first brought to it. . . .
> Dignity is the incipience of inception, and thus it is also not a character of beyng but rather It [*Es*] itself, however in its downgoing essential occurrence.
> As the downgoing inception dignity is beyng inceptively.
> Dignity is the unconcealment of concealment that preserves its inceptiveness by holding itself purely in the intimacy of inception, by staying far from this intimacy and out of it [*aus ihr her fernbleibende*], and by returning into inception and turning toward it. (GA 70: 38–39)

Dignity designates the way in which in the other beginning (the downgoing) beyng occurs inceptively. Heidegger characterizes dignity as the movement of beyng's inceptive occurrence that I described above: arising out of concealment and staying turned toward it. That Heidegger relates the notion of dignity to beyng was already the case in *Contributions*, but in the earlier volume he would speak even more often and continuously of the *Herrschaft des Seyns*, the sovereignty or dominion of being (GA 65: 58, 62, 76–77; C: 46–47, 50, 61). In *Besinnung*, we can find a passage in which he writes: "Sovereignty is the dignity of beyng as beyng" (GA 66: 17). In *On Inception*, the notion of the "sovereignty" of beyng disappears. One could say that the notion of dignity replaces the notion of sovereignty such that the inceptive occurrence of beyng is *not* described in a language of power and dominion and not in relation to efficacy in the realm of beings, but rather in relation to a poverty of inception that is not a state of deprivation or need but a poverty that is self-sufficient and does not lack anything. At one point he even writes that poverty indicates "the fullness of beyng as event" (GA 70: 135; see also GA 70: 175).

Section 153 speaks of the self-sufficiency of dignity insofar as dignity "does not effect anything in beings and does not justify itself first out of its effects. Dignity passes over all beings and their possibilities because it lets rise up each being into its measure and thus also has to leave to each being its being cast away into measurelessness" (GA 70: 172–173).

What happens in dignity and poverty is unrelated to success in the realm of beings (GA 70: 91). Public outcome is of no importance, Heidegger says in sections 21 and 22 of *On Inception*, "indeed it becomes unessential whether the incipience of inception comes to be communicated or not. What is alone worthy of the dignity is that the saying eventuates [*dass die Sage sich ereignet*]. What is worthy of the dignity is only the thinking of beyng; that it is appropriated and nothing else" (GA 70: 39).

To the poverty and dignity of beyng co-responds an appropriated solitary saying of the event not geared toward communication. Heidegger calls it the last step of thinking: "The last step of thinking leads into the knowing of beyng in which becomes manifest that, *since* thinking, in so far as it is appropriated, belongs to the event, precisely therefore the making public of the saying of beyng cannot be essential for this thinking. The event-character of thinking demands from the latter the entrance into the stillness of pure incipience" (GA 70: 40).

It is here, in the stillness of pure incipience, that thinking (which "beyng appropriates for itself") "honors" (*würdigt*) the dignity (*Würde*) of inception (GA 70: 40).

Beyng does not need what is public and yet, if it is to occur in its dignity, it needs a site; unconcealment must happen. This requires a thinking-saying response such that thinking is disposed or attuned to the poverty and dignity of being.

Inceptive Thinking, Da-sein, and Humans

In part II of *On Inception*, Heidegger meditates on beyng-historical thinking, emphasizing the few and unique ones who are appropriated into saying of beyng. But he also emphasizes the transitional character of beyng-historical thinking, saying that such a thinking first must be prepared (GA 70: 93). He calls beyng-historical thinking a "downgoing thinking" that cannot be compared to a historiographical apocalyptical mood (*historische Untergangsstimmung*)

(GA 70: 94). Beyng-historical thinking occurs as *Austrag*, as a carrying out of inception through the remembering or turning into (*Erinnerung* has the word "innen," which means "in," that we find as well in *Innigkeit*, intimacy) the first beginning and thinking ahead into the other beginning (GA 70, section 77).

What Heidegger writes in this part of *On Inception* often sounds more transitional than inceptive, like something he could have written in earlier volumes as well. He even retrieves the concepts of "throw" and "projection" that go all the way back to *Being and Time*, when he writes, "Being must throw itself *to* [zu-werfen] thinking. Thinking must be dislodged into this throw [*Zu-wurf*] and thus become itself projecting [*Ent-werfendes*]" (GA 70: 111).

Heidegger then thinks the same relation between being and thinking (in *Contributions* this is one of the meanings of the turning [*Kehre*] of the event) as *Anspruch und Antwort*, that is, claim (in the sense of being addressed) and response. The address comes through the word "of" (in the sense of "belonging to") beyng to which the essence of humans responds by fathoming and becoming steadfast (*inständig*) in Da-sein. Thus Da-sein is brought into its essential happening (*erwest*) (GA 70: 112). "All this," says Heidegger "er-eignet sich," is appropriated (middle voice).

I noted at the beginning of this chapter that Heidegger does not address thinking when he thinks the event as inception in the first part of *On Inception*. Here lies the more radical approach to the event in 1941. Once he turns to the role of thinking, however, what he writes recalls his earlier articulations of the event, which could let the reader lose sight of how he is now attempting to move away from a primary emphasis on thinking and the human. A close reading of some passages in the third part of *On Inception*, which address Da-sein, show how Heidegger struggles with a proper articulation of the relation between beyng and humans. In section 100 he writes:

> To "think" [Da-sein] at once out of the abruptness of inception: out of being (-*sein*), out of unconcealment (Da-) and out of the appropriation of the human who is steadfast in Da-sein and grounds it into beings.
> Da-sein at once coming from "being" and from "the human;" but to think being as inception, but to think the human as sacrifice of belongingness into the event. (GA 70: 124)

Although Da-sein should be thought at the same time out of being, uncon-cealment, and the appropriation of humans, still it is beyng that occurs as inception and humans belong to the event. In other words, in terms of inception, beyng retains a certain priority. Heidegger emphasizes this as well in the next section, in which he speaks (not of Da-sein but) of the relation of beyng to humans, and says how the clearing of the there (Da-) precedes (comes "before") any determination coming from humans.[15] He reminds the reader that what "human" means is determined first by the appropriation of humans into their being and cannot be presupposed when we speak of the relation between beyng (or being) and humans (GA 70: 125).

He then develops the relation of beyng to humans further by playing with the notion that the human essence oscillates (*schwingt*) in beyng. He emphasizes in the notion of *schwingen* a "being elevated" and "carried" in the appropriating throw of beyng.[16]

In this oscillating, human being is differentiated as a being from other beings but also "is placed and thrown in his essence into the differentiation of being against beings." Beyng not only determines human beings but also other beings as well as the way we relate to beings. Indeed all this "simultaneously": the "turnings toward beings" are "pervasively carried [*durchschwungen*] by beyng, the in-between that holds sway, that is *at the same time* the clearing for all beings into which beings arise. This says: beyng *already* determines non-human beings and determines at the same time in the oscillation the relation of humans toward beings and the being assailed of humans by beings" (GA 70: 126; emphasis added).

That beyng determines humans and nonhuman beings co-originarily is decidedly different from what Heidegger writes in *Being and Time*. In this early work he attributes to Da-sein (understood as the being or existing of humans) the character of discovering or disclosing beings. In *Contributions* he already thinks Da-sein as the in-between of the turning relations of the event, but as I showed, the relation of Da-sein to beings appears in a certain sense secondary to the relation between humans and gods.[17] Now, in *On Inception*, the becoming being of beings is thought more originarily.

Da-sein, then, should be thought more from beyng than from humans, although the notion of Da-sein always includes human being. Da-sein is "not properly" (*nicht eigentlich*) a determination of humans, writes Heidegger, but "only in the essential consequence" (*in der Wesenfolge*) and in another way and of another essence than traditionally conceived human subjectivity (GA 70: 129). Da-sein means the time-space of the grounding of the truth of being into beings: "Da-sein, understood in the completely other sense of *Being and Time* and thought *more* inceptively than there, is the essential occurrence of the time-space for all being of beings" (GA 70: 130).

Let me now turn to the question of how humans are appropriated by and drawn into being inceptively.

Attunement and Language

Section 108 lists a number of concepts that might be read as an outline of how humans are drawn into or included into beyng (*einbezogen in das Seyn*):

Being
Appropriation (of Da-sein)
Voice [*Stimme*] (word of beyng—concealment—keeping silent)
Attunement [*Stimmung*]
Demand of courage [or sending of mood, *Zu-mutung* means both]
Gathered mood [*Gemüt*]
Indwelling [*Inständikeit*—previously translated as "steadfastness"]
Condition [*Befindlichkeit*] (bodily being) (understood differently as in *Being and Time*, where it was equated with attunement)

Heidegger then puts these different aspects together into one sentence: "Da-sein is the gathered mood of being attuned by the voice of beyng" (GA 70: 131).

The essential determination of human being rests in Da-sein that is appropriated through the silent voice of beyng that attunes Da-sein such that Da-sein is "the re-sonating [*Wieder-klang*] of beyng" (GA 70: 131). From here human being that dwells in being-there is attuned inceptively. That Heidegger highlights *Befindlichkeit* (which is often translated as mood and usually means the condition in which one finds oneself to be) as bodily being (there are only very few places in which he refers to bodily being in Da-sein!) indicates that he would see the human "body," as attuned out of Da-sein as well.

What resounds in attuned Da-sein, the silent voice of beyng, points to the concealed and abyssal dimension of beyng, and this must also mean, beyond beyng, into the beingless. I am adding the notion of the beingless here in light of the word *Zumutung* that Heidegger uses precisely in relation to the thought of the beingless (GA 70: 122).[18]

The notion of *Zu-mutung* and the word *Gemüt* share the word "Mut," which means courage but also (in its root meaning) mood, and Heidegger finds in this semantic root a resource for articulating the various attunements (*Armut, Sanftmut, Langmut, Anmut, Großmut, Schwermut, Gleichmut, Unmut*, and *Mißmut*) that point to dimension of beyng as they resonate in Da-sein.[19] What gathers all these attunements for Heidegger is the *Gemüt* (the prefix "Ge-" has a sense of gathering), which accordingly means the gathering of disclosive moods in Da-sein; and I would like to emphasize again at this point that Da-sein does not primarily mean the human being insofar as it is primarily determined by beyng. Thus he also speaks of attunement as "the essential occurrence of beyng" (GA 70: 133).

It is difficult not to think of attunement as something pertaining to humans conceived as subjects, and we need to remind ourselves repeatedly that for Heidegger attunements are "located" in beyng and that Da-sein requires a way of thinking not anchored in "things" as "substances" but in experiencing be-ing as event. Thus we are called, again and again, to remind ourselves how it is that we come to an understanding of our being in disclosive moments (everyday absorbed being-in-the-world is not what Heidegger addresses in his inceptive thinking). We find ourselves in being, in Da-sein; we find ourselves always already attuned such that the source of these attunements are neither "we" (understood as subjective beings) nor some represented or objectified "being" separated from human existence. Attunements or dispositions precede subjectivity and we come to be who we are and to think and act through them. It is not an accident that the German word for determination that Heidegger likes to use is *Bestimmung*, which again has the word *Stimme*, voice, in it, just as the German word for attunement, *Stimmung*.

If we follow Heidegger's thinking of the event as an inceptive disclosure of be-ing, it also becomes clear that prior to some disclosure or meditation on a "self" comes—together with attuned being—language.

In the years during which Heidegger works on *On Inception* and *The Event*, the years his thinking more radically "goes under," meditations on poetry and language intensify. This is the case especially, as we will see, in *The Event*. The move away from a more Nietzschean language of power and resistance and toward a thinking beyond power in the stillness of being, removed from the ravings of machination being, goes along with an intensified reading of Hölderlin. In the winter semester 1941/1942, Heidegger gives a lecture on Hölderlin's *Andenken* and in the summer semester of 1942 he gives a lecture course on Hölderlin's *Der Ister*. In *On Inception*, Heidegger dedicates part IV to the issue of *Auslegung* and the poet (Hölderlin).

Exposition (*Auslegung*) and Poetry

Auslegung is commonly translated as "interpretation" and literally means "laying out." In what follows I will use the word "exposition" since Heidegger contrasts *Auslegung* to *Interpretation*, the latter taken as a name for a "historiographical" approach that reduces what it interprets to current self-serving interests (GA 70: 147).[20] Heidegger's reflections on *Auslegung* clearly are connected to the reading of Hölderlin. As Heidegger writes in section 128 (the first section of part IV), the task for him is to find an exposition that allows access to Hölderlin's words, in order to "ground" "something inceptive," that is, a historical beginning. Heidegger's reflections on how to expose Hölderlin's poetry seem to stand in contrast to his insistence earlier in the volume that it is "unessential whether the incipience of inception comes to be communicated or not" (GA 70: 39). This contrast is perhaps mitigated (but not removed) when Heidegger writes that "the saying and thinking must be made *approachable* [*zugänglich*], i.e. it must be possible that from it an impetus to meditation arises. This does not mean, however, that it should be 'understandable'" (GA 70: 147). To be "understandable" implies for Heidegger a reduction of something to the common language and conceptualities, whereas approachability leaves room for meditation and transformation.

Still, when it comes to exposing Hölderlin's poetry, communication is clearly a desideratum.

In the next section Heidegger proceeds to say more about what explication consists in, discussing exposition not only in relation to Hölderlin's poetry. Heidegger is trying to meditate, here, on what is at task in his thinking, that is, in his reading of the history of being and his thinking of the event as inception.[21]

Exposition is the task of inceptive thinking in the other beginning and is "the laying-out [*Heraus-legen*] of that which retains in itself, in its *initial* (inceptive) essence, estrangement [*Befremdung*]. The laying-out brings into the open, yet in such a way that it does not take but leaves to what is inceptual the estrangement" (GA 70: 148).

Estrangement is essential if Heidegger wants to avoid an "understanding" that makes use of already-formed concepts and ways of thinking. Furthermore, "what is inceptive" is implicitly strange since it is an originary happening of truth that unsettles us from (or occurs as one is unsettled into) customary ways of thinking and being. To let inception occur, then, "has the character of setting away and at a distance" and this is also what exposition is to carry out. In setting at a distance, exposition "opens up through saying the in-between and is the saying of beyng itself" (GA 70: 149).

Heidegger differentiates three aspects of "beyng-historical exposition": "the exposition of the history of being," and by this he means the exposition of metaphysics; "the exposition of beyng as history, *as* inception," which is the saying of the event, that is, the other beginning; and exposition that gathers the first two aspects, which is "the exposition in *transition* from the first into the other beginning" (GA 70: 149). He then notes how the exposition of the history of being "comes closest" to a historiographical explanation. In fact, viewed from "without" they seem to be the same. Yet in contrast to a historiographical interpretation, "the historical exposition says that which in each case disposes over [*überstimmt* normally means "to overrule" but Heidegger clearly wants to emphasize *Stimmung*, attunement here] the poet, thinker, and sculptor and remains inaccessible. What disposes over [them] grants the attunement of their determination, the voice of which they only apprehend like an echo, but which they let resound ahead for those who follow" (GA 70: 150).[22]

Thus, in his reading of the great philosophers and poets (who all in some way are inceptive since their words and thinking ultimately are granted by historical beyng even when they are not able to think this granting) Heidegger's exposition tries to apprehend the disposition guiding their thought, a disposition that resonates in their thinking words for the one who can listen beyond what is spoken or written and apprehend what is inceptual in the thinking of the philosopher, the saying of the poet, or the sculpting of the artist. The truth of such exposition cannot be proven but is decided only out of the exposed word (GA 70: 152).

Although Heidegger speaks of "the truth" and "the word," this does not mean that there is only one saying that can expose the truth and the word. The prevalence of the singular in Heidegger—if we read Heidegger with Heidegger—has to do with his sense of the uniqueness of being (*Einzigkeit*) that is tied to its always unique happening. Since the point for Heidegger is *not* to speak *about* truth or about the word of the poet or thinker, but rather to let truth and the word eventuate (in the exposition), what is thought always happens uniquely in the moment it discloses for and in thinking—when and if an originary disclosure happens.

The notion of the truth of an exposition is complicated not only by the multiplicity of sense (*Vieldeutigkeit*) inherent, for instance, in the poetic word (GA 70: 153, section 135, and GA 70: 166, section 148), but also by errancy. Heidegger not only questions his expositions of Hölderlin's hymns, how they could be erring (GA 70: 159, section 139), but also reflects more broadly (in section 136) on the possibility of erring that is inherent in every attempt at inceptive thinking and where he reminds himself and the reader (if he has a reader in mind here) that thinking ahead into inception "only rarely is inceptual": "In all that is inceptive . . . it easily occurs that, who has to think and poetize in its realm, mistakes himself [*versieht sich*] in that which has already been consigned and allocated to him, and yet is a still uncontained property" (GA 70: 155).

Heidegger also points out how one can easily think that the path one has taken could be taken as some kind of "starting point" that makes everything else possible, which would be a demand of a more traditional systematic thinking. One is driven not to see that inception initiates its essence in itself and thus cannot be posited as a rigid point of departure (GA 70: 155).

Heidegger then proceeds to meditate more specifically on Hölderlin's poetry, the explication of which arises, he says, "out of knowing the history of being" (GA 70: 156), and prepares the other beginning. We get a more specific indication of how Heidegger reads Hölderlin out of the history of being in section 138, titled "The Holy and Beyng." The holy and beyng "both name the same [*das Selbe*] and yet not the same" (GA 70: 157). They both make known "what holds sway (heals) and occurs essentially *before* the gods and humans"; they both name the other beginning. They name inception in such a way "that inception hovers as the clearing in-between of the de-cision as the carrying out of all consignment of gods into the godhead, of humans into humanity, of earth and world to their essential occurrence" (GA 70: 157). And yet, although Hölderlin names the event, he does not think it and the in-between of gods, humans, world, and earth. Hölderlin does not reach the knowledge of the history of beyng even if he makes this knowledge possible: "The presentiment of the holy experiences the abandonment of the 'earth' by the 'world' and the remoteness of the gods and the errancy of humans. But this abandonment is not recognized as the abandonment of beings by beyng, and beyng is not thought as that which lets loose and letting loose is not thought as refusal" (GA 70: 157).

This is why Hölderlin can easily be misunderstood and interpreted metaphysically, says Heidegger. This is also why Hölderlin's poetry needs the thinker (Heidegger) as the one who thinks ahead and thus first opens up the time-space of the poetry and grounds it in the question of being as the question of the truth of beyng (GA 70: 159). Although the poet is the one who first founds (*stiftet*) being, he needs the thinker who explicates and thinks what is opened up in the poetic word. Heidegger, however, is also aware that "thinking never reaches what is poetized in the essence of its words and in its own historicality" (GA 70: 160).

Heidegger will think even more extensively about the relation between thinking and poetry in *The Event* as he searches ever more deeply for a thinking-saying that lets eventuate the truth of beyng as the incipience of inception.

The More Inceptive Articulation of the History of Beyng

Heidegger's reflections on how to explicate Hölderlin's poetry and on his own lecture courses suggest that—although in his most radical attempts Heidegger tries to think the event without any expected effects and not in view of any public—he was still concerned about the preparation of the other beginning for a people. This suggests some linear form of time: preparing a time to come. Such linearity is also suggested by his explication of philosophers in the history of metaphysics. Indeed, in a passage I quoted above, Heidegger says that the exposition of the history of being "comes closest" to a historiographical explanation. Part V of *On Inception*, however, reveals his attempt to think as well the "history of beyng" more inceptively, which also means, nonrepresentationally and not in a linear way, but rather out of the event as inception, which does not aim at effects or effectiveness.

Section 152 of *On Inception* begins with the question: "What happens in the history of beyng?," a question that Heidegger immediately deconstructs by pointing out that it already operates in the differentiation between an occurrence and that which occurs (i.e., "something," a "what"), which misses precisely beyng and *its* history. Since beyng is not *a* being, that is, not a "what," the appropriate answer to the question of "what" happens in the history of beyng is: "Nothing happens" (*Nichts geschieht*); "inception initiates" (GA 70: 171); "the event eventuates" (GA 70: 172).

The history of beyng cannot be explicated by something (some circumstance or occurrence) happening in it. It cannot be described but only indicated (GA 70: 173). It is nothing but the occurring of the event as inception, which Heidegger explicates again as "the taking-on-to-itself" (*An-sich-nehmen*) of the clearing (that is both the "proper" and "property" *Das Eigene und das Eigentum*—of beyng) and the taking-on-to-itself of departure. "Thus inception is the essential occurrence of being itself, which protrudes into and rises out of its own abyss"

(GA 70: 172; see also section 153). Heidegger then evokes the dignity of inception, its self-sufficiency; how it remains abysmally remote from beings; how it does not effect anything in the realm of beings but simply provides a clearing for them and lets them arise according to their own measure and measurelessness (GA 70: 172).

The history of beyng, thought inceptively, is the event in the other beginning. Yet how should one think (thought from inception) what appears to the many as the history of being, namely, representable "events"?

What appears is only "a ghost of being," Heidegger writes: "The glaring of transparency, which appears to lie—as the true being—in all beings, obscures the simple radiance of inception. Beyng as event has not yet appropriated for itself its essential clearing. Beyng remains unknowable and sends only the ghost of being [*das Gespenst des Seins*]—which is delivered to disdain as something abstract—into the public realm. This is the impenetrable protective wall, because what is without dignity can never touch dignity" (GA 70: 173).

The history of beyng remains protected in its dignity precisely because it is impenetrable to the public that despises "the ghost of being" as something abstract and far from life. (I suspect that Heidegger is thinking about how his own thinking is being judged.) The truth of history does not lie in what becomes public but in concealment.[23]

In section 153 Heidegger meditates anew on "the history of being" but now writes being with an "i." Although he is not always consistent in the differentiated use of "y" or "i," the continued use of "i" in this section when speaking of the history of being, indicates that he is thinking of the history of the first beginning. However, even the history of the first beginning must be thought in terms of its inceptive occurrence. "The history of being (unconcealment, concealment, letting go into 'semblance' and into the distorted essence)," Heidegger writes, "cannot be brought under a rule" and is not to be thought as a process (GA 70: 174). He is especially concerned to differentiate himself from Hegel here, who still thinks in the domain of objectivity for the representing subjectivity. But still, the questions Heidegger asks himself a little earlier in the section remain pressing: "But how shall the history of being be experienced? Does this experience not imply the insidiousness of all historiographical calculating, in so far as knowledge [*Kenntnisse*] is at all necessary? Or does being itself still let itself be creatively thought without any historiographical addition?" (GA 70: 173).

Heidegger does not find an answer to these questions and yet insists on the necessity to think inceptively and overcome all historiography. He takes up the different approaches to history again in section 159. Here he adds a third way of thinking that lies in-between a historiographical explanation and an appropriated beyng-historical thinking, and this is *the world-historical account—how each fundamental stance in beings provides the ground for the character of beings* (for example the Christian God as highest and first reality) (for example, the human being as the one who stands for himself and effects and plans) [*sic*]" (GA 70: 179).

Heidegger refers here to his own interpretation of how the being of beings is disclosed and thought in the Middle Ages and modernity, an interpretation we also find in his lecture courses. He notes how the three ways of thinking history "at first" "run through each other" and disguise each other and how the path of the less inceptive explications of history have to be taken because the third path can only be appropriated inceptively, that is, it cannot be willed but only granted. Clearly, thinking the history of being as inception must remain rare and, where and whether Heidegger's saying carries this out, must also remain a question to the reader of *On Inception*.

Still, Heidegger does not let go (even in his more inceptive interpretation of the history of beyng as a nonlinear event) of the way he traces the history of being (metaphysics) since *Contributions*. Section 154 outlines this history again, but in the form of questions:

> Must there not open up in the history of being the relation of being and humans?
>
> Must there not being itself leave itself to this relation and thereby to the semblance that it [being] first is established through humans and in a human way?
>
> Is beingness as ἰδέα not the beginning of this letting loose in which being conceals itself into appearance and appearing [*Schein und Scheinen*]? (GA 70: 176)

The questions proceed all the way to the necessity of the plight of the lack of plight in order to find a more inceptive relation to being. But then Heidegger adds a somewhat perplexing question: "Is the history of being as metaphysics not the testing [*Erprüfung*] of the capacity of humans to Da-sein?" (GA 70: 176).

Why think in terms of "testing" here? Why this idea that humans need to prove themselves?

According to the "logic" of the history of being that Heidegger recounts since *Contributions to Philosophy*, metaphysics must first find its consummation in the "utmost surrendering to beings . . . in the outcasting of the truth of beings into the forgottenness of being" (GA 70: 176). The utmost plight of the lack of plight is necessary for entering into a more inceptive, authentic relation to beyng because only in the utmost plight the withdrawal of beyng (the withdrawal as which beyng occurs) and thus the nothing pertaining to being and with it concealment and unconcealment, downgoing and departure, that is, the event as inception, can be experienced and thought. After this reminiscence, in section 156 Heidegger gives himself some leeway to consider again the "depravity of the era" (and some comments he makes here sound very much like polemics in his *Black Notebooks*). But otherwise, in the remainder of part V of *On Inception*, he mainly focuses on the difference between history and historiography and the difficulty of thinking history not in terms of a sequence.

The problem of sequential thinking and the struggle to not only differentiate historiography from history but to think beyng-historically emerges as well in the context of the question of the first and other beginning (or rather "inception," since the German word is always *Anfang*) and of beginnings.[24] "Between the beginnings clefts [*Klüfte*]; their [the beginnings'] protruding is the same; that [is] not something general but in each case unique" (GA 70: 181).

Heidegger explains in an earlier section "that each beginning is separated by a cleft from the beginning and that this cleft does not first exist by itself but originates in inceptiveness" (GA 70: 61). He also writes: "Each cleft from beginning *to* beginning determines itself in each case out of each. Each beginning is in its uniqueness the history [*die Geschichte*]" (GA 70: 64).

Heidegger is aware that to speak of beginnings (in plural) somehow views them "from without" (GA 70: 64) and thus he moves in and out of a somewhat representational way of thinking. The challenge for us also is to keep representation at bay when we attempt to interpret the sentence fragment "Between the beginnings clefts." The notion of cleft (which he uses already in *Contributions*) relates to the notion of the abyss that thinking needs to be exposed to in order to inceptively think the beginning such that through the other the first beginning also first opens up inceptively. Perhaps one could think of the cleft as the "clefting" of the in-between into which Heidegger's thinking finds itself dislodged, which is the more originary, abyssal dimension of beyng. From here he thinks either back into the first or ahead into the other beginning.

In Da-sein beyng always happens uniquely in the same way in which we can say that each disclosive moment in our lives is unique. The notion of uniqueness (*Einzigkeit*) is essential for Heidegger's thinking of the event, as the issue is to be appropriated into the event, such that, when thinking finds itself appropriated into carrying out the event, beyng is experienced in each case in its uniqueness, a uniqueness that is left once one attempts to represent the event. The thinking "of" the event in its uniqueness thus must occur as a repetitive attempt at letting itself be appropriated by tuning in to the dignity and poverty of beyng. Heidegger will continue to intensify this exercise in *The Event*.

Notes

1. I am translating *Über den Anfang* with "On Inception" and not "On Beginning" for reasons that will become clear further down. I will, however retain the customary translation "beginning" (and not "inception") when speaking of the first and other beginning. Readers should be aware that the German word in all these instances is the same: *Anfang*.

2. I will not comment on this part because Heidegger here repeats the stance he takes already in *Contributions* toward *Being and Time*, namely, as attempting to articulate being in the language of metaphysics and as being preparatory for the "leap" into the truth of beyng as event.

3. This section contains material developed in a lecture course I gave at the Collegium Phaenomenologicum in 2013 and that was published in another version in my essay: "Heidegger's Reticence: From *Contributions* to *Das Ereignis* and toward *Gelassenheit*," *Research in Phenomenology* 45, no. 1 (2015): 1–32.

4. Peter Hanly, who is translating *Über den Anfang*, made me aware of this translation. In previous publications, I translated *Anfängnis* as "initiation."

5. "Bewahrt" contains the word "wahr," "true."

6. See also section 77, 95–98, where Heidegger speaks of "carrying out the beginnings" in remembering and thinking ahead.

7. The abbreviation (f.b.) means "first beginning" and (o.b.) means "other beginning."

8. In *On Inception*, Heidegger tends to write "being" and not "beyng" when the emphasis is on arising, clearing, or presencing in relation to the first beginning. The first beginning is still thought inceptively, that is, being is not thought metaphysically but more originarily than metaphysical thinking that takes beings and not being as a point of departure for questioning.

9. Note how Heidegger writes being with an "i" although he could just as well have written it with a "y," since usually, when thinking the event of appropriation, Heidegger writes *Seyn*. Perhaps he is writing "being" because the emphasis here is on appearing and beings and not on withdrawal.

10. Heidegger points out this differentiation between the beingless and the abandonment of beings by being in section 98 (GA 70: 121).

11. That Heidegger indicates here that "inception, downgoing, departure" belong to being (written with an "i") confirms my sense that there is no separation between "beyng" and "being" but rather a different emphasis (downgoing and arising).

12. "The beingless 'is' the prior-inceptive and the post-inceptive and this not insofar as it has the character of inception but insofar as it only 'becomes' a being in the inception and ceases to be [*entwird*] in the downgoing. . . . only here the innermost nihilation [*Nichtung*] of being itself is revealed, that in itself it is not only concealment and refusal but the disappropriation in the manner of downgoing [*untergänglich die Enteignung*]" (GA 70: 122).

13. At the entrance of the temple of Apollo at Delphi is written μηδέν ἄγαν, "nothing in excess." This is a principle of life advocating for moderation. The "nothing" shelters being from excess.

14. See, for instance, GA 70: 19, 92. I will say more about the notion of *Verwindung* in my discussion of *The Event*.

15. "The relation of beyng to humans, however, harbors in itself beforehand, before there comes into play a determination coming from humans, the appropriation of the clearing of the there [Da-], which occurs essentially as Da-sein" (GA 70: 125).

16. "Das Tragen und Hin- und Her- heben ist das Schwingen. , , , Die Getragenheit ist das Schwingen im Schwung der Geforenheit aus dem Zuwurf, in den das Seyn sich das Menschenwesen er-eignet" (GA 70: 126).

17. See section 267 of *Contributions*, where Heidegger writes that the encounter between gods and humans is the origin for the unsettlement characterizing the relation to beings.

18. One might also bring into play the notion of death that Heidegger reflects on in section 120, where he speaks of death as downgoing and as *being* utmost beginning, utmost concealment.

19. Heidegger writes: "Poverty [*Armut*] and the fullness of beyng as event / Gentelness [*San-ftmut*] and the stillness of beyng / Forebearance [*Langmut*] and the while / Gracefulness [*Anmut*] this threefold mood as the shining of inception (the magnanimity of the forbearance for the dignity of the poverty of appropriation) / Magnanimity [*Großmut*] beyng as conceal-ment (dignity) / Melancholy [*Schwermut*] and the abyssal character of beyng / Equanimity [*Gleichmut*] and the fracturedness of beyng / Lack of mood and ill-mood [the distorted es-sence in beyng]" (GA 70: 135).

20. In *The Event*, Rojcewicz translates *Auslegung* with "interpretation."

21. Heidegger writes: "The meditation on exposition does not serve the establishment of a 'theory of interpretation,' but only carries out the attempt to let exposition become more stead-fast. Meditation is itself an exposition, not the exposition of an exposition, but the entering into [*das Sicheinlegen in*] its essence" (GA 70: 149).

22. Heidegger here uses words related to *Stimme* and *Stimmung* (voice and attunement or disposition): "Das Überstimmende gewährt die Stimmung ihres Bestimmens, dessen Stimme sie nur wie einen Nachklang vernehmen, aber vorausklingen lassen den Nachkommenden" (GA 70: 150).

23. In section 160, Heidegger writes that the basic trait of history is concealment (GA 70: 181).

24. Here I would like to remind readers that I am keeping the English word "beginning" when speaking of the first and other beginning, even if I otherwise translate *Anfang* with "inception," since to speak and write of the first and other beginning has been customary in interpreta-tions of Heidegger's texts for so long.

7　Hovering in Incipience

A Critical Engagement with Heidegger's
Über den Anfang (*On Inception*) (GA 70)

M<small>Y EXPOSITORY READING</small> of *On Inception* in chapter 6 was already infused with some perplexity regarding Heidegger's trajectory of thought in this volume. Where is he going? How should we understand this "downgoing into departure" and this "letting pass by" of the machinational deployment of beings; how should we understand this with respect to history; not only with respect to what Heidegger calls history but also with respect to what was happening historically in a more "ontic" sense? How should we understand the arising of the notion of the "beingless" in this context and where does this lead us with respect to the question of the "simultaneity" of and difference between beyng and beings? These are the main questions I will pursue in this chapter.[1]

Heidegger's Thinking of History

A change with respect to history occurs when Heidegger lets machination pass by. One may say that by doing so, he removes himself farther from "history" more commonly understood. In *Contributions*, he would stress that history happens as a decision and this decision was at the same time cast as the decision of the history for a people. This narrative, that suggested indeed a moment in "history" when the event would happen, when truth would be grounded; this narrative now (in *On Inception*) seems gone, and what he calls history (*Geschichte*) is even more removed from a more common notion of history. It is far removed from the efficacy of beings, from political organizations, institutional practices, and from the advancement of military tanks or air strikes. (It does, however, involve the "coming into being of beings" and I will reflect more on this later in this chapter.)

Considering that Heidegger's attempt in the poietic writings has always been to think nonrepresentationally and out of a sense of being, responsive to an appropriating call of beyng, in *On Inception* he appears to have made "progress." There are moments when he articulates the incipience of inception, the "taking-to itself and catching of what is appropriated," moments that have left linear thinking behind. When he articulates the incipience of inception thus, the narrative of the history of beyng as a transition from the first to the other beginning recedes and we are left with nothing but the articulation of a "coming to be out of itself in departure into the abyss"; a middle voice event with no imaginable agent, subject, or object, or a linear time line.

Yet what is this "history" that has been so much stripped from any concrete thing or event, from any human entity? Where does it happen? And why does Heidegger insist upon thinking history more and more inceptively, more and more removed from the concrete happening of things?

Certainly, Heidegger does not let go of the narrative of the transition from metaphysics to the thinking of the event all together, and at the end of chapter 7 I also highlighted a struggle in his attempt to think history nonmetaphysically. He makes a clear differentiation between history and historiography, but what is less clear is the extent to which he or indeed anyone can think "purely" historically in an inceptive way (in Heidegger's sense). Before pursuing this question further, however, I would like to reflect more on Heidegger's insistence on thinking purely in a *geschichtlich* way. What is so wrong with *Historie*?

In *Besinnung*, where Heidegger meditates more extensively on historiography and technology, he points out (among other things) that *Historie* entrenches in the subject the relation to beings and that it evades history in the sense of a decision rooted in beyng (GA 66: 183). The historian in the traditional sense displays history before his mind's eye, looks at and represents the past as a series of events, of historical facts that can be used for explaining the present. I can nicely picture some German professors in this context, and a sense of self-complacency and mastery among his colleagues that must have bothered Heidegger as well. But philosophically speaking, the problem is that the neo-Kantian division between world and subject (neo-Kantianism was very much alive during Heidegger's career) and the turn to constitutive subjectivity as the site of truth, infused the academic understanding of history as well.[2]

What is lost in a subjectively rooted approach to history is a sense of the strangeness and otherness of history (its noncontemporaneity and removedness) as well as the insight that it is not we who "have" history but history that has us and mostly escapes our grasp. Yet who wants to give up a position of power, the power of the one who masters the knowledge of the past, and to acknowledge instead how histories we hardly know lay claim on us, how we are subject to and marked by lineages we embody and that are fundamentally strange to us?

One may, of course, question whether Heidegger really renounces a position of power in his view on history. Is not the gesture of capitulating in the face of the abandonment of beings by being and of submitting oneself to the withdrawal of being, of renouncing "loud publicness" for the sake of the solitary path of the stillness of beyng, is this not still a form of power, a giving oneself to and thus participating in the greater or rather, deeper, most hidden power? Is this not yet another guise of what Nietzsche calls the aesthetic ideal? I am reminded, here, as well of what Deleuze writes in his book on Spinoza: "Humility, poverty, and chastity become the effects of an especially rich and superabundant life, sufficiently powerful to have conquered through and subordinated every other instinct to itself."[3]

Heidegger's emphasis on the dignity of beyng could as well be constructed as the last resort of self-affirmation of someone who has lost everything: all is lost . . . yet there remains dignity in poverty.

Yet what do we gain when we read Heidegger this way? That we put ourselves in a position of power with respect to his estranging way of thinking?

There is a fundamental vulnerability one is exposed to in acknowledging to the fullest what thrownness entails, and that one cannot escape what has happened and also perhaps what will not happen. Nietzsche's *amor fati* bespeaks this vulnerability as well. At the same time, in loving our fate we may not simply be passively undergoing it. Perhaps there is something like *amor fati* at work in Heidegger's ability to let machination be, and in finding in that "letting-be" another time-space of being and thinking. (Humor might be another venue for accepting one's fate and taking a more "active" stance in it, but Heidegger does not quite seem the type for this kind of humor.)

To be historically, *geschichtlich sein*, would entail then, in contrast to the historiographical (*historisch*) viewpoint, an acceptance of historical being, of whatever is given, of the "gift" of being; it would entail an undergoing of history rather than a mastery of it. Perhaps we could read in this vein the inceptive departure that Heidegger speaks about in terms of the most proper essence of the history of beyng. One could, of course, also remain suspicious of Heidegger's "going under" and find in it a flight from the world and a retreat into some kind of "interiority." Such thinking, however, slips all too easily into a differentiation between world and subject that is precisely what Heidegger's thinking has allowed us to leave behind.

Still, the question remains: Where does history happen if we follow Heidegger's thought that history is nothing but the happening of the event as inception? Since history still requires a being (*Seiendes*) to happen and it does not happen with machinationally deployed things, the only space or time-space where it happens is when thinking happens. History happens in Heidegger's thinking only as long as he is thinking; it happens in a thinking that at the same time strives to leave all subjectivity behind and to be responsively attuned to "what" gives itself to thought.

However, "what" gives itself to thought when thinking occurs most inceptively, is not an "it," is nothing substantial, but is the event of the coming to word of the event. Unless Heidegger meditates on the first beginning, which rests upon his interpretation of some canonical texts of the Western tradition; and unless he interprets what happens around him in terms of machination and lived experience.

This belongs to history, too, but only insofar as it can be gathered in thinking the event as inception.

* * *

I remember when I first read Heidegger's lecture course *Introduction to Metaphysics* from the summer semester of 1935. I read the lecture course in light of *Contributions*. The dramatic account he gives there of the Greek beginning of philosophy—taking recourse to the chorus in Sophocles's *Antigone*—was fascinating: The Greeks were exposed to the overpowering power of nature (φύσις) and found themselves compelled to come to a stance in the midst of it. They had to hold on to what showed itself—to beings—and they came to cultivate a stance toward beings such that thinking and being were de-cided, fissured. From now on, thinking would relate to beings as *Gegen-stand* as what stands against thinking, and later (in modernity) beings would be what are *vor-gestellt*, placed in front of thinking. I remember distinctly the sense I got that the pathos at work in Heidegger's account was his pathos, a German pathos.

The account we get in *On Inception* of the first beginning appears largely to have been stripped of this more dramatic pathos; the *Fortgang*, the leaving that marks the movement of the first beginning when beings are left to themselves, is as quiet and "subterranean" as the departure into the abyss in the other beginning (although I must confess that the notion of the *Aufstand* of beings Heidegger uses in section 9 when speaking of the beginning of metaphysics—*Aufstand* literally means standing up against and is used in the context of rebellions—is reminiscent of his earlier depiction of the forcefulness of the presence of beings) (GA 70: 27).

Staying in Inception

The conclusion my previous reflections suggest is that only in a thinking of the event as inception, that is, in Heidegger's thinking, history occurs inceptively; only in thinking, the event finds a site. We might add that beyng or history also happens in Hölderlin's thinking, but there (as we will see in chapter 8) it occurs differently. Since Heidegger lets go of the idea that the event could happen for a people anytime in the foreseeable future (in a *Black Notebook* of that time he speculates on history happening "at the earliest in 2300" GA 96: 225; Ü XIV: 92). It is important that a site for it be maintained in thinking, that thinking immerse itself always anew into that abyssal time-space of inception. This is, I believe, why Heidegger is concerned about finding constancy and a "stay" (*Bleiben*) in the event by thinking the event always anew in meditative exercises that seems to be marked by constant repetition.

There are two sections in *On Inception* where Heidegger meditates on beyng as *Bleiben*, staying (or remaining). In section 10 he speaks of an ambiguity (*Zwei-*

deutigkeit) in the notion of "staying" depending on whether presencing (beyng) is taken into the egress (the downgoing marking the transition to the other beginning) or presencing is solidified into something present. Heidegger speaks of ambiguity and not of two senses of "staying," which confirms again that he thinks the incipience in which first and other beginning are not yet decided. I wonder about the temporality of this inception, the temporality of what he addresses as a staying, which means for him that incipience is not left (GA 70: 28). This staying should be distinguished from lasting and continuing (*Dauern* and *Fortwähren*), writes Heidegger. (We may assume this is because both suggest some form of linear time.)

When we think "staying" in terms of "not leaving inceptiveness," this is when we think "historically against all metaphysical habituation" (GA 70: 28). True *Geschichtlichkeit* is thus extrapolated from all linear thinking of time. Heidegger refers to Hölderlin and how it cannot be decided whether in Hölderlin's notion of "staying" (this refers to the last verse of the poem *Andenken*: "Yet what remains the poets found" [Was bleibet aber, stiften die Dichter]) is thought beyng-historically or metaphysically (this stresses again the ambiguity of "staying"). Beyng-historical staying "consists in the return into inception, in departure. The latter is the most intimate not-leaving inception because inception has left behind all intrusion of a leaving" (GA 70: 28). Heidegger performs this return over and over again and yet always differently. He has to perform it again and again because inception as he thinks it, although it is not a product of thought, happens only through thought. (Why am I reminded here of Descartes who in his first meditation finds the truth of his existence only as long as he is thinking it? Perhaps despite the greatest difference with respect to the thinker of self-consciousness, Heidegger's thinking also exhibits a strange proximity to the latter in the concentric force of a dispossessed thinking practiced in solitude and in staying with nonbeing.)

In section 20 Heidegger proceeded to think as "*Ausbleiben*" the purest [*reinste*] way of staying [*bleiben*] because it is inceptive and outgoing." Ausbleiben usually means that something does not happen or fails to appear. As usual, he wants us to hear the word more literally such that the "bleiben" is emphasized. I will translate it as "staying away." He writes: "Staying away is the pure unconcealment of the arriving (the not yet and never arrived and arrival-like) egress. Such arrival has strayed from all beings and has caught itself in purest staying away" (GA 70: 38).

We need to remind ourselves here, that because staying applies to inception, it does not indicate primarily a "human" temporal dwelling or the temporalizing of human be-ing, although inception requires human steadfastness or indwelling (*Inständigkeit*) for a clearing to happen. One might compare this staying to the notion of time-space that Heidegger develops in section 242 of *Contributions to Philosophy*. Here Heidegger speaks of the abyssal ground (the *Ab-grund* belonging to the truth of beyng) as a staying away (*Ausbleiben*). I interpreted this in chapter 2 in relation to the abandonment of beings by beings. Staying away is a "leaving empty" and thus simultaneously an opening up, an attuning or disposing disclosure. The emptiness transports into the arriving future and breaks open a happening past, that is, the staying away is a spatializing and temporalizing, a remembering expectation that opens up the decision over beyng (GA 65: 383–384; C: 303). Beyng and history are not yet decided here but they become decidable in the time-space of the abyss.

Whereas in *Contributions* the staying away marks the temporalizing and spatializing of the time-space of decision over history or lack of history, in *On Inception* Heidegger thinks the staying away as opening up the arrival of the egress and as the site where history truly happens. His thinking found a stay in the staying away.

But again: What kind of history (*Geschichte*) is this "dimly lit" happening?[4] What about Heidegger's idea only a few years earlier ("The Origin of the Work of Art," for instance) that history happens in the openness of a world? Where did the world go? And where did beings go that, according to his thought in *Contributions*, are what shelters truth (out of Da-sein)?

Still in section 20 of *On Inception* Heidegger writes that the staying away has parted from beings (die *Verabschiedung des Seienden*) (GA 70: 38). Such parting does not effect anything with respect to beings and yet it allows beings to be "elevated above themselves" and to arise in the openness otherwise refused to them: "The parting first brings beings (in the manner of the event, not as a nexus of effects) into the rareness of their essential simplicity and first-time-character [*Erstmaligkeit*] proper to beyng" (GA 70: 38).[5]

It seems paradoxical: beings, by parting from beings, first rise into the open. If we compare this thought again to *Contributions* we may say that in *Contributions*, the time-space of the abyss is yet to be grounded into beings, it yet needs to find a concrete site through the sheltering of truth in beings. In *On Inception*, on the one hand, Heidegger seems to make a similar move, the staying away parts from beings (this is analogous to the abandonment of beings by being). On the other hand, this parting now somehow lets beings arise into the open (whereas before beings did not yet shelter truth). What beings arise into the open here? What beings besides the words of the thinker?

This brings me again to the question of the relation between beyng and beings (the question of the simultaneity of and difference between beyng and beings), which now needs to take into account the beingless (or nothingless) as well.

Beings and the Beingless

The way Heidegger engages or addresses beings changes with *On Inception*. What changes as well is their "place" in the thinking of the event. Especially when we think of that passage in which he says that beings (as the beingless) are somehow older than being (GA 70: 121), it appears that the simultaneity of being and beings that he spoke of in *Contributions* is radicalized because we can in no way think of beyng as the source or generator of beings. What is also radicalized, though, is the difference between beyng and beings. We can make sense of this to some extent: Precisely by not clinging to things and by thinking of things merely as what is posited by subjectivity and useful for the deployment of power, that is, by letting things go, by turning away from them and tuning to no-thingness, beings simply emerge as beings and leave us exposed to a dispropriation (*Enteignis*) that resonates in our relation to things. This appears akin to a mystical practice: to let go of worldly things in order to find a union with . . . not God in Heidegger's case, not Being as some kind of presence, but a movement of departure that clears, opens up beyng permeated by nothingness. Again, the poem "Der Cherbinische Wandersmann" [The cherubinic pilgrim] by Angelus Silesius comes to mind and now with its second line as well: "The rose is without 'why'; it blooms because it blooms / It pays no attention to itself, asks not if it is seen."

Poverty and dignity are what Heidegger finds in the departure to the beingless.

I had suggested in chapter 5 that perhaps this new attunement in Heidegger's thinking was connected to the war, especially when considering the text in which he speaks of the strangeness of the war (*das Seltsame des Krieges*). There are, however, many ways in which we find ourselves removed from our engagement with things and things emerge in their strangeness or (let me use another word here) *indifference*. Depression makes that possible, but also a simple contemplative mood. "In-difference" is a fruitful word in thinking with Heidegger the difference between beings and being and the beinglessness of beings, especially if we hyphenate the word. In *Living with Indifference*, Charles Scott explores different forms of indifference, always highlighting the middle-voice character that events of indifference bear.[6] In a paper written in his honor, I explored the bodily dimension of indifference, arguing that we can be attuned to indifference of things and events because we bear indifference with us in our bodies.[7] What I had in mind is the experience of our body not so much as the body we live in, the *Leib* and *Leiben* Heidegger addresses, for instance, in the *Zollikon Seminars*, but rather the "thing quality" of our bodies, in which our bodies, the same bodies we live through, appear in their strangeness: these hands I call mine, this nose, these organs, the growing of hair and aging of skin. This sense of our indifferent body is not the same as the body under objective scrutiny of a scientist, since in this latter case the body is removed from its singularity, from the "mineness" to which my indifferent body in some strange way still adheres.

"My" indifferent body is an "other" belonging to "me" (or "I" to it) that echoes the otherness of all singular beings I may or may not encounter, beings in their indifference to "me," to my desires and hopes. (Merleau-Ponty's chiasm of touching touched flesh can be made fruitful for thinking the indifferent body.) Am I here still thinking with Heidegger, though?

It nevertheless seems to me that the notion of the beingless as "prior" to be-ing and thus not effected by "Being" [sic] brings Heidegger's thinking to the brink of thinking an otherness he previously could not think insofar as his thinking was held in a tension (the draw of beyng's withdrawal that needed to be with-stood) that could not allow for the indifferent happening of things. Perhaps the change has to do with maturing as well, with outgrowing a Sturm und Drang phase that in Heidegger's case drove him to embrace for some time Nietzsche's pathos and also a national socialist pathos.

It seems to me, furthermore, that in some respect thinking the difference between beyng and beings along the notions of the beingless and nothingless brings Heidegger closer to Derrida's *différance* since the beingless is not even nothing (and thus the "nothingless"). There is a "surface-quality" to the beingless since "it" is without depth, has no voice, carries no attunement. (Or does it?) The beingless is as silent as the "a" of *différance*.[8] Just as the "a" of *différance*, the word "beingless" is a marker marking nothing. One can draw even one more parallel between Heidegger and Derrida in this context. When Derrida introduces his no-tion of difference in the 1960s, giving Heidegger's notion of the ontological dif-ference a more Nietzschean bent, Derrida places difference in the context of the epoch of metaphysics coming to an end and embracing this end similarly to the way in which Nietzsche embraced active nihilism as a strength. In *Margins of Philosophy*, Derrida suggests an affirmation of Nietzsche's "active oblivion,"[9] which contrasts, of course, with Heidegger's struggle against the forgetting of being in the mid- and late 1930s. But now, in *On Inception* Heidegger seems to have found a way to embrace this forgetting—not by practicing it himself, but by affirm-ing the abandonment of beings by beyng, by affirming machination as something that does not need to be withstood but that must be left to be.

Still, the proximity between Heidegger and Derrida has its limits.

For Derrida we can never simply leave metaphysics, hence the necessity to question its limits and expose its operations if we want to make room for what is excluded in metaphysical discourse. Heidegger believes in the possibility of the return to a beginning, or rather to *the* event of inception, to the event *as* incep-tion, and he believes that some of us can dwell in inceptiveness and stay on the hither "side" of the metaphysical primacy of beings and of thinking in the poverty and dignity of beyng. What he says about the beingless he can only know and say in being.[10]

Transformation: Death and Inception

Transformation for Heidegger happens in a return to inception underneath the deployment of beings; it cannot occur through beings. Beings are beingless and nothingless until an "in-between" is cleared and being comes in-between and lets beings arise as beings.[11] Even if beyng does not effect beings, even if the beingless is in a certain way earlier than being, beings "are not"—until the event occurs and a clearing is appropriated. For Heidegger, now, at the end of metaphysics, this requires the downgoing that he associates with death. It is through death (understood beyng-historically out of Da-sein) that humans go under and "are" most inceptively (GA 70: 138–139, 142). Heidegger is rethinking his earlier thought in *Being and Time* that only in being toward death is being as such disclosed. Now he writes: "Death *is* downgoing and that *is* utmost beginning, *is* utmost concealment, *is* being" (GA 70: 139).

Is there still a Christian lineage at work here in Heidegger's thinking: transformation through death? On the other hand the idea of death and rebirth is more ancient than Christianity and not limited to the West, perhaps because any human can witness the cycles of life and death. But still this cycle of life could be seen as a change in and with beings. For Heidegger, however, the issue is not the life cycle of plants and animals or even the human species. The issue is one of history. Does this not mean that it addresses primarily being "for humans" even if Heidegger "dehumanizes" his thinking of beyng more and more? No stone, no bee, no dog, no tree cares for the history of beyng. We may say with Heidegger "beings simply are beings." And yet, are we not beings, too? What about the changes happening with the bodies we call ours (growth or growths, and decay)? What about the "material" changes into which we are physically interwoven? Climate, habitat, buildings, rhythms of events marking our daily lives? How should we think these with Heidegger? Are they even a question for him? The move he makes is always the same (although it occurs in different ways): All beings in our epoch are always already machinationally determined. How we relate to them is determined by how beyng occurs as withdrawal and abandonment. There is only one way to open a time-space for beyng that may allow beings to become "more being" (*seiender*): the removal into the abyss and thus to the incipience of inception such that beyng finds a site in the thinking of inception, in the words of the thinker that may at best let resonate the beingless. Only the "sacrifice" of those who go under and venture the abyss, keeps up the hope for an other beginning.

Only a few years ago, when I was reminded of a poem by Petrarca based on Ovid's *Metamorphoses*,[12] did it dawn on me that there was a kind of transformation Heidegger could not or would not think. The metamorphoses the poet describes occur through physical transformations that he addresses also as "transfigurements." The soul of the transfigured lags behind, so to speak, as he or she finds him- or herself transformed into a laurel or a dog by the beloved. The transfiguration is in no way anticipated; it simply occurs. In some way this is a human experience we all go through as we find our bodies change and we need to adapt to the new (alien) physical figure. It is experienced perhaps more intensely in unexpected traumatic events like the sudden death of a loved one or else in the "transfiguring" experience of art.[13] But on a more inconspicuous level any new place we go to requires an adjustment of our being in relation to the place. The way this relation plays out in each case is of course imbued with histories and lineages that we can perhaps only barely grasp, but still, there is a certain "precedence" of the physical setting or constellation, one might say.

Did Heidegger perhaps touch on thinking a transformation through beings when he speaks of the priority of the beingless and the coming-in-between of being into the formerly beingless? We may also ask whether the transformation in his thinking—the move to letting the abandonment of beings by being be—could not be described in terms of a transfigurement or transfigurements. Should his thinking be understood not only or simply as responding to or attempting to respond to the silent call of beyng but as a response to things and events (beings) changing?

I believe so, but in doing so have departed to a considerable extent from Heidegger's thinking. To think of the transformations in his thinking as being determined not only by the silent call of beyng, that is, out of an attunement with no apparent origin that at the same time is "historical" in some way—to think of these transformations as being determined as well by the transformation of "concrete" things and events requires that one take the simultaneity of beyng and beings further than Heidegger did and that one let go of the narrative of the history of being that is gathered, in 1940, in his narrative of "the" inception.

The inceptive dimension of being and thinking that Heidegger sought out in his poietic writings implied an active "looking away" from things. It unfolded more and more as a disciplined practice of staying with no-thing but the word of inception, the silent, inceptive word. This brought him finally to a collection of thoughts he deemed worthy of the simple title: *The Event*.

Notes

1. I will treat some themes from *On Inception* that are carried further in *The Event* (e.g., such as the notion of dignity, and language) in chapter 9.

2. Gadamer takes this to task in *Truth and Method* in his critique of a historical consciousness that works analogously to aesthetic consciousness and that recognizes history as being relative to (and thus contemporary with) the subject. See Hans-Georg Gadamer, *Truth and Method*, 2nd rev. ed., trans. rev. Joel Weinsheimer and Donald G. Marshall (London/New York: Continuum, 2004), part II, 1–3. Dilthey is one of the main figures Gadamer discusses in this context.

3. Gilles Deleuze, *Spinoza: Practical Philosophy*, trans. Robert Hurley (San Francisco: City Lights, 2001), 3.

4. I am taking the notion "dimly lit" from Claudia Barracchi's essay "The End of Philosophy and the Experience of Unending Φύσις," in *Paths in Heidegger's Later Thought*, ed. Günter Figal, Diego D'Angelo, Tobias Keiling, and Guang Yang (Bloomington: Indiana University Press, forthcoming).

5. The phrasing is somewhat strange in the German too: "Die Verabschiedung bringt (ereignishaft, nicht als Wirkungszusammenhang) das Seiende erst in die Seltenheit seiner dem Seyn eigenen Wesenseinfachheit und Erstmaligkeit."

6. Charles Scott, *Living with Indifference* (Bloomington: Indiana University Press, 2007).

7. Daniela Vallega-Neu, "Bodily Being and Indifference," *Epoché* 17, no. 1 (2012): 111–122.

8. Jacques Derrida, "Différance," in *Margins of Philosophy*, trans. Allan Boss (Chicago: University of Chicago Press, 1982), 1–27. Originally published as *Marges de la Philosophie* (Paris: Les Editions de Minuit, 1972), 1–29.

9. Derrida, *Margins of Philosophy*, 136; *Marges de la Philosophie*, 163.

10. "Das Seinlose ist wißbar nur im Sein" (GA 70: 122).

11. I am writing "being" and not "beyng" in order to differentiate the notion of beyng that Heidegger thinks prevalently in terms of withdrawal from the "being" into which beings rise that Heidegger writes, in fact, as *Sein*, that is, as "being" without "y" (see GA 70: 121).

12. Francesco Petrarca, *Rime Sparse* (Milan: Mursia, 1979), poem number 23 of his *Canzoniere*.

13. See John Sallis, *Transfigurements: On the True Sense of Art* (Chicago: University of Chicago Press, 2008).

8 *The Event* (GA 71)

Humility, poverty, chastity are his (the philosopher's) way of being a grand
vivant, of making a temple of his own body, for a cause that is all too
proud, all too rich, all too sensual.

—Gilles Deleuze, *Spinoza: Practical Philosophy*

Composition and Content of *The Event*

In *Contributions to Philosophy* Heidegger writes that *Contributions* "are not yet
able to join the free conjuncture of the truth of beyng out of beyng itself" (GA 65:
4; C: 6) and that the volume contains only an *attempt* at thinking "of" the event
(GA 65: 3; C: 5). The title of GA 71, *The Event*, suggests that Heidegger believed
that he had finally written a book constituting something like a "conjuncture of
the truth of beyng," a book able to bring to language the event, to let the saying of
beyng fully eventuate in the words of the thinker. It also awakens the expectation—
not of a systematic work, since it should be clear by now that thinking "of" the
event cannot be systematic but—of a composition of some kind. And yet, already
the forewords to the volume indicate again that what follows is only "the attempt
at a responding, grounding word: the saying of the carrying out" (GA 71: 3;
E: xxiii).[1] Heidegger also speaks of it as "a path on a Holzweg," "a timber trail off
the beaten track," which means a path leading into the woods but ending abruptly
and at no specific place. There are also indications, however, that Heidegger understands what he writes in *The Event* to be at least to some extent an appropriated saying: "Each of the basic words says the same, the event . . . [and] every word
replies to the claim of the *turning*: that the truth of beyng essentially occurs in
the beyng of truth" (GA 71: 3; E: xxiii). The basic words he addresses are, of course,
not to be understood as concepts; indeed, Heidegger calls them "traces" that escape representational thinking, traces that first trace what is to be thought and
that I attempt to retrace and elucidate here.

That Heidegger understands *The Event* to be clearly a "better" or more inceptive
attempt at saying of the event becomes evident when he criticizes *Contributions
to Philosophy* in the last foreword.

The first point he makes is that in *Contributions*, "the presentation is in places
too didactic," in other words, he was still thinking—at times—of an audience, of

how to guide his readers, which implies some form of "outside view." In *The Event* Heidegger will more thoroughly disregard any audience and more radically attempt to respond to nothing but the occurrence of the event.

The second critique concerns the use of the differentiation between the beyng-historical "fundamental question" of beyng and the metaphysical "guiding question" regarding beings. This very differentiation still borrows from metaphysics in that it envisions different levels of thinking and conceptualizing. In *Contributions* Heidegger indicates the necessity of a leap from the guiding to the grounding question (and in his lectures and lecture courses, guiding his audience to follow his thinking in such a leap is always a primary concern), but as we already saw in *On Inception*, the task here is to think right away, more "immediately" out of the event of inception and to rethink from here the first beginning as well.

The final four points of critique all hinge around an overemphasizing of thinking or human being. Heidegger writes that in *Contributions*, "'the beginning' is still grasped as something carried out by thinkers and not in its essential unity with the event." Related to this is that "the event does not receive the purely inceptual essence of the abyss" and that Da-sein is thought "too unilaterally in relation to the human being" (GA 71: 4–5; E: xxiv). I pointed out already in my reading of *On Inception* how Heidegger begins to think the event not primarily in relation to how thinking finds itself appropriated, but in a middle-voice manner and such that various differentiations begins to arise. We will see how this happens in *The Event* as well.

The difference between *Contributions* and *The Event* is manifest also in the composition of the respective works. I pointed out in chapter 2 that there is a partially sequential character to the junctures organizing *Contributions*. The resonating and the interplay "prepare" for the leap into the truth of beyng (GA 65: 9; C: 10). This relates to the differentiation between guiding question and grounding question and to a certain emphasis on thinking that I just addressed: the junctures follow the movement of (Heidegger's) thought in transition to the other beginning as well as the way his readers might be guided to leap (or let themselves be unsettled) into another way of thinking and being.

One may see some similarities between the composition of *The Event* and *Contributions*, as *The Event*, too, starts with parts concerning the first beginning (part I) and the end of metaphysics (part II)[2] (the order of these is inverted with respect to *Contributions* where the resonating precedes the interplay), and, after a part titled "Verwindung," that is, the "twisting free from metaphysics in the 'descent' into the abyssal occurrence of beyng as event,"[3] "proceeds" to sections concerning the event (parts V–VII) (and then to parts that do not suggest any form of "progression").[4] There is nothing resembling the six fugues of *Contributions*, however, which "culminate" in the last god. In that sense, *The Event* is less of a "work" than *Contributions*. *The Event* also does not trace the movement of thinking from metaphysics to beyng-historical thinking. Rather, the first part already speaks more radically "from within" the event as inception. One may say that the "leap" that in *Contributions* constitutes the third juncture, has already happened in *The Event* from the start as Heidegger rethinks more radically the first beginning in its originary occurrence.

In this chapter, I will again follow to some extent the order of the parts of *The Event* (this applies to about half of the volume) as I trace some basic words and attunements in this volume. In many places, however, the language that Heidegger thinks with becomes impossible to adequately translate and very difficult to follow. More often than in previous volumes, he uses poetic sounding words and images that cannot simply be traced back to previous structures of thinking, which thus challenge a hermeneutic reading.[5] I will dedicate most of chapter 9 to the question of language and the limit of the thinkable and sayable to which Heidegger exposes the reader. This will emerge again in the question of the difference between beyng and beings.

The First Beginning

As the editor of *The Event* indicates in his afterword, Heidegger had used the first part of *The Event* for the lecture course of the winter semester 1942–1943. There are indeed many sections that read like notes, and a thorough interpretation of these passages would require that one look at his lecture courses on Parmenides and Heraclitus. My main concern, however, is to show how Heidegger thinks the first beginning, as it were, on the hither side of its development into metaphysics, which occurs in the way he finds an experience of ἀλήθεια (and with it above all of λήθε, concealment) at work in Anaximander, Heraclitus, and Parmenides. My interpretation will go only as far as to show where Heidegger situates the occurrence of inception (the premetaphysical first beginning) in these three thinkers. I will then look at what he now calls *Entwindung*, which is the movement of arising in φύσις that eventually leads to the *Fortgang*, to leaving, or going forth, into metaphysics, and the abandonment of beings by being.

In a number of sections Heidegger seems to remind himself how he ought to proceed in the exposition of the first beginning. "The first beginning is recollected in thinking ahead to the other beginning" (GA 71: 30; E: 30). In other words, Heidegger exposes the first beginning in view of the other beginning that it harbors and makes possible. The task is "to show that the first beginning is outside of metaphysics, but at the same time becomes what lets metaphysics arise" (GA 71: 31; E: 23; translation altered). In section 74 "On the Presentation of the First Beginning" Heidegger lists a number of steps that start with:

> I. Immediately taking up the series Anaximander—Heraclitus—Parmenides each of these for himself.

II. Each already different—also in implicitly thinking ahead and in reference to metaphysics. (GA 71: 55; E: 44)

In each of these philosophers the exposition aims at showing how ἀλήθεια resonates in their thought, although in each case in different ways. Heidegger finds in the experience of ἀλήθεια the most inceptive moment of the "first" philosophers, and it precedes their notion of φύσις such that also φύσις should be understood in relation to ἀλήθεια (GA 71: 14; E: 7–8).

What Heidegger does in *The Event* is not the exposition he talks about (the exposition clearly was aimed at the lecture courses he prepared or gave). We find, however, several sections devoted to Anaximander who, according to Heidegger, "thinks more inceptually than Heraclitus and Parmenides" (GA 71: 71; E: 58).

Anaximander

Anaximander's fragment says in Diels's translation (which I am translating into English): "From whence things have their coming to be, there they must as well perish according to necessity; for they pay penalty and must be judged for their injustice according to the order of Time."[6]

Heidegger translates (I am again translating into English): "From whence, however, the arising occurs for each present being [*Anwesenden*] the departure into it (as the same) emerges according to the compelling need; for every present being gives (from itself) jointure [*Fug*] and also estimation (acknowledgment) one leaves to the other, (all this) out of the overcoming [*Verwindung*] of what is out of joint according to the allotting of the temporalizing through time" (GA 71: 39).

For Heidegger, although the saying of Anaximander does not speak of ἀλήθεια, ἀλήθεια is still experienced as the "whereto" of the arising and the "away-from-where" of departure of beings. The whereto and away-from-where is "presencing" (*Anwesung*) (GA 71: 39). Φύσις occurs in or as presencing and culminates, says Heidegger, in a transition (*Übergang*) that "does not let itself be taken by a solidification of what is present. The transition *preserves* [*wahrt*] the *apeiron*" (GA 71: 37).

So, in Anaximander's thought, there does not occur the primacy of present beings (this would be metaphysical), but an emphasis on the ἀλήθεια occurrence of arising and perishing. Heidegger is tempted to interpret Anaximander's *apeiron* similarly to ἀλήθεια (he asks in section 54: "What if the Anaximander's *apeiron* was the ἀλήθεια?") so that just as the λήθε in ἀλήθεια means concealment, the πέρασ in *apeiron* means limiting in the sense of closure. The πέρασ/λήθε would be "a constraint within confines, on account of which what is present could never place itself purely in the open realm of its presence" (GA 71: 36; E: 27). This constraint occurs in a solidification of singularized semblance, that is, present beings. The "a" would be the removal of that constraint and thus a freeing.

(GA 71: 36–38; E: 27–29).[7] This means that in Anaximander, beings are not solidified into their singular presence but remain freed toward limitless being, the *apeiron* that retains a sense of coming to be and passing away, of unconcealment and concealment.

Heraclitus

Heidegger says less about Heraclitus but refers to the famous fragment DK B123 "φύσις likes to conceal itself" (ἡ φύσις κρύπτεσθαι φιλεῖ [GA 71: 21; E: 14]), in which we can easily hear with a "Heideggerian ear" a sense of concealment and thus of the λήθε of ἀλήθεια.

Heidegger also mentions fragment DK B16 that also takes a prominent role in his lecture course of the summer semester of 1934. He translates it there as follows (in my translation into English): "How could one remain concealed [λάθοι] to what indeed never goes down [μὴ δῦνον]?"[8] In a fragmentary note (section 35 of *The Event*) Heidegger relates the δῦνον in this fragment to φύσις and translates φύσις as "always arising." In the just-mentioned lecture course on Heraclitus, Heidegger interprets the fragment as saying that humans cannot escape what never goes down (*das Untergehende*) (GA 55: 46), and "going down" means "entering into concealment" (GA 55: 49). Thus humans stand in unconcealment, in ἀλήθεια, and the reference to λάθοι seems to indicate at the same time a sense of concealment that Heraclitus has.

In *The Event* Heidegger also notes how λόγος (and he must be referring to Heraclitus's λόγος) is an originary gathering in the sense of "staying-with-oneself— concealment as *unconcealment*" (GA 71: 26; E: 18). Heraclitus's "premetaphysical" λόγος becomes the primary theme of Heidegger's lecture course of the summer semester of 1944, in which he discusses fragments DK B50, B45, and 112. He interprets λέγειν as a gathering determined by ἀλήθεια, by what is unconcealed and its unconcealing (GA 55: 258). When Heraclitus tells us in fragment 50 that one should listen not to him but to the λόγος, in Heidegger's interpretation this presupposes a sense of unconcealing, of ἀλήθεια or truth. Listening to the λόγος seems to echo (but ultimately the echo goes in the other direction) Heidegger's sense of listening/belonging (*gehören*) to the event.

Parmenides

Heidegger begins the first section of the first part of *The Event* with an implicit reference to Parmenides,[9] which I am quoting at length:

> Ἀλήθεια essentially occurs as the beginning.
> True-ness [*Wahr-heit*]
> Truth is "the goddess," Θέα.
> Her house is well rounded, not closed, never (trembling) dissembling heart but, instead, disclosing illuminating of everything. Ἀλήθεια is in the first

beginning the concealed—*true-ness*: the concealing preservation of the cleared-open, the bestowal of the rising up, the permitting of presence. *Truth is the essence of being.* (GA 71: 9–10; E: 3–4; translation altered)

By hyphenating *Wahr-heit*, Heidegger lets resonate (through the "wahr") the semantic field we find in the word "be-wahren," that is, to preserve or safeguard. The house of the goddess truth preserves what is cleared. Already in the first beginning ἀλήθεια is "the concealed" as she illuminates everything, "bestows the rising up" and allows presence. (To see this becomes possible, of course, only through the other beginning.)

Heidegger has a number of sections (notes) on the notion of δόξα in Parmenides, the path of δόξα is a third path next to the inaccessible path of nonbeing and the path of being. According to Heidegger, δόξα in Parmenides means not simply semblance and opinion (as in Plato) but appearing/shining (*Erscheinen*): "46. Δόξα—*gleam, shine, radiance.* Emerging out of itself and yet remaining with itself—continuously radiating out from itself and yet nothing given away or lost. Gleaming—shining not only away from itself and an emergence, but also beckoning back into something dark, concealed, inaccessible. *Shining—the radiance of the self-concealing*" (GA 71: 32; E: 24).

In the first (premetaphysical) beginning, being gives itself into appearing (δόκειν) such that this appearing also "beckons back" into the concealed, the λήθε of ἀλήθεια.

Already in the lecture course of the summer semester 1932 Heidegger reads δόξα in Parmenides as more originary and closer to truth. He highlights the double meaning of δόξα "as the character *of what appears [in] itself,* a look that offers itself" and "as the character of the *comportment* toward the appearing" (GA 35: 184–185).[10] At the same time, in Parmenides, the appearing and the comportment toward it are not yet separated in a way that the appearing would become a *Gegenstand*, something standing opposed to a perceiving. Νοεῖν (perceiving) and εἶναι (being) in Parmenides "are named in the belonging to being." This, for Heidegger, is decisively different from "the harnessing of ἀλήθεια and νοῦς under the yoke of ἰδέα," which happens with Plato, marking the beginning of metaphysics (GA 71: 11; E: 5).[11]

Twisting Out (*Entwindung*) and Leaving (*Fortgang*)

Heidegger's reading of the premetaphysical beginning is made possible by the *Verwindung*, the twisting free from metaphysics and the descent into the beginning or inception. This is why he uses the unusual phrasing: "Erinnerung in den ersten Anfang," recollecting "into" the first beginning. I have been indicating, so far, how, in Heidegger's reading in Anaximander, Heraclitus, and Parmenides, truth, unconcealing-concealing, in some way remains preserved although it is not thought as such. This is because truth occurs primarily as unconcealing such that being has the character of φύσις (arising) and gives itself into shining (δόξα). Heidegger calls this movement of arising *Entwindung*, twisting out, and differentiates it from the leaving (*Fortgang*) into metaphysics that it makes possible.[12] The arising twisting out "is not a tearing away, because the essence of ground (the event) indeed remains that which disposes" (GA 71: 29; E: 21). The leaving occurs once the ἰδέα takes precedence over ἀλήθεια, which requires τέχνη, an apprehension of what becomes present in the look (δόξα) such that what is present is held fast and even set forth and produced (ποίησις) (GA 71: 71; E: 58–59), In *Introduction to Metaphysics* Heidegger describes this in terms of the differentiation of being and thinking that initiates the classical understanding of truth as the correspondence between thing and intellect (GA 40, ch. 4C).

In the twisting out that occurs in and as the first beginning, this differentiation has not yet happened. Νοεῖν remains inseparable from εἶναι or φύσις.

In the first part of *The Event*, Heidegger thinks and speaks of the inceptive twisting out as well in ways that are far more difficult to follow. The subpart E, "Underway toward the First Beginning," may be read as an attempt by Heidegger at articulating the "twisting out" in a way that is more radically attuned to the event as inception. The poetic-sounding words that came to Heidegger here may make a little more sense later, once I lay out (as far as this is granted to me) Heidegger's thinking of the event in terms of "the wreath of the turning," but I would like to bring them up here in order not to gloss over the more puzzling and estranging moments in *The Event*. Section 71 is titled "Der Entsturz [not "Einsturz"!] der Ἀλήθεια aus dem Welt-Gebirg und der Anfang des Seins-Geschickes." Translating this is a significant challenge; here is my attempt: "The fall [not collapse!][13] of ἀλήθεια out of the world-harbor and the beginning of the destiny of being." Each word requires an explanatory footnote. Both "Entsturz" and "Welt-Gebirg" are neologisms. "Entsturz" combines the "Ent," which we find also in "Entwindung" (which has the sense of "out of") and "Sturz": "Fall." "Gebirg" usually means mountain range, but to make some sense of what Heidegger writes here, we ought to hear the word more literally as combining "Ge," which has a sense of gathering, and "bergen," sheltering, and so I translate *Gebirg* as "-harbor." That the falling out of the world-harbor is not the collapse of ἀλήθεια that initiates metaphysics is indicated by what Heidegger writes, which I may roughly summarize in Heidegger's own estranging words as follows: The harbor is a locale in which eventuates the gathering lighting up (*Gelicht*) and gathering resounding (*Geläut*). These "echo through the fourfold in the harbor of the world" (GA 71: 51; E: 40).[14] In the falling out (*Entstürzen*) ἀλήθεια takes with it a shimmering of the lighting and a waft of the sounding. Φύσις and λόγος occur essentially in the lighting and sounding of the harbor of the world. (That Heidegger is not thinking here the collapse of ἀλήθεια is indicated by the fact that ἀλήθεια is not covered over yet but still shimmers and resounds.) Initiated herewith is the destiny (*Geschick* literally means gathering-sending) of ~~beyng~~ (and this is the first time Heidegger crosses beyng out). Eventually the lighting is taken into what presences (δόξα) and is gathered by apprehension such that the bringing forth enters the realm of the "positing-to-and-in-front-of-itself." Ἰδέα takes the place of the lighting. (This is the moment of "collapse" of ἀλήθεια.) Heidegger writes: "*Incipit comedia.* Ἀλήθεια is forgotten" (GA 71: 52; E: 41).[15]

What follows in the text is a list of manifestations of machination (masks of machination, the creation of personality, the "blind screaming of the personal 'you'," the "*wild flight from* thinking") that are carried by a tone of a crass crescendo that is taken back and modulated differently in the rest of the section.

I believe that an in-depth reading of this section of *The Event* would also have to take into account the dynamics and sounding of what Heidegger writes here. This could be a chapter on its own.

Resonating (*Anklang*) and Passing By (*Vorbeigang*)

"The Resonating" is the title of the second part of *The Event.* In *Contributions* Heidegger highlights how in the acknowledgment of the compelling plight of the forgottenness of beyng, the essential occurrence of beyng resonates. Beyng resonates as refusal. The guiding attunements of the resonating are shock and diffidence. The resonating is the "first" opening of the truth of beyng and with it comes a meditation especially on the first beginning in its ending.[16] I pointed out earlier that in *Contributions* "the resonating" and "the interplay" (although they open up and meditate on historical beyng itself) have a preparatory function as they prepare for the "leap" into the truth of beyng (GA 65: 9, 82; E: 10, 65). Heidegger also highlights the necessity of acknowledging the plight of the abandonment and the withstanding of the refusal as which being occurs.

In *The Event* "the resonating" is, similarly to *Contributions*, a "first" indication of the truth of beyng and of the transition into the other beginning, but in *The Event* the resonating is not "only" preparatory for a leap (indeed, Heidegger drops the notion of leap) and also carries a different attunement or mood. The resonating indicates the transition to the other beginning as "a mode of inception" "against the leaving of the first beginning into metaphysics" (GA 71: 75; E: 63). This "against," however, has a quite different quality than in *Contributions* where Heidegger seems to evoke a resistance against machination and denounces the unleashing of beings into machination. Now, in *The Event*, the relation between the abandonment of beings by beyng in the will to will and the "twisting free into inception" is one of "passing by": "The demise and the transition pass each other by; according to the law of the letting go [*Loslassung*] of being into its extreme distorted essence, (i.e. into the will to willing), beyng lets the distorted essence go on. Beyng overcomes the dominance of the distorted essence not by 'engaging' with it and overpowering it but, rather, by letting go the distorted essence into its demise. The abyssal sort of overcoming is the letting go of that which is to be overcome into the fanaticism of its distorted essence" (GA 71: 84; E: 70–71; translation altered).[17]

"Letting go is nothing negative," Heidegger adds. The letting go of beyng into the will to will is precisely what allows beyng to open up in its most inceptive occurrence, that is, it allows for the twisting free into inception. To want to break the will to will would mean to want to master it, writes Heidegger a few sections later. Instead, the appropriate comportment, the one whereby one does not try to master but dwells in the event of inception and thus also in the letting go (*Loslassung*) of being into its demise, is "the releasement [*Gelassenheit*] of forbearance" (GA 71: 87; E: 73; translation altered).[18]

Heidegger addresses the passing by of the abandonment of beings by beyng and the twisting free into the beginning as "constellation" evoking the sense of stars ("stella" means star in Latin and "Stern" means star in German) passing each other. He speaks of the "Kon-stellation" of "Unstern" and "Vorstern" and "Irrstern." The "Unstern" is something like a "non-star," a star that is not properly a star. It addresses the "Unfug"[19] "the disjuncture of the machinational demise" (GA 71: 85; E: 72; translation altered). The "Vorstern" is the "fore-star (of the downgoing into the inceptiveness of the joining [*Fug*] in the event)" and the "Irrstern" is the "errant star of the earth" that strays between planetary devastation and the concealment of the beginning (GA 71: 85; E: 72; translation altered). Heidegger speaks of the errant star and also uses the adjective "irrsternlich" ("errant-star-ringly") in contexts that address machinational being and the demise of the first beginning. The straying of the errant star takes the form of godlessness, unbounded order, and will to will (the will to will is a will to order), devastation (*Verwüstung*), lack of plight, forgottenness of errancy, and so on.[20] Heidegger thus still speaks about the demise of metaphysics and how it plays itself out, and yet we are to let this demise pass by as we twist free into the abyssal inception.

Metaphysics now appears as a *Zwischenfall*, which literally means "a falling in-between" that Rojcewicz translates as "episode" (but we should not forget that for Heidegger, this "episode" is still a necessary event in the Western history of being). This notion of "episode" and the notion of the constellation of the "passing by of abandonment and the twisting free into inception" undo a linear sense of time and evoke a strange contemporaneity of ending and inception, as well as of first and other beginning. History (*Geschichte*) is not a linear passing by of occurrences, but a *Geschicht*.

Geschicht is a neologism Heidegger forms that lets resonate the notion of "Schicht" that in common German means "layer," but according to the dictionary of the brothers Grimm (which Heidegger loved to consult) etymologically derives from "sich schicken, fügen, ereignen," that is, sending, joining, happening, and thus is synonymous with history in the sense of destiny. What appears to us as a series of stages is—thought inceptually, that is, from inception or from the event— "the *Geschicht* of the appropriating event" (GA 70: 76; E: 64).[21]

Differentiation, Difference, and the Beingless

In section 181 Heidegger attempts to think the whole joining or dispensation (the German word here is *Fügung*) beginning with the "passing by." The "sequence" in which he thinks here, to a certain extent corresponds to the sequence of parts II–IV in *The Event*, since part II, "The Resonating" (in which Heidegger thematizes the "passing by") is followed by part III, "The Differentiation" and part IV, "Twisting Free." In the passing by (in which the devastation and the downgoing "don't know of each other") diverge the abandonment of beings by being on the one hand, and "the differentiation" on the other hand. With the differentiation metaphysics is overcome and a transition (twisting free) into the "turning" of the truth of beyng takes place.

In chapter 6 I laid out to a certain extent how Heidegger thinks the differentiation (of being and beings) in relation to "the difference" that occurs as departure into the abyss in *On Inception*. With the differentiation of being and beings (that occurs as the arising into being of formerly beingless "beings") opens up the more originary difference (departure, dispropriation, beinglessness) in which or out of which this differentiation of being and beings happens. This bespeaks a nexus of events familiar to us from *Contributions*: Metaphysics has forgotten or cannot think the ontological difference it presupposes and this ontological difference rests on the withdrawal as which beyng happens such that in this withdrawal beings take precedence over being. The departure into the abyssal truth of beyng requires a letting go of beings (of the precedence of beings) and out of the withdrawal of being or the abandonment resonates the appropriating event.

Now, in *On Inception* and *The Event*, Heidegger articulates refusal and eventuating in a more differentiated way as he finds a withholding (*Vorenthalt*) that is more originary than the withdrawal of beyng leading to the abandonment of beings in metaphysics and somehow "older" than the appropriation of beings into being. This withholding is "the inceptive dispropriation" (*die anfängliche Enteignung*) that he bespeaks as well through the notion of "beinglessness" (*Seinlosigkeit*): "The beinglessness (of beings) is the inceptual event of the dispropriation; the inceptual dispropriation in the sense of *withholding*. This dispropriation is the inceptual, not yet twisting out, essencing back [*noch unentwundedes Rückwesen*] into the groundless inception" (GA 71: 132; E: 112).

In the inceptual dispropriation, inception (a coming into being, a twisting out) has not yet happened. Such dispropriation can be thought now "in carrying out the difference into departure." "The difference differentiates being and the beingless" (GA 71: 132; E: 112). Letting go of machinational beings and with it of all beings, beinglessness can be thought as what precedes the coming into being of beings. The inceptual event is precisely the differencing of beyng from the beingless.

Let me remind readers that the beingless is not the nothingness belonging to being or beyng. Nothingness belongs to beyng insofar as beyng occurs as withdrawal or as presencing. In coming into being or withdrawing resonate the not yet and no longer, an abyssal lack or concealment; beyng always implies these. (One can approximate this by thinking of how we experience death or departure or an unimaginable future.) Heidegger relates the beingless not to being/beyng but to beings, to things in the largest sense. The beingless is beings before they come into being; it precedes any sense of loss or departure or expectation. The beingless is the nothingless.

I reflected on the difficulty of thinking the beingless and the difference (in which beyng differentiates itself from the beingless) in chapter 6. In *The Event*, Heidegger points out that the difference (of beyng and the beingless) is accessed through the differentiation between being and beings (although the difference is more "inceptual" than the differentiation):

> A. *First of all point into the difference and specifically on the basis of the differentiation. . . .*
> B. *The exhibition of the difference as departure. . . .*
> C. *The difference and the twisting free of beyng.* (GA 71: 122–123; E: 104)

These three points are followed by further aspects of the difference (carrying out the difference as pain, metaphysics, Da-seyn, historicality, the first beginning) in sections that outline the difference. Given that the last point concerns "the first" beginning, it is clear that we are not dealing here with a sequence to be followed, although points A, B, C seem to suggest a certain path in the thinking that "follows" (*folgen*) the differentiation of being and beings into the inceptual difference.[22]

Twisting Free into the Wreath of the Turning (*der Kranz der Kehre*)/Joining into the Juncture

In chapter 6 we saw how Heidegger differentiates the twisting out (*Entwindung*) in the first beginning from the twisting free (*Verwindung*) in the other beginning such that the one inception bears within it the different occurrences (arising and departure).

Indeed the twisting out can be thought only through the twisting free that is the downgoing into abyssal inception that Heidegger now more fully articulates in terms of conjuncture, joining (*Fuge, Fügung, Gefüge*) and turning (*Kehre*).[23] He thus takes recourse to notions that were central in *Contributions* but that he did not develop much in the other poietic writings. I noted in chapter 4 that he does not speak of the "turning" either in *Besinnung* or in *Geschichte des Seyns* and instead speaks of the "carrying out" (*Austrag*) of the encounter of gods and humans and the strife of world and earth. I suggested that this might have to do with an attempt at articulating the relations unfolding in the event not in terms of a relation between beyng and humans (call and response) and to move away from articulating the event primarily in relation to humans (even if humans are first appropriated in the event). Now, in *The Event*, the notion of turning reappears along with some new concepts and it is approached not by speaking of the role of humans or thinking but in relation to the twisting out and twisting free. Heidegger now speaks of the event as a winding (*Gewinde* relates to *Verwinden* and *Entwinden*) and of the "wreath" (*Kranz*) of the turning.

In section 181 Heidegger thinks the relation between different forms of "twisting" (*winden*) and turning (*kehren*) following the overcoming (*Überwindung*) of metaphysics. The details of the movements he is speaking of here are difficult to follow but the words he highlights show connections that give at least some indications as to how he is thinking here. He is saying that the overcoming of metaphysics is the transition into the turning (the essential occurrence of the truth of beyng in the beyng of truth), which is a return (*Rückkehr*) of the turning into "Da-seyn" (the clearing of the truth of beyng that is the ground of the essence of humans), which is the twisting free of beyng into the event. Heidegger then writes: "What is the twisting free, however? It is just the twisting up [*Einwindung*] into the winding (wreath) of the event, such that beyng and its turning purely and essentially occur in the event. Thereby the twisting free is a circulating in the event, wherein a constancy prevails which is itself determined out of the event" (GA 71: 141; E: 121).

In twisting free, metaphysics (the prevalence of beings out of the differentiation of being and beings) is overcome such that beyng returns (*zurückkehrt*) into its "junction" (*Fug*). The constancy Heidegger speaks of here makes me wonder again about the temporality of the circulating in the event. It is reminiscent of the "staying" he speaks of in *On Inception*, which has not the sense of duration.[24] It is important for him that the twisting free into the event not be understood like a Hegelian sublation (*Aufhebung*) and that all thinking in terms of "dialectics" be held at bay: "The twisting free is not sublation into the absolute; instead, it essentially occurs in the conjoining [*Fügung*] toward the abyssal character of the inception" (GA 71: 142; E: 121; translation altered).

Heidegger elaborates on this conjoining with cognates of the same word, which can only be approximated in English:

Fügung: ist Fügen als Ereignis des Gefüges des Zeit-Raumes des Abgrundes, ist Sich-fügen in den Fug des Anfangs. Das Sich-Fügende west im Fug. (Conjoining: is joining as event of the conjuncture of the time-space of the abyss, is compliance into the juncture of the inception. The complying joining essentially occurs in the juncture.) (GA 71: 142; E: 121; translation altered)

Fug means "fitting connection." This fitting connection is not sublation, that is, the difference (*Unterschied*) remains in departure (*Abschied*). Complying (*Sich-fügen*), Heidegger elaborates two sections later, means both unfolding the conjuncture and thus joining into the juncture.[25] I believe that with the notion of "complying" he is rethinking and transforming the notion of the thrown projection, that is, it relates to the movement of thought that he now articulates in terms of following, complying, thanking, and so on (I will come back to this later in the chapter).

Ereignis and Its Cognates

After twisting free into the wreath of the turning of the event (part IV), Heidegger proceeds with part V, titled "The Event: The Word-Treasure of Its Essence." He adds: "For the introduction into 'The Event.'"[26] In this part that also physically takes up the center of the volume, he attempts to "delimit" more clearly the "otherwise still fluctuating use of words" (GA 71: 147; E: 127; translation altered). The words he elucidates here are all cognates of *Ereignis*. The movements he articulates as he delimits different cognates of *Ereignis* all surge from the "center" of the event thought as *the* inception (the one inception that gets articulated into first and other). Perhaps he is thinking here out of the "wreath" of the turning. I will highlight only a few central points for each word that Heidegger explicates.

1. "*The event* [*Ereignis*] says the explicitly self-clearing incipience of the inception" (GA 71: 147; E: 127). This is not the beginning of a sequence of events exterior to the event. Rather in the event, in the incipience of inception, are harbored appropriation and what is appropriated.

2. "*The appropriating* [*Ereignung*] (the appropriating eventuation) is intrinsically counter-turning [*gegenwendig*]." Heidegger thinks both at once (in their counter-turning) arising and downgoing. When the event clears itself there comes into the clearing the difference toward beings (arising) as well as the downgoing into inception. Heidegger then unfolds the counter-turning of the appropriating in terms of *Ver-eignung* and *Übereignung*.

3. "*Propriation* [*Ver-eignung*] is the preservation, by way of departure, of the event into the abyss of its intimacy with the beginning" (GA 71: 149; E: 129; translation altered).[27] The emphasis here is on how in the event concealment is cleared and thus preserved. "Propriation points toward what is most proper to the event, which is the inception" (GA 71: 150; E: 129).

4. "*The consignment [Übereignung]*. It is appropriation in such a way that the event allows the clearing to occur essentially as the in-between of time-space so that the 'there' eventuates and Da-seyn is as the essential occurrence of the turning (i.e. the truth of beyng as the beyng of truth)" (GA 71: 150; E: 129). The emphasis now is on the clearing of the "there" (the Da) in Da-seyn in which the downgoing becomes "historial" (*geschichthaft*). (Heidegger thus keeps the sense of how Da-sein or Da-seyn is a historial site.) It requires humans that Heidegger brings into play in the next word elaboration.

5. "*The assignment [Zu-eignung]*.[28] This word says that the event consigns itself to the essence of the humans and prior than to all other beings confers itself on this essence" (GA 71: 150; E: 130; translation altered). Human beings thus maintain a special role in the occurrence of inception (compared to other beings). Humans have the task to preserve the truth of all beings (and we will see that language is essential for this). Heidegger now thinks human being in the turning from and to the event in its abyssal inceptuality. He says how in consigning itself to the human being, the human essence is "included" (*einbezogen*) into being and calls this movement *die Aneignung*, "arrogation."

6. *The arrogation (die An-eignung)*.[29] "The arrogation directs the human into the propriation and disposes [*stimmt*] him for the belongingness into departure" (GA 71: 152; E: 131; translation altered). Heidegger relates this departure to our relation to death. Following the movement of departure requires a unique relation to death since death reaches into the "extreme possibility" of beyng itself. At the same time, in this relation to death, that is, in departure into the abyss, humans first find their proper essence (*das Eigene*).

7. *Properness (Eigentlichkeit)* (the same word that is often translated as "authenticity" in *Being and Time*) is not found in a movement to itself of human being *out* of a horizon of being (as in *Being and Time*) but rather in the return *to* the inceptual essence of being (which, as we just saw, has all to do with our relation to death), in staying within the inceptual event. Heidegger develops further the "properness" of humans in their belonging to the event by bringing into play language. Being a "self" occurs through a response (*Anwort*) that is the word of language that answers to the word of beyng. The word of beyng is silent (*lautlos*) and occurs as the attunement (*Stimmung*) that claims the human essence. In responding humans correspond (*entspricht*) in their counter-word (*Gegenwort*) to the silent word of beyng that simultaneously assigns and arrogates the human essence. By remaining steadfast in the response "humans adhere to that wherein they are arrogated. This adherence to the appropriated essence is properness, i.e. being as self" (GA 71: 156; E: 134). At the end of fairly long elaborations on properness (on the proper human being) Heidegger brings into play the gods. He emphasizes that we are in a godless age and that the gods remain excluded (*ausgeschlossen*) from an immediate relation to beyng. In order to comport themselves

to (human) beings, "they require that the clearing of beings, as beings, be steadfastly preserved, built, and disposed in historical humanity" (GA 71: 161; E: 138). This thought announces the next cognate of *Ereignis* that brings into play the relation between humans and beings.

8. *The eventuation* (*die Eignung*). "In the properness of the historical human being, there eventuates to the previously beingless (beings) *the eventuation* into beyng" (GA 71: 161; E: 138). Heidegger emphasizes the uniqueness of human being and destiny. Only out of this unique belonging of humans to beyng, only in human responsiveness can beings eventuate through knowing, acting, shaping, grounding, and building.

Heidegger then further develops the essence of beings in terms of *Geeignetheit*.

9. "*Appropriateness* [*Geeignetheit*]. The word says that beings have been admitted into their inceptually fitting being" (GA 71: 163; E: 140), that they have entered the eventuation. Thereby beings do not occur for humans but are assigned to the incipience of inception; they occur "toward the event" "out of the 'absence' [*Absenz*] (i.e. here, departure)" of humans (GA 71: 164; E: 140). Each being is unique and singularized in a way that is completely distinct from the metaphysical determination of single beings in terms of the schema of singular and general. To the singularity of beings released into their appropriateness Heidegger contrasts the dispropriation of beings (dis-propriation here has a less originary sense than in the passage discussed above).

10. *The dispropriation* of beings "withdraws beings from the assignment to the beginning" (GA 71: 165; E: 140); it appropriates the abandonment of beings by being (GA 71: 166; E: 141). Heidegger spoke of "dispropriating" in this sense already in *Contributions*: "In this era, 'beings' . . . are dispropriated of beyng" (GA 65: 120; E: 95).

Heidegger ends his list of cognates of *Ereignis* with *Eigentum*, a term that gathers all essential determinations (cognates) of the event.

11. *The domain of what is proper* (*Eigentum*) is the name of "the time of entry of the truth of beyng into the appropriated inaugural essence. In the domain of what is proper, the inceptual unification of the difference and the departure eventuates towards the abyssal unity of their oppositional essence" (GA 71: 169; E: 144). This "unity" of the *event* cannot be represented, Heidegger emphasizes, but must be experienced in terms of the "that being is" out of the inceptual pain (*Schmerz*) to which belongs equiprimordially "the shock of the abyss and the delight of departure" (GA 71: 169–170; E: 144). "The domain of what is proper is the consummation of the event, in which guise the uniqueness of beyng eventuates into the more inceptual beginning" (GA 71: 170; E: 145).

The synopsis of the different moments and movements of the event that I have just given and that Heidegger gathers in section 184 (part V) of *The Event* can of course only serve as an indication of how Heidegger at a certain time in his poietic writings attempts to bring together all that constitutes the event. If we follow what Heidegger writes, we would have to experience the pain he speaks about and find ourselves assigned to and arrogated by the event in an originary experience of language. What I have been doing in my synopsis thus cannot claim to be a saying of the event. But in this section, Heidegger himself at times seems to recur to what sounds like explanations of what he is attempting to think. The section serves as an "introduction" to the essential vocabulary of the event. A look at the shorter sections (186–194) of part VI, titled "The Event," shows how the "vocabulary of the essence" of the event is not at all set in stone as Heidegger plays with different outlines of the event, for instance using cognates of *Rührung* (*Anrühren, be-rühren, her-rühren, rühren*) that seem to be inspired by rethinking inception as an event that moves, touches, stirs. He also makes notes in which he thinks of the event as sending (*Schickung*), fate (*Ein-fall* literally means "what falls in"), and *Er-eigen, er-eugen, eräugen*, which relate to eyes (*Auge* means eye), catching sight or showing.

What I would like to draw attention to, here, at the end of my synopsis of section 184, is how "the domain of what is proper" to the event includes appropriation and what is appropriated, that is, it includes Da-sein (now written as Da-seyn), humans, gods, and beings.

It may be noteworthy, however, that Heidegger does not speak about earth and world and that the gods are barely mentioned and do not appear central here, whereas in *Besinnung* and *Die Geschichte des Seyns*, the four: humans and gods, earth and world take precedence even with respect to the notion of turning. The emphasis in *The Event* lies undoubtedly in inception out of a movement of downgoing and departure and (in the first half of the volume) a thinking together of twisting out and twisting free.

The second half of *The Event* is more concerned with questions of attunement, Da-seyn, human being, and language. I will thus turn to these themes that have also been broached to some extent in chapter 6 of *On Inception*, where Heidegger already introduces a different emphasis on the role or place of the human in the event as he thinks *out of* the event of inception *and into* it. In relation to the human being this is the movement of "assignment" and "arrogation" outlined above. Our proper essence is found in downgoing and departure and the consignment of Da-seyn.

Da-seyn and Human Being

In *The Event*, Heidegger begins to write also Da-seyn with a "y." He does not do this consistently (and sometime writes Da-sein when he could very well have written Da-seyn) but when he does use the "y," special emphasis is placed on how Da-seyn belongs to the essential occurrence of the event as inception (GA 71: 209;

E: 179). It is one more way in which Heidegger shifts the emphasis away from human being, although humans find their essence out of Da-seyn (or Da-sein) by being steadfast or indwelling (*inständig*) in Da-seyn, and although humans maintain a both necessary and special role in the clearing of beyng in and as Da-seyn. He notes how "at first" Da-sein is said in terms of "human Da-sein" (obviously thinking of *Being and Time* here) but that one ought to clearly distinguish the fact that Da-sein (projected out of being) *can* be determined by taking human being as a point of departure, from the fact that "primarily and properly, Da-sein, even if not unrelated to human being, must be spoken of out of an experience of beyng, thus in terms of the history of beyng" (GA 71: 206–207; E: 177).

"All beyng is Da-seyn," says Heidegger in section 217, and this means: "beyng, in its dispensation into the junction, still makes known this inceptual essence, namely, that beyng essentially occurs as the truth of beyng" (GA 71: 207; E: 177).

Da-seyn means *that* beyng occurs as *truth* of beyng. The "Da-" in Da-seyn does not indicate a "here" or "there,"[30] but names the appropriated openness: that being occurs as truth of beyng. And Da-seyn names the turning: the truth of beyng is the beyng of truth and vice versa. The *truth* of beyng (unconcealing concealment) occurs as this truth *is* (through human steadfastness); in turning, the *beyng* of truth (and with it human steadfastness) occurs in the abyssal truth of beyng (in the clearing of the "there"). Heidegger thought this turning relation already in *Contributions*.[31] In *The Event*, however, the emphasis is on how in Da-seyn the downgoing finds a site and becomes historical (GA 71: 206; E: 176). "And experience [*Er-fahrung*] is related to this and only to this inceptive Da-seyn,[32] to Da-seyn that belongs to inception; to let experience be attuned out of this [Da-seyn]" (GA 71: 209; E: 179; translation altered).

When, appropriated in the event, humans experience the event, they find themselves consigned to preserve (*verwahren*) the event.[33] *Verwahren* has the word "wahr" (true) in it and Heidegger now (in *The Event*) likes to use also the antiquated noun *die Wahr* (sometimes together with the antiquated word "die Hut" which carries a sense of preserving and caring) when elucidating what constitutes this preserving.[34] (This whole nexus of meaning is highlighted as well in several instances in which Heidegger writes *Wahr-heit* with a hyphen.) According to the dictionary of the brothers Grimm, *Die Wahr* means "attentiveness" (*Aufmerksamkeit*), which is another word Heidegger privileges in *The Event* especially when speaking of inceptive thought. The way Heidegger describes the role of humans in *The Event* is, then, not much different from *Contributions* in which he would speak of "the future ones" as grounders and preservers (or "stewards," *Wächter*) of the truth of being. It is noteworthy, however, that he now appears to put the emphasis almost exclusively on the preserving and not on grounding in the sense of building. This is consistent with the "poverty" (*Armut*) of the essence of humans that he refers to already in *Besinnung* in the context of moving away from a language of empowerment and that he repeatedly refers to in *The Event* together with the notion of "nobility" (*Adel*) (GA 71: 191, 212–213, 235–236). The human essence has nothing "in itself" that it brings to the event or to beyng. When humans are truly consigned to their essence, they "follow" the event in an experience that has the character of *Behutsamkeit* (solicitousness) and *Aufmerksamkeit* (heedfulness) and that is, says Heidegger "the pain of carrying out the differentiating-departing downgoing into inception" (GA 71: 190; E: 162; translation altered).

The Experience: The Pain of Departure—Carrying Out the Difference

When Heidegger thinks of the role of humans in the event (now thought as the incipience of inception) he seems to have in mind most of all the role of thinking or, to be more precise, how (his) thinking experiences the inception, how it finds itself attuned (disposed) by beyng in what he calls "the pain of departure" (*der Schmerz des Abschieds*) in carrying out the difference (*der Austrag des Unterschieds*).[35]

Of course, Heidegger does not understand pain in the usual sense; pain is not a subjective state of being; it is rather a pain pertaining to the historicality of beyng or a "beyng-historical pain" (*ein seynsgeschichtlicher Schmerz*) (GA 71: 218; E: 187). It gathers the differencing as which the event occurs: "Pain holds steadfast (*instāndet*) in the inceptual difference of the event-related opposition between the departure and the difference" (GA 71: 49; E: 39).

Let us recall that difference names the event of differencing of beyng from the beingless (the originary dispropriation) out of which beings rise into being (twisting out);[36] but it also (and in the other beginning above all) names the departure, the letting go of the primacy of beings in the downgoing into the abyss (twisting free). Pain gathers both and in each case addresses the differentiation from beings. It is the originary unity of the horror of the abyss (*der Schrecken des Abgrundes*) and the delight (*Wonne*) of departure (*die Wonne des Abschieds*).[37] Heidegger does not explain these notions further but they may remind us of how in *Contributions*, restraint (which is the prevalent disposition in this earlier volume) gathers both shock and diffidence. *Wonne*, though, is very different from diffidence; it carries a sense of sensual joy, a joy that perhaps he experiences as he releases into the experience of the event as appropriation.

Pain and the carrying out of the difference are linked as well to death insofar as death mirrors the originary dispropriation as which the event occurs. Heidegger speaks of death in section 202 as "the departure-like abyss with respect to the beginning" (GA 71: 193; E: 165). Departure is the movement that leaves behind beings, which is precisely what occurs when we face death. At the same time, in departure and death, beyng lights up in a more originary way.[38] Thus, for Heidegger, the pain in death is "not 'one' pain among others, but is the essentially occurring abyss of pain, taking pain as the essence of the experience of being" (GA 71: 194; E: 165–166).

Inceptive Thinking (Following, Heedfulness, Questioning, Thanking, Knowing)

Heidegger characterizes inceptive thinking not only as experiencing in terms of carrying out the pain of departure. He often speaks of thinking in terms of *Folgsamkeit*, which contains the word *folgen*, to follow, and usually means obedience (GA 71: 190, 247–248; E: 162, 214).[39] He often says how thinking follows the twisting free or the departure into the abyss. Such following is a kind of heedfulness (*Aufmerksamkeit*) (GA 71: 243; E: 210), a concept to which he devotes several sections (sections 320–324). The first of these is also one of the two only places in *The Event*, where he speaks of the Germans: "Heedfulness [*Aufmerksamkeit*] is the future German term for the future mode of essential, i.e. inceptual thinking, a mode grounded by the Germans. It is the other, more inceptual term for 'philosophy'" (GA 71: 289; E: 251).[40]

Heidegger meditates on the notion "Merk" in *Aufmerksamkeit* (making use of the usual dictionary by the Grimm brothers). "Das Merk" means " the sign" and he elucidates this in terms of "that by which something 'emerges' for us, by which we 'notice' something, i.e. experience it, i.e. are struck by it" (GA 71: 290; E: 251).

The emphasis is on receptivity and not on an "active" or "willfull" seeking; thinking is rather a thanking than a questioning. In *Contributions* Heidegger would often speak of the future ones as "seekers" (*Sucher*),[41] and place emphasis on questioning in the context of the question-worthiness (*Fragwürdigkeit*) of beyng. There are still places in *The Event* where he speaks of the questioning of inceptive thinking but then he redefines what questioning means: "*Inceptive questioning* is the carrying out of the difference in the pain of the experience of departure" (GA 71: 237; E: 205).[42] He more emphatically asserts, however, that in beyng-historical thinking questioning, in the strict sense of the word, is futile (*hinfällig*): "The carrying out is thinking. In this thinking 'questioning,' too, is overcome" (GA 71: 237; E: 204). A few paragraphs later in the same section he writes: "The futility of all questioning must itself be carried out in the carrying out of the pain of departure. *The carrying out is essentially more steadfast in the abyssal ground* than any questioning" (GA 71: 238; E: 205; translation altered).[43]

Inceptive thinking is not a questioning (in the strict sense) but a thanking (*Danken*): "The steadfastness of reception is thanking" (GA 71: 222; E: 190).[44]

Carrying out the difference is a thanking (section 258). In thanking thinking responds to the bestowing and granting as which the event occurs. At some point Heidegger thinks of thanking as a counter-gift (GA 71: 314; E: 272).

> Steadfastness in the assigned proper domain of poverty is the nobility of thanking.
> Thanking is not an addition to beyng-historical thinking but belongs to the distinctive character of the pain of the experience of the event. (GA 71: 235; E: 203; translation altered)

Heidegger does not want this thanking to be confused with some kind of submissiveness and thus adds: "Thanking is the high spirits [*das Hochgemute*] of the great courage [*des hohen Mutes*] which acknowledges the risk to the distinctive character of carrying out" (GA 71: 235; E: 203; translation altered).

The notion of courage (*Mut*) has always been important for Heidegger, and I pointed out already in chapter 7 on the volume *On Inception*, how he finds in the semantic root of "Mut" that in older German also means "mood" or "spiritedness" (it may perhaps be compared to the Greek *thumos*) a resource for articulating various attunements of thinking (*Langmut, Armut, Großmut*, etc.). In section 200 of *The Event*, he links *Mut* to *Anmut* which usually means grace or charm, but the context suggests a more literal sense of "bestowing" courage: The consignment of human being into the truth of beyng "fits [humanity] for courage [*Mut*], i.e. for the knowing (knowing of beyng) preparedness for the truth of beyng. The appropriating event is the inceptual vouchsafing [*Zu-mutung*] of courage.[45] The appropriating event vouchsafes courage to the human being and is itself grace [*Anmut*]. As this grace, it is the favor of the inception but also harbors the danger of disgrace and presumption [*Übermut*]" (GA 71: 192; E: 164; translation altered).

I am adding these remarks on courage to what Heidegger says about thinking as following and thanking in order to counterbalance a sense of unquestioning religious piety one may get in this context. That courage is demanded as well means that the "thanking thinking" is not simply "passive." Furthermore, the "danger of disgrace and presumption" reminds us of the exposedness and abyssal character as well as of the tentativeness of Heidegger's thinking. This tentativeness should be kept in mind as well when interpreting his references to the "knowing" of beyng that (as he says at one point) is also "ignorance" (*Nichtwissen*, not-knowing) of inception (GA 71: 249; E: 215),[46]

Word, Claim (*Anspruch*), Saying (*Sage*), and Language

Inceptive thinking occurs as a saying through words. Ultimately it is in the thoughtful word that thinking carries out the twisting free of beyng, and in

The Event Heidegger meditates more than in previous volumes on the notions of saying and "the word." He rethinks the thoughtful word (*das denkende Wort*) as well as the thoughtful saying more radically than in *Contributions* out of the incipience of inception, so much so that he will speak of "the word" or of "the Saying" (*die Sage*)⁴⁷ primarily as the word or Saying *of* beyng or of the event.⁴⁸ The thinking word and saying (*das Sagen*) is "but" an echoing of the word of beyng, a response. I will thus first turn to how Heidegger thinks the word of beyng or of the event.

The Word

"The event is the inceptual word, because its assignment [*Zueignung*] (as the unique arrogation [*An-eignung*] of the human being into the truth of beyng) disposes [*stimmt*] the human essence to the truth of beyng. Inasmuch as the appropriating event is in itself this disposing, and since disposition eventuates as an event, the inception that occurs as event (i.e. beyng as abyssal in its truth) is the inceptually disposing voice [*stimmende Stimme*]: the word. The essence of the word resides in the inception that occurs as event" (GA 71: 170–171; E: 145; translation altered).

Heidegger writes of the word as the disposing or attuning voice of beyng.⁴⁹ It is thus not a being (a word-thing) but an event. It is more the "not-yet-said" or "to-be-said" than the said, the coming to language (but not itself language) of what eventually may find a site in Da-sein through (also silently) spoken or written words. The singularity of *the* word (not words) of beyng rests in the singularity of beyng, that beyng *is* not generally or specifically but always uniquely.

Heidegger makes clear that the word of beyng should also not be understood as a meaning that has yet to find an uttered word. Both word-sounds and word-meanings are derivative of the soundless word of beyng (GA 71: 171; E: 145).

As he describes how the coming to meaning and sounding occurs, he brings into play the beingless: "But all sounding is the echo [*Widerhall*] of the fact that beings, previously beingless, enter into the eventuation toward beyng and persist therein. The echo of the inceptual voice of being originates such that being breaks on beings, which are themselves first lit up through the appropriation to being. In the inceptual voice of the disposition occurring through the event, there is neither speaking out nor silence" (GA 71: 171; E: 146; translation altered).

The expression "Sein bricht sich am Seienden" reminds of how waves break on the rock. Sounding words and meaning are echoes of a soundless eventuation that disposes and determines human being and at the same time lets appear (come into being) beings as such. All beings come to be through the word of beyng. Anything that appears to us *as such* appears by virtue of the coming to language of beyng.

The Claim

Heidegger speaks of the event of the inceptual word also as *Anspruch* (claim) and as *Sage*. He not only says that the disposing or attuning (*stimmend*) inceptual word (of beyng) determines (*bestimmt*) but also that it claims (*beansprucht*) human being: "We are still unable to apprehend that this claim [*Anspruch*] of the beginning is an addressing [*Ansprechen*] and a claiming [*ein in den Anspruch nehmen*] that eventuates in what is speechless" (GA 71: 171; E: 146).

    Sprechen means "to speak," and *Spruch* "a saying" or proclamation (as in "the saying of Anaximander"). In common German, *Anspruch* and *Ansprechen* are used in the sense of claiming or laying claim that does not necessary involve speech. Heidegger is rethinking that aspect of the event of appropriation that in *Contributions* he would call the throw (*Zuwurf*) or call (*Zuruf*) of beyng (to which humans respond projectively in Da-sein). The notion of claiming, however, bears the same movement as the arrogation (*Aneignung*), a movement that does not end in human being but that takes human being to itself (the movement), indeed appropriates human being such that the proper of humans is found more radically in abyssal beyng than he had articulated it in *Contributions*. To translate *Ereignung* as appropriation makes more sense in *The Event* than it did in *Contributions* since the German word *Ereignung* has more a middle-voice character (as in "it happens") than the sense of "taking something for one's own use."[50]

The Saying

Just as the word and the claim, the "saying" of inception inceptually belongs to inception and occurs in silence:

> The saying is itself the incipience of the inception. The saying brings the inception dispositionally into the word (not vocables) and also silences the inception. . . .
>   The saying "of" the inception recollectively appropriates [*er-eignet erin-nernd*] the thoughtful word and confers (grants) and refuses speech. The latter always is the re-illumination of the starry brilliance of the beginning. (GA 71: 297; E: 258; translation altered)

A little later in the same section (336), Heidegger writes: "The recollecting appropriating occurrence of inception shall be heard steadfastly in its attuning [*Stimmen*]: The Saying is the *granting* and *refusing* saying [*das Zu-sagende und Versagende*] of the voice that stirs the abyssal ground. The Saying recollects and, by recollecting, in advance takes the recollected into the departure of the downgoing. Out of this that is recollected, the projection of thoughtful speech is projected" (GA 71: 298; E: 259; translation altered).

In *Contributions*, Heidegger thinks "saying" as the saying of the thinker. Surely such saying is appropriated in the event but still it is the appropriated and responsive saying of the thinking, and not the granting and refusing Saying of the silent voice of beyng. In *The Event*, what Heidegger used to call "saying" (*Sagen*) he now calls "speech" (*Rede*). The passages of section 336 I just quoted are, however, puzzling, since he speaks of the saying as a recollecting and it is difficult not to understand recollecting as something proper to human thought. Yet the German word for recollecting, *erinnern*, has the literal sense of "taking something in" and thus indicates the same movement as the claim and arrogation I referred to above. The response of thinking is one of following the (re)collection or arrogation and thus going down into the abyssal incipience of inception out of which emerge—in the poverty of beyng—language and speech.

Toward the end of section 336, Heidegger brings together the notions of saying, word, claim, and speech (language) as follows: "The saying, in that it says the inception, places the inception into its history. The saying as saying (granting, announcing, forbidding, refusing [*zu-sagend, ansagend, unter-sagend, versagend*]) takes the word into the claim [*Anspruch*] and consigns something essential into the proclamation [*Spruch*] and thus into the language which, as the speech of thinking, maintains itself in the clearing of beyng, without immediately knowing either the latter or the former as such" (GA 71: 300; E: 260; translation altered).

In the notion of saying (*Sage*) Heidegger invites us to hear not only disclosive granting but also a withholding or refusing. The word suggests a gathering of the "to be said and not to be said" that claims steadfast thinking such that this claim finds a site through the spoken word of the thinker or the poet.

Thinking and Poetizing

The largest part of the last section (XI) of *The Event* is devoted to the relation between thinking and poetizing. Not only is the relation to poetry essential for beyng-historical thinking but the encounter more specifically with Hölderlin's poetry allows Heidegger to delimit further what is proper to beyng-historical thinking.

I discussed in chapter 6 the essential traits of the relation between (Heidegger's) thinking and (Hölderlin's) poetry as Heidegger sees them in 1941/1942. Hölderlin's poetry poetizes the holy and thus founds (*stiftet*) beyng, but the time-space of beyng that the poet founds first needs to be grounded by thinking. The thinker (the inventive thinking of beyng) first will allow the word of the poet to be heard.[51] Thinking and poetizing need each other.

They share a number of traits: both occur as a thanking but in different ways;[52] both find themselves disposed, yet respond in different ways;[53] both are historical in an originary sense, but in different ways;[54] both occur through the word, but in different ways (GA 71: 323; E: 281); finally, "what is to be poetized and what is to be thought are *the same*" (GA 71: 325; E: 282), namely, the truth of beyng, but in different ways, such that the poet poetizes the holy and thinking thinks the inception.

Although thinking and poetizing intimately belong together, in this intimacy they also are most apart (*getrenntest*).[55] Sometimes Heidegger uses the word *Ent-stiften* (de-founding) in order to mark that thinking is "set out from the domain of poetry, separated from the essence of poetry" (GA 71: 239; E: 206; translation altered).[56]

In section 373, Heidegger lists essential (related) differences between poetizing and thinking. I will point out the ones he refers to most also in other sections.

1. Whereas in saying the holy the poet founds the dwelling in the familiar (*im Heimischen*), the thinker grounds the abyss of beyng and thus steadfastness in the unfamiliar (*im Unheimischen*). Heidegger phrases this as well as follows: "Poetizing is a becoming at home out of what is unfamiliar." "Thinking is a becoming at home in the unfamiliar" (GA 71: 330; E: 286).

2. Whereas poetry prepares the advent of the gods, thinking "is the venture of experiencing godlessness" (GA 71: 329; E: 285). Heidegger also writes of how thinking searches for the "un-holy" (*das Heil-lose*) and speaks of the abyss as "the abyss of the un-holiness."

3. Whereas poetizing occurs through image-words (*das bildende Wort*), thinking occurs through the imageless word.

Heidegger indeed often mentions the imagelessness of the thinking word. In section 243 he elucidates this by remarking how concepts arise out of dispositions and therefore do not need either the sensory (*das Sinnliche*) or images. He admits that there remain residues of images in what disposes but says that these residues are not determining with respect to the imageless concepts (GA 71: 220; E: 189).

4. Whereas "poetizing is, in finding, the naming (the naming), . . . thinking is, in seeking, the questioning word" (GA 71: 329; E: 286). Whereas the poet reciprocates the greeting in order to be saved as the one who has been greeted, the thinker "'questions' i.e. carries out the departure" (GA 71: 330; E: 286).

We see here that Heidegger brings in questioning again as a main trait of thinking in distinction to poetizing. When he earlier highlights thinking as a thanking in distinction to a questioning he seems to bring thinking closer to poetry. But from the other differentiations between thinking and poetizing one can make sense of the fact that at this point he does not let go of the notion of seeking and questioning all together. Thinking goes down into the abyss, into the unfamiliar and un-holy. The imageless thinking word does not rest in the naming of the familiar but remains exposed in and exposes the unfamiliar. The thanking in which thinking occurs renounces the holy "out of the necessity of

honoring what is question-worthy." The renunciation of the holy comes from ex-
periencing the dignity of what is question-worthy, Heidegger writes in section 372.
"To thank is to pass by ungrounded being and to pass by the power of beings"
(GA 71: 328; E: 284).

Notes

1. "Das Sagen des Austrags." Translation of "Austrag" altered.
2. This is the order indicated by Heidegger in the table of contents. The first part, however,
was in another place from the rest of the manuscript since Heidegger used it to prepare his lecture course of the winter semester 1942–1943, *Parmenides and Heraclitus* (GA 71: 343; E: 297).
3. *Verwindung* is usually translated as "overcoming" or "twisting free," but when one looks
at how Heidegger thinks *Verwindung*, neither of these translations seems to fit.
4. These are "Da-seyn" (VIII), "The Other Beginning" (IX), "Directives to the Event" (X),
and "The Thinking of the History of Being (Thinking and Poetizing)" (XI). *The Event* consists
of a total of eleven parts.
5. See Daniela Vallega-Neu, "At the Limit of Word and Thought: Reading Heidegger's *Das
Ereignis*," in *Internationales Jahrbuch für Hermeneutik* (Tübingen: Mohr Siebeck, 2013), 77–91.
6. Hermann Diels, *Die Fragmente der Vorsokratiker* (Berlin: Weidmannsche Buchhandlung, 1903), 81. Drawn from Martin Heidegger, *Grundbegriffe*, a lecture course Heidegger gave
in the summer semester of 1941, which is contemporaneous with *The Event* (GA 51: 98).
7. In GA 55: 110, Heidegger translates φύσις κρύπτεσθαι φιλεῖ as "Das Aufgehen dem Sichverbergen schenkt's die Gunst." In English: "The arising gives favor to self-concealing."
8. Daniel Graham translates this fragment as follows: "How would one escape the notice
of what never sets?" (in Daniel Graham, ed. and trans., *The Texts of Early Greek Philosophy*
[Cambridge: Cambridge University Press, 2010], fragment 136).
9. See the lecture course of summer semester 1932, *Der Anfang der Abendländischen Philosophie* (GA 35: 103ff.).
10. Perhaps there is a relation between Heidegger's reading of δόξα in Parmenides as being
more originary, and Heidegger's thinking of errancy as belonging to the essence of truth such
that he distinguishes errancy from distortion (see chapter 4).
11. In this context, see also the lecture course of the summer semester 1935, *Introduction to
Metaphysics* (GA 40, esp. 117).
12. I am translating *Entwindung* and *Fortgang* differently from Rojcewicz, who translates
Entwindung as "disentanglement" and *Fortgang* as "advancement."
13. Compare Rojcewicz translation in E: 40.
14. Heidegger uses the word "fourfold" here, but nothing in the context of this passage suggests that he is already thinking of the fourfold of earth and sky, gods and mortals.
15. Metaphysics is the beginning of comedy? It certainly contrasts with the more "tragic"
character of the downgoing into the abyss in the other beginning.
16. *Contributions*, sections 50–80.
17. I am translating *Loslassen* with letting go and not "releasing" because of the latter's connotation of "freeing." "Letting go" is more neutral.
18. Rojcewicz translates "die Gelassenheit der Langmut" as "the tranquility of patience."
19. *Unfug* in current German means "mischief," but Heidegger is undoubtedly playing with
the semantic root of "fug" that we find in "Fuge," "Gefüge," "Fügung," and so on.

20. *Contributions*, section 112.

21. Rojcewicz translates *Geschicht* as "historiality."

22. See GA 71: 126, 128; E: 107, 109. At times, Rojcewicz translates *folgen* as "obedience."

23. Under the heading of part III, "The Twisting Free," Heidegger writes among other things: "The joining of the conjuncture of the junction in inception" [Die Fügung der Fuge des Fugs im Anfang] and "The joining also in its whole *Durchfängnis* [literally the state of being caught throughout] is the twisting free into the windings of the event" [Die Fügung auch in ihrer ganzen Durchfängnis ist Verwindung in das Gewinde des Ereignisses].

24. See chapter 5, section "Staying in Inception."

25. Section 183.

26. I am translating "Wortschatz" not as "vocabulary" but more literally.

27. Rojcewicz's translation of *Ver-eignung* as "expropriation" is misleading. Furthermore, expropriation is sometimes used as a translation for *Ent-eignis*.

28. Rojecwicz renders *Zu-eignung* inappropriately with "arrogation."

29. Rojcewicz translates *Aneignung* as "adoption." One would usually translate it as "appropriation" in the more common sense.

30. See *The Event*, section 227.

31. See GA 65, esp. sections 190 and 191.

32. Hyphenating *Er-fahrung* highlights the inchoative "er-" as well as the "path" character of experience.

33. GA 71, section 196. I believe Rojcewicz makes a mistake in this section when he translates the *Wesen* of humans as "entity."

34. Rojcewicz translates *die Wahr* as "safeguarding" and *die Hut* as "protecting."

35. Rojcewicz translates *Austrag* as "enduring." "Carrying out" is a more literal translation that keeps the sense of spacing the German word has.

36. Another way Heidegger phrases the carrying out of the difference is by saying: "beyng itself differentiates itself against beings as it clears them" (GA 71: 247; E: 213; translation altered).

37. See, for instance, sections 94, 257. Rojcewicz translates *Wonne* as "bliss."

38. Compare Heidegger's account of being-toward-death in *Being and Time*.

39. Rojcewicz translates *Folgsamkeit* as "submissiveness."

40. Heidegger speaks of the Germans as well in section 127. Here he addresses "the highest danger for the advent of the West . . . in the fact that the Germans are succumbing to the modern spirit" (GA 71: 93; E: 78).

41. The grounders of Da-sein are *Sucher*, *Wahrer*, and *Wächter* (seekers, preservers, and guardians). See GA 65: 17, 230, 294, 298, 304.

42. See also GA 71: 278; E: 242.

43. Compare also section 264 on the issue of question-worthiness and the futility of questioning.

44. In sections 306 and 372, Heidegger speaks of thanking as a questioning.

45. In more current German this word has the sense of demanding something overly courageous of someone.

46. See also GA 71: 113; E: 96, where Heidegger notes: "Inceptive ignorance—patience—forbearance; thanking."

47. In order to differentiate the word *Sagen* ("saying," understood in terms of the thinking-saying) from *die Sage* ("Saying" attributed not primarily to thinking but to beyng), I will capitalize "Saying" when referring to *Sage*.

48. One may say indicatively that the "of" in the phrase "the word of beyng" connotes more a subjective than an objective genitive. However, Heidegger still found this designation of

"subjective genitive" misleading with respect to how inceptive language happens as the word of being. For a more in-depth analysis of the role of language in Heidegger's poietic writings, see Krzysztof Ziarek, *Language after Heidegger* (Bloomington: Indiana University Press, 2013). Ziarek discusses the word "of" being on pages 62–64.

49. See also section 314 of *The Event*.

50. One of the problems of translating *Ereignung* as "appropriation" in *Contributions* is precisely this sense of taking something for one's own use.

51. See GA 71, sections 245–346.

52. See *The Event*, section 365.

53. See ibid., section 352.

54. See ibid., section 364.

55. Ibid., section 368.

56. See also GA 71: 243, 327; E: 210, 284.

9 At the Brink of Language

A Critical Engagement with Heidegger's *The Event* (GA 71)

Oh, what are you anyway, my written and painted thoughts! It was not long ago
that you were still so colorful, young and malicious, so full of thorns and
secret spices that you made me sneeze and laugh—and now? You have
already lost your novelty, and I am afraid that some of you are ready to
turn into truths: they already look so immortal, so pathetically decent
and upright, so boring!

—Friedrich Nietzsche, *Beyond Good and Evil*

The Event

I vividly remember the day I received *Das Ereignis* in the mail in our cottage in
Turlock, California, as I was surprised to find myself immediately reading the
book (something I did not do either with *Besinnung* or with the other volumes
following *Contributions*). I did not know that I had awaited the publication especially of this volume. What book would Heidegger find worthy of the simple title
The Event? I remember reading with growing puzzlement sentences I could
not understand. I found myself estranged by the text and thus also enticed by
it. What I found most enticing is that the "picture" I had made for myself of
Heidegger's *Contributions to Philosophy* crumbled. His words were fresh again,
strange again—indeed stranger than I had ever found them!—and I was filled
with new resistances and puzzlements, bewildered by words with repetitive
sound-variations.

That was about six years ago. Meanwhile I found plenty of "structures" of
thinking, movements of thought that I somehow can articulate. I can to some
limited extent "explain" how Heidegger thinks, follow many more of the subtle
differentiations he makes, sense shifts in mood and tonality. But what gets easily
lost in this explanatory approach to the text is that which he struggled with most
intimately in his poietic writings: a thinking and saying that does not solidify into
concepts and categories but that remains always fresh; a saying of beyng without ground. I wanted to give myself some leeway in the chapters following the

exposition of Heidegger's poietic writings, to engage his texts more freely and not simply within the traditional academic context, searching around the edges of my resistances to his texts, opening questions to which I do not have answers. I am not sure how successful I have been with this but, on the other hand, "success" is not the point here.

In this chapter that engages more freely and critically Heidegger's *The Event*, I will begin by reflecting on his work with language and on the question of "poietic" language more generally. I will again question his more radical "descent" into the abyssal dimension of the event when he thinks of the event as inception (I already engaged this dimension in chapter 7 when discussing the notion of the "beingless"), this time with a focus on the religious dimension I find at work here. Lastly, I will turn to what follows Heidegger's descent into inception in 1940/1941, namely, the thinking of the fourfold, that is, the projection of a cosmology in thinking about "things." The question is, whether finally, after the radical descent into "the abyss" in the years 1940/1941, he reemerges by thinking even more radically than before the "simultaneity" of beyng and beings. But first, let me turn to the issue of language.

Coming to Thought and Coming to Language

How can one engage Heidegger's thinking in its most original dimension, that is, in that work with language and thought that defies traditional philosophical thought and language? By thinking. The thinking I have in mind here is precisely not arranging ready-made concepts in one's mind. It is rather an art that requires an open space of indeterminacy, a not-knowing, a waiting and responsiveness to what gratuitously begins to take shape as a thought and thus emerges "poietically." What do we say, though, when we say that a thought takes shape gratuitously? Does this mean that it comes from nothing? And what would "nothing" mean here? Nothing in the sense of a certain withdrawal or reserve (a "not yet" or "no longer") belonging to beyng? This "nothing" would be something we can be attuned to, something we can listen to. But then there is also what I might call a more radical nothing that I find in Heidegger, which would be the nothing beyond being, the beingless. This nothingness does not resound. For Heidegger, this "beingless" is a "nothingless" and it is not an origin. "It" somehow falls into beyng, into the event of coming to be, such that something becomes a being. One may say this more appropriately in the middle-voice manner: a falling into beyng occurs of what at that moment emerges as a being. As, for instance (and for Heidegger above anything else), a word or a thought.

Often, when a word or thought comes to us, it is a telling word; it tells us something perhaps about someone else and or about ourselves. It tells us about what was already there, already happening, but we did not "see" or notice. Such a word un-covers, dis-covers something. Often, when this happens, there is some-one listening there. We find ourselves saying something to someone, something that "comes up" gratuitously but that, perhaps, would not have come up if the other had not been there. Then there is the sense that there is still so much more to be said in the telling word that no words can capture. We let this "so much" reverberate until it fades away or perhaps some chatter or occurrence forces itself in, interrupts the happening and takes us somewhere else.

Do words really come from nothing? Is there not always already so much there but only hidden from us, unnoticed? Hidden in "our" flesh or in the flesh of the world, as Merleau-Ponty calls it? This is indeed one of the main points of dif-ference between Heidegger and Merleau-Ponty. Merleau-Ponty always thinks in the fullness of being whereas Heidegger seems to always seek out an originary nothingness in order to find in the most inceptive inception, away from all beings, *almost* purified from all intrusion (errancy always remains), the other beginning of a destiny for a people.

Yet what are we saying when we say that there is always already so much there? Should we say, with Heidegger, that this is representational thinking, an imaginative representational thinking that covers over the originary occurrence of coming to be and withdrawing? For Heidegger, the task is to think in Da-sein, in an originary disclosive moment in which the word and things more fully "are." Or, rather—since he says that only beyng *is* whereas beings are not—what may be sought is a fuller moment of beyng in which what occurs in this moment (beings or things) is more fully something that *is*.

In Da-sein we are dislodged from everydayness, an everydayness that Heideg-ger now understands in terms of machinationally determined modes of relating to things. Da-sein, on the other hand, is the disclosure of beyng in its singularity. Meanwhile (according to Heidegger) machinational "life" goes on. So, in a cer-tain way, there always is "so much going on" but which for Heidegger is precisely what is to be left alone.

When Heidegger thinks of the occurring of a more originary language and thought, he thinks of it as it occurs in his solitary practice of thinking. His think-ing concentrates, gathers into an experience of departure, letting go of beings, letting echo only the sayings of some Ancient thinkers; his thinking gathers in a λέγειν turned toward the unsayable, turning in the turning of the truth of beyng, circulating in the wreath of the turning. Sometimes his meditative practice leads him to think through sound-meaning variations like *Ereignis, Ereignung, Eigen-tum, Enteignung, Vereigung*; or *Stimmen, Stimmung, anstimmen, bestimmen, Stimme*; or *Rühren, Anrühren, Berühren*; or *Mut, Langmut, Zumutung, Anmut, Gemüt*; or *Wahrheit, Wahr, bewahren, verwahren*; or *Fug, Fügung, Gefüge*; or *Anklang, Ein-klang, Widerklang*; or *Wort, Antwort, Gegenwort*; or *Überwinden, Verwinden, Gewind, Einwinden, Entwinden*; or *Sage, Zusage, entsagen, versagen*.

At one point in *The Event* Heidegger answers to "the indignation at the supposed play with word-meanings." What looks like mere invented word games, however, "in essence only is the counter-tone [*Gegen-klang*] of the appropriation" (GA 71: 299; E: 259). Appropriation (*Ereignung*) occurs through attunement (*Stimmung*), which Heidegger addresses as well as the silent voice (*Stimme*) of beyng. At this inceptive level there is not yet sound, not yet language, not yet meaning.

I wonder about the moment of transition to the thought or word of the thinker, which Heidegger sometimes addresses as a break. I held back the following passage from *The Event* that occasions a series of reflections for me in this respect. In section 289 he writes:

> The thinking word is the proclamation [*Spruch*] of the experience of departure. The proclamation is a breaking [*Bruch*] of the silence of the appropriated clearing. From whence and how silence here? The sound-less [*das Laut-lose*] as the non-sensible [*das Un-sinnliche*]. The sound-lessness of beyng.
> The proclamation is the word of the response to the claim [*An-spruch*] of the inception. (GA 71: 263; E: 227; translation altered)

Two main questions spark my interest here. One is the issue of the breaking of silence and the other the question of sensuousness.

In chapter 6 I quoted the following passage: "But all sounding is the echo [*Widerhall*] of the fact that beings, previously beingless, enter into the eventuation toward beyng and persist therein. The echo of the inceptual voice of being originates such that being breaks on beings, which are themselves first lit up through the appropriation to being. In the inceptual voice of the disposition occurring through the event, there is neither speaking out nor silence" (GA 71: 171; E: 146; translation altered).

Being breaks on beings like an ocean wave breaks on a rock. In this break a word comes to be. This is the moment at which the beingless and nothingless (word) enters into the clearing of being. In *On Inception* Heidegger called this the moment of a *Dazwischenankunft*, the moment of the coming in-between of the clearing in the becoming being of the beingless (GA 70: 11). Only in this moment does the event come into the open. Without the broken echo of the thinking response in the thinking word, there is no clearing, there is no turning in the event, no thing, no sense.

The imagery of the breaking in which the word comes to be is reminiscent of two poems by Stefan George that Heidegger discusses in his late essay "The Word" from 1958.[1] In one of the poems ("In the Stillest Peace . . .") George writes in the last stanza:

> As when the sea
> With shrill scream
> With wild crash

Once again thrusts
Into the long-abandoned shell. (GA 12: 217)[2]

The shell is, in Heidegger's interpretation, the ear of the poet. The word requires the ear of the poet. Only then, thrusting into and echoing in (as it were) the poet's ear, does the word first emerge. Just as Heidegger thinks that only in the response to the voice of beyng does the word emerge. Certainly, the "shrill scream" of the ocean stands in stark contrast to the silent voice of being, but the poem starts with the stanza:

In the stillest peace
Of a musing day
Suddenly breaks a sight which
With undreamed terror
Troubles the secure soul.

So George also has the sense of a preceding stillness. The other poem by George, "The Word," ends with the stanza:

So I renounced and sadly see:
Where word breaks off no thing may be.[3]

Here the sense of the breaking is, however, different from the thinking we find in *The Event*. In Heidegger's interpretation, George is saying that where the word breaks off (*gebricht*—not *bricht*), there is no thing, that is, the thing is only by virtue of the word.

That Heidegger finds a sense of break in the arising (or coming in-between) of the word is a clear indication that there can never be the "pure word of beyng" uttered by the thinker. Indeed, there cannot be a pure event of the truth of beyng in which somehow a pure revelation of beyng as such happened. Beyng will never be *in* a word although it only happens with the word. With "the word" or "words"?

We saw how Heidegger thinks the silent word of beyng (to which thinking responds) necessarily as a singular (because of the singularity of the truth beyng in its eventuation) but he also speaks of the "thinking word" (that responds to the silent word of beyng) in the singular, probably in order to distinguish what is said in the thinking word from the many words that we can "objectify." Yet, in section 332 of *The Event*, Heidegger says that the word (in singular) of inceptual thinking "has the plurivocity (*Mehrdeutigkeit*) of the inception" (GA 71: 255; E: 255). We cannot expect the thinking word to be univocal, or to have a univocal meaning because the inception itself is not univocal. Thus, not only the word of beyng but also the word of thinking is essentially plurivocal. Sometimes he even speaks of a disposed indeterminacy (*bestimmte Unbestimmtheit*) of inception (GA 71: 217; E: 187). Singularity, then, has nothing to do with a clearly definable essence or substance. The thinking word is a gathering of plurivocity echoing the plurivocity of the inception. And still, plurivocity does not mean multiplicity. There is multiplicity only when we think in terms of beings.

Does this mean that the thinking word is not a being (*ein Seiendes*)? Would only (written or spoken) words in which the word resounds be beings? Or should we distinguish different "levels" or ways of thinking of words and beings? (Let us not forget that although in English we use the plural "beings" in order to distinguish *das Seiende* from *das Sein*, Heidegger uses the singular also when speaking of what we translate in the plural as "beings.") The thinking word echoes the plurivocal silent word of beyng. Such echo sounds only when the sound breaks on the rock, when being breaks on a being, when words are spoken or written silently or loudly.

Derrida denounces as metaphysical the self-presence of the spoken word, the word in silent self-presence that binds the signifier to one supposed signification that dominates the signifier. If we take into account that Heidegger speaks of the word of being as plurivocal (*mehrdeutig*) and sometimes even undetermined (*unbestimmt*), his sense of the word seems to escape Derrida's critique.[4] On the other hand, though, Heidegger resists a disseminating multiplicity. In Derrida, allowing the primacy of the written word is part of the movement of dissemination that his deconstructive thinking performs. The breaking of the word is always a shattering that produces a multiplicity of signifiers with no preceding unity of being.

I have always thought that there is even a stronger sense of dissemination when we speak out a word, and that one can keep more of a sense of unity in relation to a word "only" written, a word one has not yet shared. Think, for instance, of the common experience of how one is disappointed by someone or falls in love with someone and thinks over and over in his or her mind how to confront and tell him or her, writing perhaps letters one will never send. The moment of actual voicing one's feeling, the moment one speaks out to the other, is a break of a peculiar kind. Once spoken out to the other, the word has become its own being, a word whose effects we cannot predict, a word we cannot simply take back or burn—unseen by anyone—like the written word we wrote on a page in our solitary room. There is, however, an experience of breaking also in silent writing, as I write these words, for instance. There still is a break, breaking open. Once the written word is read by someone, the break seems again stronger and of a peculiar kind, different from the spoken word. Yet, is it not the case that every word (even if typed on a computer) is a mark, leaves a mark where there was no mark even if I can erase or "delete" this mark? Indeed, attempting to write more freely in response to Heidegger's poietic writings, as I am doing here, not only bears a sense of break but also comes with a sense of risk, the risk of saying nonsense, the uncertainty of whether these words will be heard or not, and not knowing how they will be heard. It is certainly much easier to do a textual interpretation where one has something to hold on to, textual evidence one can present (and I am aware that I am taking recourse to this as well here).

I wonder, in this context, about those words Heidegger writes in *The Event*:

> *The saying of the inception*—its expression and presentation can only be simple. Here, this means: emerging out of the one and the unity of the beginning: in the manner of the event.
>
> Any discovering, any teaching, but also any awakening, any thrusting must stay away; in the same manner any "ordering" of "contents." Only the pure word that rests in itself must resonate. No listener must be presupposed and no room for the listening-belonging (*Gehören*). (GA 71: 297)

Here Heidegger is speaking of "his" saying of the event. Now he emphasizes again unity (a unity, we now know not to imply univocity). The "pure" word must resonate; no listener must be presupposed. No one, no thing, no text to hold on to. Only the experience of departure into the abyss. Courage (*Mut*) is required here, as Heidegger so often says, as he writes words he knows will be estranging to the ones who read them.

Then he writes about staying here (*bleiben*), about finding an abode in the unfamiliar, *das Unheimische* literally means the "un-homey," circulating in the wreath of the event, echoing the silent voice of beyng, breaking and then only letting resonate with every word the silent voice of being. In order to stay in this distant proximity to the event, in this "unhomeyness," Heidegger had to learn to push away or let go of beings.

Is this not a form of epoché Heidegger performs, an epoché that opens the time-space of his solitary thinking/saying? Is the "pure" word of beyng a "purified" word of beyng? Is there a metaphysical gesture at work here in this notion of "pure"?

This epoché that I do indeed see Heidegger performing at times (think of all the places where he says how *not* to understand something) seems to me to be crossed by another main move in his thinking, a concentric force that bends back, as it were, words that otherwise would "spiral out." Through repetition and iteration, through gathering and concentration, his thinking bends toward the silent voice of being, every time anew, every time slightly differently, performing both the singularity and irreducible plurivocity of what he attempts to think.

Letting go of beings, departing into the abyss, the silent voice of beyng resounds without sound in the thoughts of the thinker.

What about the fragmentary thought I quoted above, which speaks of the sound-lessness of the voice of beyng as "non-sensible"?

The sensible-intelligible distinction is metaphysical, certainly, and Heidegger understands thinking in attunement to undermine this distinction. But how should we interpret, then, his remark: "The sound-less as the non-sensible. The

sound-lessness of beyng" (GA 71: 263; E: 227). The sound-lessness of beyng implies also a lack of sense for Heidegger; sense comes with sound, comes with a
sensing in the double sense of the word, even if the thoughtful concept of inception
is "imageless," as Heidegger always emphasizes. Indeed attunements, dispositions, and movements of thought are what allow one to follow his thinking,
especially if one attempts to keep simple objectification or representation at
bay. I am always reminded in this context of how David Hume writes: "where we
cannot find any impression, we may be certain that there is no idea."[5] He certainly interprets sensing metaphysically (on the basis of a metaphysical understanding of a human being and largely in terms of representational thinking) but
he did touch upon something true here that obviously also struck Kant who
writes how a concept without sensible intuition is "blind." It seems to me that the
sense of sense (in the double sense of the word) is a fundamental guideline for
Kant's *Critique*. It is as if one can find this sense of sense distilled and stripped of
representation (as much as that is possible) in Heidegger's thinking.

Yet there is a moment in Heidegger's thinking where utter finitude comes
into play (and this takes him far away from Hume and Kant): non-sense at the
edge of sense: death, dis-propriation, the beingless. Should we count among these
the silent voice of beyng as well? Heidegger writes that "it" (which is no thing) "is
neither speaking nor keeping silent [*weder Verlautbarung noch Schweigen*]"
(GA 71: 171; E: 146; translation altered). It is prior to language, prior to an articulation of something. But why call "it" "voice," then? Because it is the attuning/
disposing, he says. It is an attuning to which thinking replies such that this attuning resonates and finds sense in the responsive thinking word. The attuning
emerges in departure into the abyss, in letting beings go, and thus a differencing
occurs such that in dis-propriation is appropriated a clearing, and the beingless
comes in-between, that is, a being comes into being. However, in *The Event*,
Heidegger tends to think the coming-into-being of a being in terms of the egress
(into presence) marking the first beginning. The other beginning, instead, is
marked by departure and downgoing, a movement he announces in his very first
foreword to *The Event*.

The Ultimate Descent

The first foreword to *The Event* is a quotation from Sophocles's *Oedipus at Colonos*
taken from the following context.[6]

Having blinded himself after discovering that he had killed his own father
and married his own mother, finally exiled from the city of Thebes, old Oedipus
wanders around with the help of only his daughter and half sister Antigone in
order to find a place where he can die. Finally Oedipus and Antigone reach Athens and, more specifically, the temple of the Eumenides at Colonos, where a quite

mysterious death awaits Oedipus. An Oracle had told him about his final destiny and after long wanderings, having heard where he had arrived (namely, at the place an Oracle had foretold), he finally knows what awaits him. At that point, Oedipus asks a stranger to call for the king of Athens, Theseus, because he, Oedipus, could help Theseus reap great gains.

It is then that the stranger asks the old blind Oedipus (I translate Heidegger's translation): "And what is, then, of a man who cannot look [*blepein*] the warrant?" And Oedipus answers: "Whatever we might say, we see in all that we say [*horan*]."[7] Heidegger interprets this passage as saying that the man who cannot look does not see beings; he is blind for beings. Whereas the phrase "we see" means: to have an eye for being, for the "destiny" and "truth of beings." This seeing of being is, according to Heidegger, "the sight of the pain of experience" and "the capacity to suffer, up to the affliction of the complete concealment of the departure [*Das Leidenkönnen bis zum Leid der völligen Verborgenheit des Weggangs*]" (GA 71: 3; E: xxiii). Blind for beings but seeing being, Oedipus suffers the complete concealment of departure.

The way Oedipus dies, or rather, "goes away into complete concealment," is also quite mysterious. After receiving the signs from the sky (Zeus's thunder), Oedipus, who up to that point is depicted as not being able to go one step without the help of his trusted Antigone—this blind Oedipus gets up and walks ahead alone and quite assuredly to his destiny. He *knows* where he is going. It is a god who summons Oedipus to his final destiny. What happened in the end, nobody knows. Sophocles writes: "It was some messenger sent by the gods, or some power of the dead split open the fundament of earth, with good will, to give him painless entry."[8] Thus Oedipus suddenly disappears into the earth, leaving no trace, no corpse behind.

So much links this scene from *Oedipus at Colonos* to the movement of Heidegger's thinking especially in *On Inception* and *The Event*. Blind for beings because he blinded himself, Oedipus follows a divine call, walks alone and "knowingly" to his destiny, and goes under, leaving no trace behind. In 1941/1942, Heidegger performs in thinking his most radical descent into the event thought as inception, thinking even beyond being the beingless, describing the movement of thinking as a departure into the abyss. Heidegger, too, speaks of a knowing of inceptual thinking so much that he begins to move away from thinking of the appropriate response to beyng as a questioning and rather speaks of following and thanking. The thinking response to beyng is imageless since he has worked year after year to hold representational thinking at bay, as if he was progressively blinding himself, until he no longer needed to resist machinational beings and simply could let go, could let the raging of will to power in World War II go, could see the necessity of the abandonment of beings by beyng with more serenity, as it were, abiding in the poverty and dignity of beyng.

What about the divine call Oedipus follows, though? Heidegger distinguishes the event of appropriation from the gods. The soundless voice of beyng is not a divine voice. Or is it? I wonder whether a sense of "gathering" we find in Heidegger's turn toward the silent voice of beyng does not carry an intrinsic religious dimension.

The last section of *Contributions* is titled "*Language* (its origin)" and it begins thus: "When the gods call the earth, and when in the call a world echoes and thus the call resonates as the Da-sein of the human being, then language exists as historical, as the word that grounds history" (GA 65: 510; C: 401).

Language exists as historical only "when the Gods call the earth." This does ascribe a divine dimension to the originating of language, which can be gathered as well from Heidegger's reading of Hölderlin.[9] But the origin of language that Heidegger thinks already in *Contributions* in terms of silence and that he experiences in the necessity for thinking to fathom the abyss, this originary silence seems to go beyond language and it is in exposure to this abyssal silence that he sees "the thinker" to go farther than "the poet."

When distinguishing thinking from poetry, Heidegger highlights repeatedly that thinking dares to experience godlessness and seeks what is un-holy. Perhaps in his descent into the abyss in 1941/1942, Heidegger is also farthest away from the gods. On the other hand, already in *On Inception*, he does make the connection between the holy and beyng, saying that they are the same and yet not the same. He also writes that they both precede the gods, that is, make them possible (GA 70: 157).

In *The Event*, Heidegger says more about godlessness,[10] and remarkably little about the gods. He speaks of "the last god" only in section 254. In addition, in one of the forewords concerning *Contributions*, he only mentions how in this earlier volume "The thought of the last god is still unthinkable" (GA 71: 5; E: xxiv). (What this means is not clear to me.) What he says about the last God in section 254 in some way resembles what he says about the last god in *Contributions*: he still needs to be decided; first the time-space of his appearing needs to be prepared. Yet he also says things that he did not say (perhaps would not have said) in *Contributions*: He speaks of the decision of the last god's essence in terms of him *being*, that is, in terms of a *seiender Gott*. He also speaks of him as the "highest god" with whom essentially occur all gods that have been (*alle Gewesenen*) (GA 71: 229–230; E: 197).[11] He then ends this section on the last god with the enigmatic sentence: "The last god first grounds the essential occurrence of that which, badly calculated, is called eternity" (GA 71: 230; E: 197).

Not only this last sentence remains enigmatic for me. What would a "being god" be? He (again: why a "he" god?) would certainly not be a being either like a human or like other beings. And why does Heidegger still hold on to this thought of the last god since he will let go of him eventually? It would have been more consistent with the descent into the abyss to stay with godlessness.

Even in that case, though, one still could have spoken of a religiosity in Heidegger's thinking, a religiosity of its own kind perhaps. If we take into account what he said in a television interview with Thai monk Bhikku in 1963, Heidegger could say indeed that thinking in response to the silent voice of beyng is a religion. In the interview he says: "Religion means, as the word says, a bonding back to powers, forces, and laws, that supersede human capability. [Heidegger gives as examples communism and Buddhism.] I would say that no human being is without religion and that every human being is in a way beyond himself, that is, deranged [*verrückt*]."[12]

The last phrase, Heidegger says with a certain mischievous smile on his face. (In his writings his humor does not transpire as readily.) The apparent primary meaning of the word *verrückt* he uses is the literal one: "being un-settled," "dislodged." But there is no doubt that he was loving the play with the more common meaning: being insane.

The notions of poverty, dignity, and nobility to which Heidegger takes recourse so often in his thinking of *The Event* do not let any humor transpire and also have a tone (at least to my ear) closer to Christian piety than to Greek religion. The passages in which he speaks more out of an attunement resonating in these words are among the most difficulty to follow for me, perhaps out of resistances I have to lineages I do not wish to treasure, perhaps simply because I belong to another time.

Toward the end of my dissertation written on the notion of grounding in Heidegger's *Contributions* and Derrida, the tonality of my thinking started leaving what I would call a Sturm und Drang phase that loved the abyss. I began having a different "intuition" or "sense" of the historical time I lived in. The image that arose for me one day was that of a morning after a great battle, a morning also after the mourning of the losses that occurred in this battle: fresh, crisp air, a spacious emptiness, stillness without melancholy. It is a space in which things and events can begin to emerge again, in a certain simplicity, perhaps, without a unifying bending back or an overarching order. From this vantage point, the "bending back" and with it, a certain "religiosity" in Heidegger's thinking became more apparent.

Where to Now? A New Cosmology and the Emerging of Things

The bending back into the inceptual abyss reaches a peak in 1941/1942.[13] The emphasis on the incipience of inception (on departure and the abyss) takes Heidegger away from thinking of the event as the encounter of humans and gods, and the strife of earth and world. He does not so much think ahead into the sheltering of truth (the encounter of gods and humans and strife of world and earth) into beings as he did in *Contributions* and "The Origin of the Work of Art." In his thinking path of 1941–1942, he is farthest away from the openness of a world and the coming to presence of beings. His thinking is most solitary.

But we know from the works that follow that Heidegger's thinking will take a new path, a path that will take him to writing some dialogues (the *Country Path Conversations*) and to develop what came to be known as his "topological" thinking. He will emerge from the imageless and soundless abyss with a thinking of the fourfold of gods and humans, earth and sky. Beings reemerge as things gathering the fourfold, things like a jar, and a bride.

One could, of course, emphasize how already in *On Inception* and *The Event*, Heidegger's thinking begins to take on the character of releasement (*Gelassenheit*) that allows things to become "more being" precisely by resonating with "the beingless." One could make the case that the thinking of inception overcomes the ontological difference more radically than *Contributions* does. Let me recall that in *On Inception* and *The Event*, he thinks the event as the coming in-between of being into the beingless such that the beingless "is," in a hard-to-think way, older than being, in the same way that dispropriation now characterizes the most inceptive moment of the event of appropriation. Beinglessness is lost in machinationally disclosed beings just as truth and the inceptive dispropriation get covered over. Beinglessness thus is something that needs to be preserved if the event is to occur inceptively. This is what the thinking in releasement—letting pass by machination and following in departure into the event—allows to happen. When thinking departs into the groundlessness of dispropriation, when thinking lets itself be attuned by the soundless voice of concealed beyng and becomes a receiving thanking, then, for Heidegger, beings are released into their essence.

We do not find any examples of beings that are released into their essence in *The Event*, but we do in the *Country Path Conversations* (1944), where Heidegger begins to speak not just of beings (*das Seiende*) but of things, *Dinge*.[14] He also speaks of the woods, the field, and of night and day, of earth and sky. This is the beginning of what is often called his topological thinking.[15] I like to call it a cosmological thinking as well. For many readers of Heidegger, this is where his thinking becomes more concrete. The word "concrete" comes from the Latin "concrescere," "grow together." It reminds in some way of the word *Versammlung*, gathering.[16] In this sense, Heidegger would have happily embraced the term "concrete." But his thinking certainly does not become concrete in the more common sense of the term since he does not speak of what we think of as "real" and "solid" things, of things insofar as they resist our flesh or can be measured. Consider for instance the jug of which the interlocutors of the first country path conversation speak.

The task in thinking the jug is not to represent it as an object but to let it be what or rather how it is. The interlocutors eventually come to the insight that the essence of the jug lies not in its so-called materiality but in its emptiness (GA 77: 130; CPC: 84). In relation to this emptiness they develop further relational determinations of the jug. The emptiness is emptiness of the drink so that the containing quality of the jug (*das Fassende des Krugs*) abides in the drink. The drink is further developed in relation to what is drunk, i.e. the wine that gathers earth and sky, and the one who drinks, the human (GA 77: 134–135; CPC: 87). Thus the emptiness of the jug is brought to abide in this expanse of earth and sky and the relation to the human as well. It is then that the jug is itself, the interlocutors conclude. The scholar says: "The jug abides in itself in that it turns back to itself over and through this expanse" (GA 77: 135; CPC: 88). This expanse is then identified with the open-region, the *Gegnet*, which is the essential occurrence of truth. The relation of the drink to the human furthermore brings into play the festival that also brings the human to abide. (Not explicitly named but to surmise in this context is the relation to the divine.) In the open-region that emerges from the emptiness of the jug, earth and sky and humans (and the divine) come to abide in the festival.

What is developed here is the thought of a thing, a jug, in the context of a relation to being (*Sein*), where thinking is released into a relation to the open-region such that this releasement is *vergegnet*, "enregioned." With recourse to the language of *Contributions* and *The Event*, we may rethink this by saying that thinking is appropriated into belonging to the event of appropriation in which the truth of beyng occurs such that being comes in-between the beingless and beings, in this case the jug, becomes more being (*wird seiender*).

The emptiness of the jug mirrors and in the mirroring carries with it, so to speak, the beingless that is preserved insofar as the open-region or the openness of truth is such only in relation to the emptiness. The jug has become more being through the thinking of its emptiness. This is how thinking lets this thing rest in its being.[17]

Clearly such an approach to things no longer looks at them as objects that can be manipulated. But does it let beings be what they are? Does it think beings in their singularity? Or is the singularity, the *Einzigkeit* of being that Heidegger attempts to evoke, not rather the singularity of a moment in which is contemplated being in departure, a moment that has left the singularity of things behind? Is he opening up for us the possibility of a deeper or more essential relation to things or is he missing the relation to things when he lets "pass by" machinationally determined beings?

The provisional answers I have for myself in relation to these questions are twofold. On the one hand, I do not see Heidegger's thinking ever opening up to the singularity of things and events in *their* indifferent happening and this is because he will always remain faithful to the primacy of beyng. Human being occurs in the spacing between beyng and beings but within this spacing Heidegger's thinking remains bent back toward beyng and concealment. On the other hand, he does open for me a space of thinking differently of beings or things in their singularity and indifferent happening, namely, by rethinking them in terms of their temporal happening both in terms of the relational differencing through which they emerge and in terms of their "concreteness" that one may think in terms of gathering, constellations, or gravitational centers. Such thinking of beings requires of course that one let go of the gravitational pull of the primacy of beyng and the unifying discourse of a history of beyng.

Notes

1. Martin Heidegger, *On the Way to Language*, trans. Peter Hertz (San Francisco: Harper and Row, 1971). "The Word" is the only essay translated by Joan Stambough.
2. Ibid., 148. In German: "So wie das meer / Mit gellem laut / Mit wildem prall / Noch einmal in die lang / Verlassene muschel stößt."
3. Ibid., 140.
4. Ziarek expresses a similar critique of Derrida's suggestion in "Différance" that Heidegger seeks the one word for being. Ziarek stresses how the uniqueness of the word of being that Heidegger emphasizes has nothing to do with a unique name; rather the unique word is the word "as each-time singular in how the event, coming to word, lets be" (Krzysztof Ziarek, *Language after Heidegger* [Bloomington: Indiana University Press, 2013], 38).
5. David Hume, *An Enquiry concerning Human Understanding*, ed. Eric Steinberg (Indianapolis: Hackett, 1993), 52.
6. I am taking the comment on this passage from my essay "Heidegger's Reticence: From *Contributions* to *Das Ereignis* and toward *Gelassenheit*," *Research in Phenomenology* 45, no. 1 (2015): 1–32.
7. "Und welches ist von einem Manne, der nicht blicken kann, den die Gewähr? Was wir auch sagen mögen, Alles sagend sehen wir." See "Forewords: Sophocles, *Oedipus at Colonus*, vv. 73–74," in Martin Heidegger, *The Event*, trans. Richard Rojcewicz (Bloomington: Indiana University Press, 2013). In the translation by David Grene, this sentence reads: "There shall be sight in all the words I say." Sophocles, *Oedipus at Colonos*, trans. David Grene, in *Greek Tragedies*, ed. David Grene and Richmond Lattimore (Chicago: University of Chicago Press, 1991), 3:80.
8. Sophocles, *Oedipus at Colonos*, 1880.
9. See the last section of chapter 8 in this volume.
10. See especially section 123.
11. Rojcewicz mistakenly translates *Gewesenen* as "past things."
12. http://www.openculture.com/2014/05/martin-heidegger-talks-philosophy-with-a-buddhist-monk.html.
13. Most of this section takes materials from a lecture course given at the Collegium Phaenomenologicum in 2013.
14. Martin Heidegger, *Country Path Conversations*, trans. Bret David (Bloomington: Indiana University Press, 2012) (hereafter cited as CPC).

15. For an in-depth reading of Heidegger's thinking of the fourfold, see Andrew Mitchell, *The Fourfold: Reading the Late Heidegger* (Evanston, IL: Northwestern University Press, 2015).

16. In the early use of "concrete," it came to mean the quality of a substance in distinction to a quality viewed by itself. Then it came to mean something "existing in a physical form."

17. We need to continue to distinguish, here, between Heidegger's thinking of things and the being of things. Heidegger's thinking of the fourfold thinks ahead into how things may shelter and disclose a world but strictly speaking, things do not gather a world, and human dwelling does not yet essentially occur.

Conclusion

In my expository reading of Heidegger's poietic writings I traced shifts in concepts, movements of thought, and attunements. Thereby a narrative emerged that (like all narratives) does not do justice to all the nuances and particularities in his writings that escape the general "storyline" of the narrative. The narrative that emerged relates to a number of questions that guided my reading of Heidegger's poietic writings and that I outlined in the last section of chapter 1.

In this concluding chapter, I will (1) give an account of this narrative. Then I will address four interrelated clusters of themes that constitute foci of my critical engagement with Heidegger's poietic writings, and some of these also take into view the *Black Notebooks*. These clusters concern (2) the question of language and the limits of hermeneutic interpretation; (3) the relation between attunement, language, and conceptual determinations; (4) the relation between attunements, history, and the body; and (5) Heidegger's thinking in terms of the history of beyng and how its gathering power organizes, delimits, and limits the concrete engagements with things and events.

Heidegger's Poietic Writings

In my reading of Heidegger's poietic writings of the event, I traced a shift from a more Nietzschean pathos in which he seeks an empowerment of beyng and resists the machinational deployment of beings (this comprises roughly the years 1934–1939), to a more "mystical" attunement that emphasizes "letting go," "following," and "poverty," whereby machination is no longer resisted but left to its own demise. This shift begins roughly in 1939—although it is prepared earlier—but emerges more fully in 1940 and 1941. It goes along with a deemphasizing of the role of human being in thinking historical beyng as event and inception.

The notion of Da-sein (literally translated "t/here-being") addresses less and less human being (although human being always remains essential) and more and more the disclosure of truth. In *Contributions to Philosophy*, Heidegger has a stronger tendency to approach the truth of beyng as event in terms of how thinking finds itself appropriated by being, and to articulate the event as the turning relation (*Kehre*) between the appropriating throw (or call) of beyng (*ereignender Zuwurf, Zuruf des Seyns*) and the appropriated projective response of thinking (*ereigneter Entwurf, Zugehören*), thus highlighting the relation between beyng and thinking (or human being). In *On Inception* and *The Event*, Heidegger initially blends out how thinking occurs but articulates the truth of beyng as the event of inception, so to speak, out of itself. Thinking sets out from utter "dispossession," indeed from dispropriation (*Enteignis*), which resonates in the notion of the beingless and nothingless (*das Seinlose, das Nichtslose*). As regards the directionality of his thinking, the translation of *Ereignis* as event of appropriation indeed makes more sense in 1940/1941 than in 1936: the truth of beyng (thought as the event of inception) "arrogates" (*aneignet*) and appropriates (*ereignet*) thinking. He thus begins to think beyng as event in the human-less dispropriation that is like the opening of an originary abyss that draws thinking into it and bestows being. Correspondingly, he meditates on inceptive thinking less in terms of a questioning and a projection and more primarily as a following and thanking.

The "dehumanizing" happens also on the level of attunement. In *Contributions*, the grounding attunements of restraint, shock, diffidence, and presentiment, clearly relate to human being and thinking (which does not mean that they are "subjective"), to how thinking finds itself steadfast (*inständig*) in the clearing of truth. In the later volumes, Heidegger emphasizes how attunements (*Stimmungen*) arise from the voice (*Stimme*) of beyng itself: poverty and dignity now designate beyng itself (rather than thought).

Heidegger's thinking of language (that is intimately connected to attunements) follows the same "dehumanization." Whereas the question of language in *Contributions to Philosophy* is addressed primarily in the notion of *denkerisches Sagen* (the saying of thinking), in 1940–1941, the notion of Saying (I am capitalizing Saying, *Sage*, in order to distinguish it from *Sagen*) starts to play a stronger role such that Heidegger begins to think the appropriating event as occurring in a Saying that is not the saying of the thinker but of beyng itself. The Saying (that one may think in terms of the silent voice of beyng) draws thinking into the abyssal dimension of truth out of which occurs the speaking (*Rede*) of the thinker.

With respect to shifts in conceptuality, structure, and movements of thinking, I have been tracing as well the way Heidegger articulates the difference between beyng and beings in the various poietic writings. I showed how, although in *Contributions to Philosophy* he speaks of the simultaneity of beyng and beings and emphasizes how no truth of beyng occurs without beings, still beyng and beings remain sharply differentiated. This differentiation, furthermore, is tied to elements of foundational thinking that sometimes interweave with a (at least to some extent) linear conception of time.

Heidegger frames the task of *Contributions* as addressing the preparation of the other beginning of Western history of beyng through the preparation of the grounding of Da-sein as the site for the historical grounding of the truth of beyng. This historical grounding requires that truth be "sheltered" in beings (words, works, deeds) and would be marked by the passing by of the last God. Thus only through the sheltering of the truth of beyng in beings does beyng occur as event.

In this sheltering (in the occurrence of grounding) beyng and beings occur in their "simultaneity" (which does not simply mean "at the same time"). Heidegger understands his own thinking in *Contributions* as being transitional and preparatory for, although already determined by, the other beginning. His words certainly attempt to shelter truth (and as far as this succeeds would "ground") but cannot initiate the other beginning for a people. As long as this other beginning for a people is not initiated, beings remain abandoned by beyng and beyng occurs as withdrawal that, at the end of the first beginning, unleashes beings into machination and lived experience and thus into groundlessness. In terms of the history of beyng of the West, truth finds no sheltering in beings; no grounding occurs; beyng has no site and beings remain abandoned, deprived of being.

Concerning the relation between beyng and beings one needs to differentiate, then, between the historical situation (abandonment of beings by beyng) and Heidegger's own thinking effort (speaking in the "simultaneity" of beyng and beings). As concerns the latter, it, too, involves a differencing of beyng and beings. His own attempts at speaking of the truth of beyng as event requires the unsettlement from the predominance of beings that is tied to representational thinking and subjective experiences. Especially in the context of *Contributions*, he finds the necessity of a radical dislodging from machinationally deployed beings into this strange transitional time-space, where thinking holds itself in an attunement that withstands the occurrence of beyng as withdrawal and thus provides a site for the withdrawing manifestation of beyng in the (performative) thoughtful saying. Thinking thus appears to occur in the spacing "between" beings and beyng, in a resistance against representing beings, things. This resistance occurs through a radical exposure to the abyss as which the truth of beyng inceptively opens up. The attempted movement of thinking (within the spacing of beyng and beings) has traces of a foundational structure: it sets out with the dislodging into the abyss out of which beyng occurs as appropriating event that appropriates a clearing or opening (Da-) that needs to be sustained (-sein) in order "then" (but not in a linear sense of time) to be sheltered into words.

In the essay "The Origin of the Work of Art," Heidegger does attempt to trace the way from beings to beyng, that is, from the work of art to the disclosure of truth; but this way, too, requires the previous transposition into the truth of beyng.[1] "The Origin of the Work of Art" should be seen as an attempt to think ahead into how a work could shelter truth (since in terms of the Western history of beyng, this is not yet happening). I pointed out how in this attempt, a foundational thinking remains in place when Heidegger differentiates the primordial strife of the truth of beyng (unconcealing-concealing) from the strife of world and earth. Furthermore, with the primordial strife, also the relation between gods and humans seems to "precede" the sheltering of the strife of world and earth in the work of art. In other words, the truth of beyng is thought as more originary than its sheltering in beings.

In the context of *Contributions*, then, one may differentiate, on the one hand a transitional articulation of the truth of beyng as event that focuses on how thinking is dislodged into the abyssal truth of beyng and finds itself appropriated to withstand the withdrawal of beyng in Da-sein (and here thinking seems far removed from beings or things), and, on the other hand, the fuller articulation of how the truth of beyng would occur in the encounter of gods and humans (the clearing of Da-sein) and the strife of world and earth, such that this strife is sheltered in beings, and beings would become "more being" (*seiender*). Here the truth of beyng and beings would be "transformed into their simultaneity" (GA 65: 14).

So far I have provided a synopsis of the issue of the difference and "simultaneity" between beyng and beings in the context of the question of grounding in *Contributions to Philosophy*. At the end of chapter 4, I outlined how in section 70 of the next volume of the poietic writings, *Mindfulness (Besinnung)*, Heidegger speaks of three possibilities of history: either (1) the other beginning will never take place and history ends in the complete unleashing of beings into machination and lived experience; or (2) the grounding of Da-sein for a people occurs and with it another beginning of the history of beyng; or (3) what we end up with is a hybrid situation: although the grounding of Da-sein for a people does not occur, there begins the estranging history of beyng confined to the few lonely ones. I suggested that in the years following *Mindfulness*, the years marked by the outbreak of World War II, Heidegger's thinking seems to embrace more and more this third possibility, as he more radically "goes under," in solitary thinking, into the most abyssal and inceptive dimension of the truth of beyng, removed from the commonly understood "actual events" of his time.

As Heidegger begins to think the truth of beyng (or the event) in terms of inception (*Anfang*), both the difference and the simultaneity of beyng and beings are radicalized. In *On Inception* and *The Event*, his thinking of the truth of beyng in terms of inception does not suggest a linearity between first and other beginning, since he thinks out of the *one* beginning or inception either in the direction of the twisting out (*Entwindung*) into metaphysics or the twisting free (*Verwindung*) into the turning of the event, thereby articulating both first and other beginning more inceptively.

As Heidegger lets machination pass by and his thinking twists free into the "wreath" (the turning) of the abyssal event, he drops the notion of a "sheltering" of beyng into beings and instead articulates the relation between the truth of beyng and beings in terms of the coming-in-between (*Dazwischenkunft*) of the clearing (the "between") in which the formerly beingless (or nothingless) comes or arises into being. The beingless, he tells us, is "older" than being and nothingness and thus needs to be sharply differentiated from the abandonment of beings by beyng in machination. The occurrence of the truth of beyng in terms of the clearing of being thus involves right away the coming into being of (the formerly beingless) beings. I interpreted the beingless (or nothingless) as addressing something unthinkable, namely, not yet or no longer being ~~beings~~ "prior" to the event of inception ("prior" to Da-sein). Heidegger thus articulates the "simultaneity" of beyng and beings more strictly than in *Contributions* and without (or perhaps almost without) foundational thinking. Yet at the same time, the simultaneity of beyng and beings occurs in the differentiation of beyng from beings. Indeed, he writes that only beyng "is," whereas beings, even when they arise into being and are "more being" (*seiender*), properly speaking (according to him), *are* not (GA 70: 11–12).

In *The Event*, Heidegger does not develop a thinking of things in relation to world and earth, gods and humans, as he does in the earlier "The Origin of the Work of Art." Perhaps the not-yet-published volume 73 of the *Gesamtausgabe* that contains his poietic writings of 1944 will show us more about how he begins to address beings as things and how he will come to articulate things as the gathering of the fourfold of gods and humans, earth and sky. He does so, certainly, in the *Country Path Conversations* of 1944–1945. In these we get a perhaps more tangible sense of how it is that even when beings rise into being, they *are* not, as it is out of the emptiness of the jug that the relations to gods, mortals, earth, and sky emerge.

The Question of Language and the Limits of Hermeneutic Interpretation

When working through Heidegger's poietic writings more closely, the heading he gave to his collected works, "Wege, nicht Werke" (Ways, not works), acquired a new and richer meaning for me. Especially reading *The Event* made it clear for me that, viewed retrospectively, *Contributions to Philosophy* has been only one of many attempts to think and speak of the event, perhaps the most structured one when one thinks of the six junctures (*Fugen*) that somehow organize the book. However, to take these junctures and interpret the writings that follow *Contributions* according to them (as some interpreters of Heidegger have done) brings us nowhere close to how thinking happens for Heidegger in the poietic writings. Neither does a reading that tries to systematize his works with respect to words or concepts he uses.

Indeed, especially *The Event* to a large extent resists a hermeneutic approach to the text.[2] It does so specifically in two ways: the first concerns the "fore-structure" of understanding, namely, that every interpretation already moves within a horizon of understanding regarding what is questioned; and the second concerns the dialogical character of understanding. When in *The Event* Heidegger's thinking "goes under," appropriated in a dispropriation that leaves thinking exposed to an abyssal dimension of being without images, when thinking occurs no longer as a questioning but as a following, attuned by the silent voice of beyng, his thinking reaches a limit where there are no preconceptions to be found. Especially in the notion of "the beingless" (or "nothingless") that in a strange way "is" ("is" needs to be crossed out) prior to being and nothingness, Heidegger marks a non-place and non-time "prior" to language and meaning. The latter emerge in the incipience of inception, which is the coming-in-between of the clearing, of an opening in which the formerly beingless rises into being, that is, in which also words rise into being.

As one tries to follow Heidegger's thinking of the beingless, even the being-historical framing of his thinking (the history of being in its epochal unfolding) seems to be left behind; first and other beginning are not yet differentiated. Not even nothing is there in the incipient inception. And yet he thinks and writes, attempting to articulate precisely the coming-in-between of the clearing (*Da*-sein), the arising of sense at the edge of non-sense, and in such away that thinking continues to bend back to the beingless. All that thinking articulates here, is the very happening of inception in which thinking itself arises, circulating in the "wreath" of the event, finding constancy in repetitive word-sound iterations; finding "something" to say in the arising of language that becomes "something" only in the arising of language.

In this saying there are not only no preconceptions but—Heidegger seems to tell himself at some point—"no listener must be presupposed" (GA 71: 297). Thus his thinking of the event (insofar as it is appropriated in the event of inception) answers to no one, has in mind no one. It happens, at best, perhaps, freely, without why, without reason, in a middle-voice manner,[3] and yet attuned and appropriated by this freely occurring event of inception. Heidegger seems far away, here, from philosophy in any traditional Western sense.

One may remain puzzled or bewildered by many of Heidegger's "experimentations" with language in his poietic writings, by that solitary thinking that often does not even try to be communicative, but this does not take away from the fact that his engagement with language and thought at the edge of the sayable and the transformations of language and conceptuality, within a span of only five years, are quite remarkable. They show us not only that thinking for Heidegger has nothing to do with an ordering of concepts but also that emphasizing (as many Heidegger scholars do) that he had only one question, namely, the question of being, does not say much, as the question of being and with it the sense of being undergoes radical transformations. A reading that does justice to his thinking, to how it occurs always anew and never finds rest in some "outcome;" such a reading needs to enter the performative dimension of thinking and language and thus needs to work at the level of attunements and dispositions, following the movement of his thinking and seeking within or through that movement an encounter with what he writes.

Attunement and the Arising of Words and Determinations

Heidegger's thinking resists speaking "about" something, since it attempts to be poietic, to bring forth a sense of beyng that arises out of historical beyng itself. In the thinking "of" the event, there is nothing already there that thinking could describe or address. How is it, then, that his thinking finds something to say?

What gives guidance to thinking in the event of appropriation are attunements. In *Contributions*, Heidegger attributes to each of the junctures (the resonating, the interplay, the leap, etc.) "guiding attunements." He writes that these guiding attunements arise themselves out of a fundamental attunement in which these guiding attunements attune together (GA 65: 395; C: 314, section 249). One of the questions that has arisen for me, in this respect, is how attunements specifically guide Heidegger's thinking and how we ought to think the arising of words and determinations out of these attunements.

For Heidegger, grounding attunements reveal being or beyng as such and are thus differentiated from attunements relating to specific things and events. Although in his poietic writings he does not make this differentiation (he does so in *Being and Time* as well as in the 1929/1930 lecture course *The Fundamental Concepts of Metaphysics*), it seems to me to be operative in the way his thinking attempts to be responsive to an abyssal sense of beyng rather than to this or that thing or event. In order to speak the word "of" beyng, out of beyng, thinking needs to remain unsettled from the relation to this or that thing, unsettled into this strange "in-between" that has no fixity and that needs to be endured every time anew, "steadfastly" (*inständig*), as Heidegger writes. When one follows how his thinking concretely happens in his poietic writings, this "in-between" (that we find addressed as well in the notion of Da-sein) appears as a polyphonous site of unrest, from which he seeks to draw out what is to be said; every time anew.

The being or beyng that is revealed in the polyphonous grounding attunement also varies according to its historicality. Heidegger distinguishes a sense of being as presencing (first beginning) from a sense of beyng as withdrawal (other beginning). Furthermore, these senses of being ("senses" in the double sense of the word) also resound in varying modalities in his thinking, involving varying senses of power (the prevailing power of φύσις or what is beyond power and powerlessness), abandonment (machination), refusal (death), or sheer voiceless absence (in the notion of the beingless).

Regarding conceptual determinations that we find in Heidegger's poietic writings, we may distinguish especially moments when he tries to speak of nothing but how the event happens *as* it happens inceptively, from moments when he pursues a more critical meditation on the first beginning, and the latter both in terms of the history of metaphysics and in terms of its ending through the predominance of machination and lived experience. Especially in his reading of metaphysics, one gets the sense that he has more to write "about."[4] There is more to write about both in terms of philosophical texts of the Western tradition that (as his lecture courses testify) he reads with impressive rigor and imagination, and in terms of a critical analysis of what is happening in the current epoch (in terms of machination). But when it comes to Heidegger's attempts to only listen and be responsive to the soundless voice of beyng, the coming to determination of something has a different character and seems to elude one's grasp. Here he seems to want to let language itself (in terms of the language "of" beyng) speak. We saw how this attempt is carried out especially in *The Event*.

Attunements play a decisive role both in Heidegger's reading of metaphysics in terms of the history of beyng and in his deepening work with language at the edge of the sayable, that is, when he tries to articulate the event as inception. Attunements are revealing, that is, they are constitutive of truth. But it seems to me that in their polyphonies, attunements are permeated as well by opacity and indeterminacy. There is a profound link, I believe, between this opacity and indeterminacy and what Heidegger calls errancy (*Irre*). This is a link, furthermore, that he left little explored.

Already in his essay "On the Essence of Truth" (1930), Heidegger makes it clear that there is no truth without errancy. Errancy marks the relation to beings that belongs to the clearing of truth, a relation that at the same time tends to cover or dissimulate the truth of beyng. As far as I can tell, he never reflected explicitly on errancy in view of attunements; yet it is precisely here, in the intertwining of attunements, truth, and errancy, that I find the locus of what one may call Heidegger's errancies, or, for that matter, anybody's errancies. When speaking of Heidegger's errancies, I have in mind not only but perhaps especially the *Black Notebooks* and his relation to history in a more "concrete" sense: the history of things and events occurring with and around him. In order to question this relation (a questioning that necessarily operates in the differentiation of beyng and beings that one finds in Heidegger's thinking), one needs to take into account not only grounding attunements (and in his poietic writings, he seems to address attunements only in this more fundamental sense) but also "non-grounding" attunements. By non-grounding attunements, I mean attunements that do not reveal the truth of beyng as such by unsettling us from our relation to things (as grounding attunements do, i.e., for example, angst or deep boredom). Non-grounding attunements are related to more specific things or events (as the fear of something or someone or the love for something or someone). According to Heidegger, they dissimulate and conceal truth as such. In his poietic writings, he does not pay attention to these dissimulating and concealing attunements. But how can one dissociate, in the polyphony of what he calls "the" grounding attunement of the other beginning, grounding-attunements from non-grounding attunements—that is, what is truth revealing and what dissimulates truth? How can one dissociate, furthermore, the attunement of an age or a people, from more localized, "personal" attunements?

I believe that especially when it comes to Heidegger's narrative of the history of beyng, the attunements that determine (the German word I have in mind here is *bestimmen*, which relates to both voice, *Stimme*, and attunement, *Stimmung*) his thinking are rooted in history in a more profane sense than he would like[5]— not only in the sense that he is part of a philosophical lineage that sees the cradle of civilization in the Greeks, not only in the special task he saw for the Germans and for his own thinking, but also in his resistance against his own times that he voiced even more forcefully in the *Black Notebooks*.

More mysterious, perhaps, are the determinations of thinking that we find when Heidegger's thinking "goes under" more decidedly in 1940–1941 and lets go of a certain resistance against machination. I mentioned above how in those years he attributes attunements more strongly to beyng itself (nobility, dignity, poverty) and how his saying stays more intimately a saying of the event as the incipience of inception, circulating in word-sound iterations in which thinking finds some kind of constancy. Is his thinking more "purely" attuned by beyng here? But here, too, one can at least intimate connections between the attunements in Heidegger's thinking and what happened concretely with and around him. I suggested, for instance, a connection between his "downgoing" and what he addressed as the "strangeness of war" (that broke out in 1939) as well as his deepened disillusionment with the Nazi movement. But one can also sense a deep piety in the attuning words he privileges that are woven into religious lineages he does not seem to acknowledge or be aware of.[6]

Attunements, History, and the Body

Although I do affirm Heidegger's understanding of attunements as not simply being subjectively located feelings but as overcoming us and as being revelatory, and this indeed sometimes in profound ways, I suspect that he was so taken by "his" historical task that he tended to attribute the attunements determining his thinking too unilaterally to historical beyng. I believe that this blinded him to his own, let me say, more "ontic" dispositions, a blindness that emerges more evidently in the *Black Notebooks*, where he is looser with his conceptuality than in the poietic writings. His anti-Semitism is an attunement rooted in a lineage that, as Jean-Luc Nancy notes, he does not reflect on.[7] That in some instances he attributes to world Jewry a special role in the necessary devastation of the West shows how his beyng-historical thinking could be prone to errancy by integrating concepts whose provenance cannot be attributed to "the silent voice of beyng." Heidegger must have intuited this when he limited his remarks about world Jewry to the *Black Notebooks* and hardly ever mentioned even the Germans in his poietic writings.

That Heidegger was aware of a certain blindness with respect to concrete events may be suggested as well by the first foreword to *The Event*, where he quotes Sophocles's *Oedipus at Colonos*. He writes that Oedipus sees being but is blind toward beings. It is hard not to think that Heidegger somehow saw himself in this blind Oedipus. The tension between beyng and beings is one I marked throughout my expository reading of Heidegger. Furthermore, the emphasis Heidegger places on grounding attunements and his lack of attention toward attunements relating to more specific things and events (i.e., relating to beings) is linked, I believe, to his lack of attention to the body.

The fact that Heidegger hardly ever mentions the body in his poietic writings (and when he does, mostly with critical reference to Nietzsche and biologism) has to do with his attempt at thinking nonrepresentationally, but also with the importance he gave to overcoming subjectivity and subjectively oriented thinking. Yet, despite the fact that Heidegger thematizes the body only sparingly, I have always had the distinct sense that his thinking involves the lived body in a pronounced way. This certainly has to do with the importance of attunements in his thinking. Attunements relate to the lived body not simply in the sense that they are located in isolated bodies. Rather, attunements make us aware of the ecstatic, relational, and temporal constitution of the lived body. Heidegger allows for ways to conceive bodies thus also when he interprets beings or things as sheltering time-space or as gathering what he (later) calls the fourfold (world). I have developed elsewhere how his thought of the simultaneity of beyng and beings can be developed into showing how any mode of sheltering also involves the lived body.[8] Attunements could be understood, especially when we think of them in terms of dispositions, as "connective tissues" that determine bodily dispositions.[9]

However, lived bodies are not simply ecstatic and relational; they are also dense and bear sedimentations of past experiences that mostly escape our awareness. People are not only prone to be overcome by attunements; their bodies bear attunements with them as well. This is mirrored, for instance, in the particular style and character of a thinker or text. I am highlighting this in order to indicate that one cannot altogether ignore aspects of thinking that are bound to particular bodies that occur as sites of thought, that "shelter" a concrete site of being; Heidegger's attuned and disposed body, for instance, as he searches for words at the edge of the sayable or as he interprets being historically with reference to particular texts. The intimate character of Heidegger's nonpublic writings and the attunements they bear also let resonate for the reader Heidegger, the bodily thinker, and not only his "thoughts." This lets us question a differentiation metaphysics has always taken for granted: the differentiation between the thinker (a man) and his thought.[10] As much as he attempts to dehumanize his account of the event, his writing also carries "his" polyphonous voice; that open site of being that is gathered in "what" we call Heidegger. This is what makes his thinking so alive and perhaps seductive or estranging: the question of being or the think-ing of the event is happening in the text; it is a happening, an event that attunes the reader such that he or she can to some extent participate in it. We are, in turn, attuned; our bodies occur in the reading as sites of beings, carrying polyphonous attunements. And part of that polyphony occurs as dispositions arising from lineages that we embody, and of which we are scarcely aware. I believe that it is important, especially when considering Heidegger and his thinking in the politi-cal context of his nationalism and anti-Semitism, that we remain alert to the his-tories of the dispositions that inform our bodies and with them, our responses to his text. Thus Heidegger can teach us, perhaps despite himself, to be vigilant in our thinking concerning the limits that come with the embodiment of our thinking and to take into account, when we think about history, the histories of bodies, of human and other bodies that are constitutive of sites of being.

The Gathering Power of the Thought of the History of Beyng

To think of history in terms of histories of bodies is certainly something Heideg-ger did not do. From his perspective, this would be thinking in terms of beings, that is, metaphysically. Instead, the history of beyng must be (for Heidegger) articulated in the singular, a singularity that is necessary, insofar as beyng never occurs "in general" but always uniquely through a unique site of beyng, a site that is sustained in thinking—for instance, in Heidegger's thinking.

In my view, however, a view that comes out of a sensibility that is informed differently by its historical time, Heidegger did not carry through radically enough the overcoming of the ontological difference or the transformation of beyng and beings into their simultaneity. There always remains a certain gather-ing power at work in his thinking that takes very different forms at different times in his work, a gathering power that is related to various forms of negativity (abyss, withdrawal, refusal, dispropriation), to dispositions resonating in words like "restraint," "steadfastness," "forbearance," "dignity," "poverty," "gathering," and so on, and also to both his dedication to a yet-to-occur grounding of the truth of beyng in beings in the passing by of the last god, and to his turn toward thinking from inception. It is through this gathering power that Heidegger's thinking re-mains closest to metaphysical traditions.

I do not see the fact that there is no radical overcoming of the ontological difference in Heidegger's thinking simply as a failure of Heidegger but more as a limit, a limit that at the same time gives his thinking its force. For Heidegger, overcoming the ontological difference means that his thinking becomes a site of being (Da-sein) such that in thinking, beyng and beings are transformed into their simultaneity. But I pointed out above how the narrative of the history of beyng reintroduces in a different way a quasi-foundational relation between beyng and beings. Historically speaking, the grounding of beyng through its sheltering in beings does not happen and beings are not yet becoming "more being" (*seiender*). The "not-yet" of the coming (*zu-künftiges*) event finds a site in Heidegger's attuned thinking, always anew, always differently. Heidegger's own thinking thus occurs repetitively and always differently as a site of gathering, a site that at once carries out the simultaneity of beyng and beings and holds open their differencing in the "not-yet" (of the other beginning) that is as well a "no-longer" (of the first beginning). This gathering and differencing in which the thinking of beyng happens, happens only by virtue of thought's exposure to "the abyss," to death, to non-being, and this, in turn, requires a removal from a relation to commonly understood "beings." Only in this abyssal in-between (in Da-sein as it occurs in thinking) did Heidegger find truth. Thus he had to interpret everything happening around him in terms of machination. There could be no space, in his thinking, to find "truth" in small, local events since there could be no truth without the gathering power of ("his") abyssaly exposed thinking, a thinking that finds itself to be responsive to "the" historicality of beyng.

Looking ahead to Heidegger's thinking of the fourfold, for instance, to the essay "The Thing" (1944/1945), one might say that here it is not thinking but the thing that gathers the fourfold of gods and humans, earth and sky, such that there is a world in which truth happens. Heidegger writes that this is what "thing" means in old German: to gather (GA 79: 16). However, not only does he say at the beginning of the essay that humans have never truly thought of things (GA 79: 5); in the appendix to this essay, he writes: "*the thing does not thing* [gather]; *the thing does not essentially occur as thing*. . . . Thing / World does not occur as world; the event refuses itself" (GA 79: 23). This suggests that the gathering of the thing does not yet occur; that it occurs "only" in Heidegger's thinking. It is in his thinking that such gathering is held open as a possibility, not as mere possibility, but in terms of a "to come" that attunes the thinker and perhaps also the reader of this essay. As I see it, his thinking did not allow for an engagement with things and events in *their* singular happenings.

One may only speculate as to why Heidegger had to hold on to the gathering power of "beyng" and thinking. I suspect it has much to do with not only the metaphysical but also the religious traditions his thinking incorporates in partially transforming ways. As for "us" today (whoever this "us" might include and exclude), the complexity of the worlds we live in, the plurality of interweaving, connected, and disconnected lineages of people on this earth and the growing realization that a hegemonic conception of history fails to do justice to those lineages, all this leads to the necessity of different kinds of thinking, that is, kinds of thinking that respond to the irreducible plurality of forms of being.

In my own thinking, in departure from Heidegger, this has lead me to radicalize the thought of the "simultaneity" of being and beings further and to unhinge the notion of Da-sein from the narrative of the history of beyng, which implies letting go of the notion of "beyng" with a "y." This leads to disseminating the question of being and to thinking the being of beings and events in their singular and interconnected spatial-temporal occurrences.[11] Such an approach has (had) repercussions with respect to my reading of Heidegger. My approach to his texts take the direction not only of a distancing from the narrative of the history of beyng but also of reading his texts as sites of being that cannot be reduced to the unity of one thought; sites of being that for the attuned reader bear mostly hidden histories and still bear unforeseeable possibilities.

Notes

1. See GA 65, end of section 242.

2. See Daniela Vallega-Neu, "At the Limit of Word and Thought: Reading Heidegger's *Das Ereignis*," in *Internationales Jahrbuch für Hermeneutik* (Tübingen: Mohr Siebeck, 2013), 77–91.

3. The middle voice, which we find in Ancient Greece but not in contemporary European language, expresses an occurrence neither actively nor passively but rather in terms of the self-unfolding of an occurrence.

4. Heidegger writes how historiographical viewpoints keep sliding in (GA 66: 233).

5. True history (*Geschichte*) (in contrast to historiology, *Historie*) for Heidegger involves the divine.

6. David Farrell Krell, who read the manuscript of this book, insisted in his comments on the necessity of a genealogy of Heidegger's piety, a task I will have to leave to someone else.

7. Jean-Luc Nancy, *La Banalité de Heidegger* (Paris: Galilée, 2015), 43.

8. See Daniela Vallega-Neu, *The Bodily Dimension in Thinking* (Albany: State University of New York Press, 2005), ch. 5.

9. A rare allusion to the lived body (*Leiblichkeit*) in *On Inception* (1940) shows us how Heidegger was inclined to differentiate attunement (*Stimmung*) from *Befindlichkeit*, which I will translate as "disposition." This occurs in section 108, which addresses the essential provenance (*Wesensherkunft*) of humans. Here Heidegger meditates on how humans are drawn into or involved (*Einbezogen*) in beyng "by" beyng. He lists a sequence of fundamental words leading from the appropriation of Da-sein to the notion of attunement to steadfastness (or indwelling) and "Befindlichkeit [*Leiblichkeit*]" ("disposition [bodiliness]") and he adds in parentheses that *Befindlichkeit* is grasped differently from *Being and Time*, where it was equated with attunement (GA 70: 131).

10. Andrew Mitchell brought to my attention that while I question this differentiation I also operate with it precisely as I put it into question and also when I distinguish expository chapters from a more "intimate" or "personal" engagement with Heidegger's text. The difficulty here is not to fall back into crude distinctions: "thinker" vs. "man," "thinking matters" vs. "personal matters." I wish to acknowledge that regarding this issue I share a concern with Heidegger, namely, not to think in terms of represented beings and categories but rather performatively. What I do not share with Heidegger, as should become evident in the next section of my conclusion, is a prioritizing of historical "beyng" over things and events in their singular and interconnected happening.

11. See my essay "The Dissemination of Time: Durations, Configurations, Chance," *Research in Phaenomenology* 47, no. 1 (2017): 1–18.

Bibliography

For Heidegger's *Gesamtausgabe* (Collected works) and their respective English translations, see "Key to Heidegger's *Gesamtausgabe*" following the Acknowledgments.

Works by Heidegger in English Translation

Basic Writings. Edited by David Farrell Krell. San Francisco: Harper San Francisco, 1992.

Country Path Conversations. Translated by Bret David. Bloomington: Indiana University Press, 2012.

Martin Heidegger and National Socialism: Questions and Answers. Edited by Günther Neske and Emil Kettering. Translated by Lisa Harries. New York: Paragon House, 1990.

Nietzsche, vols. 1 and 2: *The Will to Power as Art* and *The Eternal Recurrence of the Same.* Translated by David Farrell Krell. San Francisco: Harper San Francisco, 1991.

Nietzsche, vols. 3 and 4: *The Will to Power as Knowledge and as Metaphysics* and *Nihilism.* Edited by David Farrell Krell. San Francisco: Harper San Francisco, 1991.

On the Way to Language. Translated by Peter D. Hertz. New York: Harper and Row, 1971.

Poetry, Language, Thought. Translated by Albert Hofstandter. New York: Harper and Row, 1971.

The Question Concerning Technology and Other Essays. Translated by William Lovitt. New York: Harper and Row, 1977.

Other Works

Aho, Kevin. *Heidegger's Neglect of the Body.* Albany: State University of New York Press, 2009.

Arendt, Hannah. *Eichmann in Jerusalem: A Report on the Banality of Evil.* London: Penguin Classics, 2006.

Babich, Babette. "Heidegger's Black Night: The Nachlass and Its Wirkungsgeschichte." In *Reading Heidegger's* Black Notebooks 1931–1941, edited by Ingo Farin and Jeff Malpas, 59–88. Cambridge, MA: MIT Press, 2016.

Barracchi, Claudia. "The End of Philosophy and the Experience of Unending Φύσις." In *Paths in Heidegger's Later Thought*, edited by Günter Figal, Diego D'Angelo, Tobias Keiling, and Guang Yang. Bloomington: Indiana University Press, forthcoming.

Capobinaco, Richard. *Engaging Heidegger.* Toronto: University of Toronto Press, 2010.

Davis, Bret. *Heidegger and the Will: On the Way to Gelassenheit.* Evanston, IL: Northwestern University Press, 2007.

Deleuze, Gilles. *Spinoza: Practical Philosophy.* Translated by Robert Hurley. San Francisco: City Lights, 2001.

Derrida, Jacques. *De L'Esprit: Heidegger et la question*. Paris: Editions Galilée, 1987. Translated by Geoffrey Bennington and Rachel Bowlby as *Of Spirit: Heidegger and the Question*. Chicago: University of Chicago Press, 1991.

———. "Différance." In *Margins of Philosophy*, translated by Allan Boss, 1–27. Chicago: University of Chicago Press, 1982.

———. *Marges de la Philosophie*. Paris: Minuit, 1972. Translated by Allan Boss as *Margins of Philosophy*. Chicago: University of Chicago Press, 1982.

di Cesare, Donatella. *Heidegger e gli Ebbrei: I "Quaderni Neri."* Torino: Bollati Boringhieri, 2014.

Diels, Herrmann. *Die Fragmente der Vorsokratiker*. Berlin: Weidmannsche Buchhandlung, 1903.

Farin, Ingo, and Jeff Malpas, eds. *Reading Heidegger's* Black Notebooks 1931–1941. Cambridge, MA: MIT Press, 2016.

Gadamer, Hans-Georg. "Destruktion *and Deconstruction*." In *Dialogue and Deconstruction*, edited by Diane P. Michelfelder and Richard E. Palmer, 102–113. Albany: State University of New York Press, 1989.

———. *Truth and Method*, 2nd rev. ed. Translation revised by Joel Weinsheimer and Donald G. Marshall. London/New York: Continuum, 2004.

Graham, Daniel, ed. and trans. *The Texts of Early Greek Philosophy*. Cambridge: Cambridge University Press, 2010.

Haar, Michel. *Le Chant de la Terre: Heidegger et les assises de l'histoire de l'être*. Paris: L'Herne, 1985. Translated by Reginald Lilly as *The Song of the Earth: Heidegger and the Grounds of the History of Being*. Bloomington: Indiana University Press, 1993.

Herrmann, Friedrich-Wilhelm von. "Von 'Sein und Zeit' zum 'Ereignis.'" In *Von Heidegger her (Meßkircher Vorträge 1989)*, ed. H.-H. Gander. Frankfurt am Main: Klostermann, 1991.

———. *Wege ins Ereignis: Zu Heideggers* Beiträgen zur Philosophie. Frankfurt am Main: Klostermann, 1994.

Hölderlin, Friedrich. *Sämtliche Werke*. Historisch-kritische Ausgabe, 2nd ed. Berlin: Propyläen, 1923.

Hume, David. *An Enquiry Concerning Human Understanding*. Edited by Eric Steinberg. Indianapolis: Hackett, 1993.

Kirk, G. S., J. E. Raven, and M. Schofield, eds. *The Presocratic Philosophers*, 2nd ed. Cambridge: Cambridge University Press, 1983.

Krell, David Farrell. *Ecstasy, Catastrophe: Heidegger from* Being and Time *to the* Black Notebooks. Albany: State University of New York Press, 2015.

———. *Intimations of Mortality*. University Park: Pennsylvania State University Press, 1986.

———. "Troubled Brows." *Research in Phenomenology* 46, no. 2 (2016): 309–335.

Malpas, Jeff. *Reading Heidegger's* Black Notebooks. Cambridge, MA: MIT Press, 2016.

Michelfelder, Diane, and Richard Palmer, eds. *Dialogue and Deconstruction: The Gadamer–Derrida Encounter*. Albany: State University of New York Press, 1989.

Mitchell, Andrew. *The Fourfold: Reading the Late Heidegger*. Evanston, IL: Northwestern University Press, 2015.

Nancy, Jean-Luc. *La Banalité de Heidegger*. Paris: Galilée, 2015.

Nietzsche, Friedrich. *Also Sprach Zarathustra*. In *Sämtliche Werke: Kritische Studienausgabe*, vol. 4, edited by Giorgio Colli and Mazzino Montinari. Munich: DTV de Gruyter, 1980.
———. *Die Geburt der Tragödie*. In *Sämtliche Werke: Kritische Studienausgabe*, vol. 1, edited by Giorgio Colli and Mazzino Montinari. Munich: DTV de Gruyter, 1980. Translated by Ronald Speirs as *The Birth of Tragedy*. Cambridge: Cambridge University Press, 1999.
Petrarca, Francesco. *Rime Sparse*. Milan: Mursia, 1979.
Powell, Jeffrey. *Heidegger and Language*. Bloomington: Indiana University Press, 2013.
Richardson, William J. *Heidegger: Through Phenomenology to Thought*. New York: Fordham University Press, 1993.
Sallis, John, "Grounders of the Abyss." In *A Companion to Heidegger's* Contributions to Philosophy, edited by Charles Scott, Susan Schoenbohm, Daniela Vallega-Neu, and Alejandro Vallega, 181–197. Bloomington: Indiana University Press, 2001.
———. *Transfigurements: On the True Sense of Art*. Chicago: University of Chicago Press, 2008.
Schelling, Friedrich. *Die Weltalter Fragmente in den Urfassungen von 1811 und 1813*. Edited by Manfred Schröter. Munich: Biedersteing und Leibniz, 1946.
Scott, Charles. *Living with Indifference*. Bloomington: Indiana University Press, 2007.
Scott, Charles, Susan Schoenbohm, Daniela Vallega-Neu, and Alejandro Vallega, eds. *A Companion to Heidegger's* Contributions to Philosophy. Bloomington: Indiana University Press, 2001.
Sophocles. *Oedipus at Colonos*. Translated by David Grene. In *Greek Tragedies*, vol. 3, edited by David Grene and Richmond Lattimore. Chicago: University of Chicago Press, 1991.
Toadvine, Ted. "Natural Time and Immemorial Nature." *Philosophy Today*, SPEP supplement (2009): 214–221.
Trawny, Peter. *Heidegger und der Mythos der jüdischen Weltverschwörung*. Frankfurt am Main: Klostermann, 2014.
Vallega, Alejandro, A. *Latin American Philosophy from Identity to Radical Exteriority*. Bloomington: Indiana University Press, 2014.
Vallega-Neu, Daniela. "At the Limit of Word and Thought: Reading Heidegger's *Das Ereignis*." In *Internationales Jahrbuch für Hermeneutik*, 77–91. Tübingen: Mohr Siebeck, 2013.
———. "The Black Notebooks and Heidegger's Writings of the Event (1936–1944)." In *Reading Heidegger's* Black Notebooks 1931–1941, edited by Ingo Farin and Jeff Malpas, 127–142. Cambridge, MA: MIT Press, 2016.
———. "Bodily Being and Indifference." *Epoché* 17, no. 1 (2012): 111–122.
———. *The Bodily Dimension in Thinking*. Albany: State University of New York Press, 2005.
———. "The Dissemination of Time: Durations, Configurations, Chance." *Research in Phaenomenology* 47, no. 1 (2017): 1–18.
———. "Ereignis." In *The Bloomsbury Companion to Heidegger*, edited by François Raffoul and Eric Nelson, 283–289. London: Continuum, 2013.
———. *Heidegger's* Contributions to Philosophy: *An Introduction*. Bloomington: Indiana University Press, 2003.

———. "Heidegger's Imageless Saying of the Event." *Continental Philosophy Review*, 2004. doi: 10.1007/s11007-014-9310-4.

———. "Heidegger's Poietic Writings." In *Heidegger and Language*, edited by Jeffrey Powell, 119–145. Bloomington: Indiana University Press, 2013.

———. "Heidegger's Reticence: From *Contributions* to *Das Ereignis* and toward *Gelassenheit*." *Research in Phenomenology* 45, no. 1 (2015): 1–32.

———. "Poietic Saying." In *A Companion to Heidegger's* Contributions to Philosophy, edited by Charles Scott, Susan Schoenbohm, Daniela Vallega-Neu, and Alejandro Vallega, 66–80. Bloomington: Indiana University Press, 2001.

———. "Thinking in Decision: On Heidegger's *Contributions to Philosophy*." *Research in Phenomenology* 33 (2003): 247–263, 281–283.

Van der Velde, Pol. *Heidegger and the Romantics: The Literary Invention of Meaning*. New York: Routledge, 2012.

Wolin, Richard, ed. *The Heidegger Controversy: A Critical Reader*. Cambridge, MA: MIT Press, 1993.

Ziarek, Krysztof. "Imageless Thinking: The Time-Space for the Imagination in Heidegger." *Hermeneutisches Jahrbuch* 14 (2015): 145–162.

———. *Language after Heidegger*. Bloomington: Indiana University Press, 2013.

Index

abandonment of beings. See *Seinsverlassenheit*
Abgeschiedenheit (seclusion), 110, 114
Abgrund (abyss, abyssal ground), 4–5, 16–17, 57, 79–80, 109, 126, 151, 161; bending back into, 177–178; departure into, 106, 173, 175–177; downgoing into, 15, 111, 113, 150–151, 163; horror of, 157–158; as negativity, 192–193; time-space of, 37, 133–134; truth and, 25–26, 58, 82, 106–107, 156, 185
Abschied (departure), 109–111, 153, 157–158; delight of, 157; difference as, 110, 150; movement of thinking as, 106, 114, 135, 169. See also *Abgrund*, departure into
abyss. See *Abgrund*
Adel (nobility), 73, 157, 177
Ahnung (presentiment), 27, 43n17, 109
ἀλήθεια (truth as unconcealing-concealing), 4–5, 29, 32, 142–147; *Einsturz* (collapse) of, 74. *See also* truth; unconcealing-concealing
Anaximander, 142–144
An-eignung (arrogation), 153, 160, 165n29, 183
Anfang (inception, beginning), 11, 14, 28, 56, 66, 86–87, 110, 111, 121, 171–172; the beingless and, 113–115; contrast with *Beginn*, 8; *Da-seyn* and, 155–156; death as, 127n18, 137; definition of, 105–109; dignity and, 115–116; event as, 107–108, 123, 125, 131–132, 146; exposition and (see *Auslegung*); extremity of, 104, 169; grounding and, 35–38; incipience of (see *Anfängnis*); staying and (see *Bleiben*); translation of, 18n16. *See also* first and other beginning
Anfängnis (incipience), 106–107, 116; dignity and (see *Würde*); of inception, 129–130, 152, 161–162, 177–178, 187
animality, 72, 83–85, 100–102
Anklang (resonating), 22, 26, 29, 141, 147–149, 173
Anmut (bestowing courage), 159
annihilation, 68–71
Anspruch (claim), 161, 162. See also *Anspruch und Antwort*
Anspruch und Antwort (claim and response), 5, 9, 22, 34, 43, 117, 151, 153, 160, 170–171

Antigone (Sophocles), 132
anti-Semitism, 92, 97, 102n6, 190, 192
appropriating event. See *Ereignis*
appropriation. See *Ereignung*
Arendt, Hannah, 71
Armut (poverty), 75–76, 116, 157, 177, 183. See also *Würde*
arrogation. See *An-eignung*
assignment. See *Zu-eignung*
attentiveness. See *Aufmerksamkeit*
attunement. See *Stimmung*
Aufmerksamkeit (attentiveness, heedfulness), 156–158
Ausbleiben (staying away), 10, 37, 133–134
Auslegung (exposition, interpretation), 120–123
ausstehen (withstanding), 27, 38, 40, 53
Austrag (carrying out, enduring), 76–79, 80, 90n31, 117, 157–159; translation of, 165n35
authenticity. See *Eigentlichkeit*

Basic Questions of Philosophy (Heidegger), 21, 74
Befindlichkeit (bodily being, mood, disposition), 119, 194n9
Befremdung (estrangement), 121
beginning. See *Anfang*; first and other beginning
being. See *Sein*
being and beings, 87, 89n15, 112, 118, 160, 170, 184; beings arising into being, 107–108, 110, 111–112, 134; co-originarity of, 52, 55, 58–61; decision between, 85–88; differencing of, 72, 81, 85–86, 109, 135–136, 183–184, 193 (see also *Unterschied*); simultaneity of, 13, 35, 46–49, 55, 85–86, 134–135, 183–186, 192–194. *See also* ontological difference; *Unterscheidung*
Being and Time (Heidegger), 1–4, 6, 9, 12–13, 23, 25, 27, 32, 35–36, 43n19, 59, 76–78, 94, 110, 117–118, 137, 153
being-away. See *Weg-sein*
beingless. See *Seinlose*
beinglessness. See *Seinlosigkeit*
beingness. See *Seiendheit*

beings, 94, 118, 134–136, 150, 168, 172; are not, 108, 137; blind for, 175; non-beings, 114; parting from, 134; release of, 178; unleashing of, 67–68, 111, 113

Berückung (captivation), 38

Besinnung (mindfulness, meditation), 65–67, 99, 120–121; translation of, 63

Bestimmung (determination), 58–59, 95, 120, 188–190

beyng. See *Seyn*

beyng-historical. See *seynsgeschichtlich*

Black Notebooks (Heidegger), x, 18n12, 60, 92–97, 189–190

Bleiben (staying), 132–134, 173. See also *Ausbleiben*

bodily being. See *Befindlichkeit*; body

body, 25, 42–43n15, 44n34, 49–52, 58–59, 94, 100–101, 135, 191; bodily being, 25, 50–52, 55, 119. See also *Leib*

boredom, 37, 43n16

break, of being on beings, 160, 170–173

captivation. See *Berückung*

carrying out. See *Austrag*

claim. See *Anspruch*

claim and response. See *Anspruch und Antwort*

clearing. See *Lichtung*

cleft, 126

coming in-between. See *Dazwischenkunft*

communism, 96

complying. See *Sich-fügen*

concealment, 4–5, 7, 25–28, 37, 41, 52, 79–80, 106–107, 110, 115, 143–145; death and, 127n18, 137; original concealment and errancy, 52, 59, 82–83. See also ἀλήθεια; unconcealment

conflict. See *Kampf*

consignment. See *Übereignung*

constancy, 37–38, 40, 132, 151

constellation, 148

counter-tone. See *Gegen-klang*

counter-word. See *Gegenwort*

Country Path Conversations (Heidegger), 178–179, 186

Da-sein (there-being), 2–4, 10, 13–14, 34–37, 40, 49–52, 114, 193; grounding and, 22, 37, 56–57, 86–87; human being and, 14, 31, 77–79, 85, 90n33, 116–120, 182–183; singularity of, 55–58, 160, 169; translation of, 13; truth of being and, 6, 14, 35, 56–57. See also *Da-seyn*

Da-seyn (there-beyng), 151, 153, 155–157

Dazwischenkunft (coming in-between), 107–108, 111, 185, 187. See also in-between

death, 59, 108, 127n18, 136–138, 153, 157–158, 174, 193; of God, 33

decision, 10, 16, 31–38, 49, 52–58, 65–67, 71–72, 78, 83, 85–88; as *Entscheidung*, 34, 71

dehumanization. See *Entmenschung*

Deleuze, Gilles, 131

delight. See *Wonne*

departure. See *Abschied*

Derrida, Jacques, 135, 172

determination. See *Bestimmung*

différance, 136

diffidence. See *Scheu*

dignity. See *Würde*

discourse. See *Rede*

disposition. See *Stimmung*

dispropriation. See *Enteignis*

dissemination, 52, 55, 58, 172, 194

divine call, 176

downgoing, 15, 109, 111, 113–115, 127n11, 137, 150–151, 155; the last, 114–115

δόξα (appearing, shining), 145–147

draft. See withdrawal, draft of being's

Durchgestaltung (elaboration), 21

ear of the poet, 171

earth, 32, 44n34, 47–48, 50–52, 61n3, 122, 177–179. See also strife of earth and world

Eigentlichkeit (properness, authenticity), 3, 153–154

Eigentum (domain of what is proper), 123–124, 154

die *Eignung* (the eventuation), 154

Einführung in die Metaphysik (Heidegger). See *Introduction to Metaphysics*

Einzigkeit (uniqueness, singularity), 24, 122, 126, 179. See also singularity

elaboration. See *Durchgestaltung*

emptiness, 37–38, 58, 86, 112, 179

encounter. See *Entgegnung*

enowning. See *Ereignis*

Enteignis (expropriation, dispropriation), 110, 113–114, 135, 149, 154, 157, 178, 183

Entgegnung (encounter), between gods and humans, 76–79, 85, 127n17, 177–178

Entmenschung (dehumanization), 100–102, 183

entrückend (transporting), 38, 80

Entscheidung. See decision

Ent-setzung (un-settling), 49

Ent-stiften (de-founding), 163

Entsturz (fall), 146
Entwindung (twisting out), 145–147, 150–151, 185; translation of, 164n12
Ereignis (event, enowning), 1, 5–6, 34–35, 66, 77–78, 99, 105–106, 123, 131, 152–155, 160; translation of, 18n11, 183
Ereignung (appropriation), 5, 6, 106, 152, 170; translation of, 161, 166n50
Erlebnis (lived experience), 30, 32, 60, 69–70, 86, 101–102
errancy, 52, 59, 80–83, 122, 164n10, 189; Heidegger's, 94–95, 97–98, 189
errant star, 148
Erschrecken (shock), 25–27
estrangement. See *Befremdung*
event. See *Ereignis*
excess, 101, 127n13
exposedness, 13, 97–100, 131, 163
exposition. See *Auslegung*
expropriation. See *Enteignis*

Feldweg-Gespräche (Heidegger). See *Country Path Conversations*
first and other beginning, 7, 32, 109, 111–112; decision over the other beginning, 31–33, 38, 56–58, 64; first beginning, 29, 42n12, 74–75, 132, 142–145; non-linearity of first and other beginning, 126, 148, 185; other beginning, 25–26, 47, 65–66, 174, 184; prior to first and other beginning, 105, 107, 133, 152, 187; transition between first and other beginning, 8, 13, 21–24, 39, 57, 85, 117, 121–123, 147–148. See also *Anfang*
forbearance. See *Langmut*
foreign, the, 96–97
forgottenness of beyng, 82, 86
Fortgang (leaving), 111, 132, 142, 145–147, 164n12
Foucault, Michel, 71, 96
fourfold, 78, 178–179, 193
Fuge (conjuncture, juncture), 20–24, 26, 64, 66, 140, 150–152, 186. See also *names of individual junctures*
Fügung (conjoining), 149–152
fundamental attunement. See *Grundstimmung*
future ones, 31, 42n10, 156

Gadamer, Hans-Georg, 19n24, 138n2
gathering, 63, 119, 144, 146–147, 157, 173, 176, 192–194
Gebirg (-harbor), 146
Geeignetheit (appropriateness), 154

Gefüge (structure), 12, 14. See also structure
Gegen-klang (counter-tone), 170
Gegenstand (object), 69, 101, 132, 145. See also thinking, objectivity and
Gegenwort (counter-word), 153
Gelassenheit (releasement), 17, 58, 148, 178–179
Gemüt (gathering mood), 90n24, 119
George, Stefan, 170–171
German people, the, 8, 31, 53, 60, 96–97, 103n10, 158, 165n40, 190
Geschicht (history in the sense of destiny, historicality), 148–149, 165n21
Geschichte (history of beyng), 7, 51–52, 85–88, 96–97, 123–126, 134, 137, 192–194; decision over, 31 (*see also* decision); definition of, 1, 54–55, 129–132, 194n5; inception and, 104, 126 (see also *Anfang*); truth and, 183–184; unity and plurality of, 55, 93
Die Geschichte des Seyns (Heidegger). See *History of Beyng, The*
geschichtliche Besinnung (historical meditation), 65. See also *Besinnung*
Gewalt (violence, coercive force), 68, 70–73
Gewinde (winding), 151
ghost of being, 124
Gleichzeitigkeit (simultaneity), 46–49. See also being and beings, simultaneity of
glow. See *Glut*
Glut (glow), 79. See also *Lichtung*
godlessness, 176–177
gods, 8–10, 28, 33–35, 153–154, 163, 176–177; humans and, 49, 66, 76–79, 85, 127n17 (see also *Entgegnung*); the last god, 28, 33–35, 56–58, 176–177
Greek thought, 4, 7, 25, 29, 67, 74, 132, 142–145
grounding attunement. See *Grundstimmung*
groundlessness, 4, 26, 70, 111. See also *Abgrund*
Grundfragen der Philosophie (Heidegger). See *Basic Questions of Philosophy*
Grundstimmung (fundamental attunement, basic disposition, grounding attunement), 3, 8–9, 43n16, 59, 94, 102, 188–190; definition of, 25–28. See also *names of individual attunements*
Gründung (grounding), 21, 35–38, 47–49, 86–88, 107. See also *Abgrund*; *Grundstimmungen*

Haar, Michel, 61n3
heedfulness. See *Aufmerksamkeit*
Heimischen (familiar), 163. See also *Unheimischen*

Heraclitus, 65, 144
hermeneutic interpretation, 186–187
Herrmann, Friedrich-Wilhelm von, 1, 20
Herrschaft (sovereignty, mastery), 71–72, 75, 115–116
Hesiod, 37
historicality of beyng, ix, 21, 45, 63–64, 99, 157, 193. See also *seynsgeschichtlich*
Historie (historiography), 1, 54, 87, 124–125, 126, 130–131
history: as *Geschicht* (history as destiny) (see *Geschicht*); as *Geschichte* (history of beyng) (see *Geschichte*); Heidegger and, 92–102; historical grounding, 13, 23, 49, 87–88, 183–184; as *Historie* (historiography) (see *Historie*); inceptive occurrence of, 132; of philosophy, 29, 53–54; possibilities of, 86–88, 185; restricted sense of, 56. See also *seynsgeschichtlich*
History of Beyng, The (Heidegger), 75–76
Hölderlin, Friedrich, 2, 8–10, 19, 33, 120–123, 132–133, 162
holy, 122, 162–164
horizon, 3–4, 59, 76–77, 153
human beings, 71, 73, 77, 84–85, 117–119, 141, 153–157, 161. See also *Da-sein*, human being and; *Entmenschung*; gods, humans and
Hume, David, 174
humor, 131, 177

in-between, 10, 16, 46–49, 53, 85, 107–109, 126, 136–137, 148, 170, 188, 193. See also *Dazwischenkunft*
incipience. See *Anfängnis*
in-decision, 33, 37. *See also* decision
indifference, 135–136
indwelling. See *Inständigkeit*
Innigkeit (intimacy), 117
Inständigkeit (steadfastness, indwelling), 27, 40–41, 73, 78, 98, 156, 158
interplay. See *Zuspiel*
intimacy. See *Innigkeit*
Introduction to Metaphysics (Heidegger), 43n27, 74, 132, 146

joy, 76
juncture. See *Fuge*
Jünger, Ernst, 84, 91n48

Kampf (conflict, struggle), 65, 78, 87; translation of, 89n8

Kant, Immanuel, 174
Kehre (turning), 5–6, 22, 34–35, 76–77, 90n31, 150–152, 156, 169, 182–183
knowing. See *Wissen*
der Kranz der Kehre (the wreath of the turning), 150–152, 169
Krell, David Farrell, 57, 84, 99

Langmut (forbearance, patience), 75–76, 90n23
language, 8–9, 16, 28, 118–120, 153, 159–162, 165–166n48, 168–174, 183, 186–187. See also *Sage*; *Sagen*; word
Lassen (letting). See *Gelassenheit*; *Loslassung*
leap. See *Sprung*
leaving. See *Fortgang*
Leib (lived body), 94, 103n8, 191, 194n9. *See also* body
λήθη (forgetfulness, concealing), 143–145. *See also* ἀλήθεια
letting pass by, 113, 129, 148, 178–179, 185. See also *Vorbeigang*
Licht (light). See *Lichtung*
Lichtung (clearing), 37–38, 73, 79–88, 99, 110, 114, 117–118, 170, 185; *die Lichtung für das Sichverbergen* (clearing for self-concealment), 80
life, 68–70, 101
listening, 9, 13, 28, 144
lived experience. See *Erlebnis*
Loslassung (letting loose, letting go), 16–17, 52–53, 147–148, 164n17
Loswurf (casting oneself loose), 5

Machenschaft (machination), 29–30, 54–55, 60–61, 67–76, 84, 86, 95–96, 100–102, 113–115, 169. *See also* letting pass by
machination. See *Machenschaft*
das Machtlose (what is without power), 67, 72–76, 99–100, 102
Merk (sign), 158
Merleau-Ponty, Maurice, 50, 135, 169
metaphysics, 36, 53, 67–69, 89n15, 109, 125, 136, 141–152, 192; inception of, 111–112
middle voice, 4–6, 24, 106, 129–130, 135, 168, 194n3
Mitchell, Andrew, 194n10
mood. See *Mut*; *Stimmungen*
Mut (courage, mood), 75, 90n24, 159, 173

Nancy, Jean-Luc, 190
nationalism, 53, 96–97, 192

National Socialism, 60, 96–97
nature, 29, 32, 43n29. *See also* φύσις
Nietzsche, Friedrich, 26, 33, 53, 64, 67–70,
    75–76, 84, 98, 101, 131, 136; eternal return, 69,
    70; will to power, 68–69, 73, 95, 147–148
nihilism, 69–70, 99
nobility. See *Adel*
Not der Notlosigkeit. See plight
nothingless, 107–108, 136, 150, 168–170, 183,
    186–187. See also *Seinlose*

Oedipus at Colonos (Sophocles), 174–176, 191
"On the Essence of Truth" (Heidegger), 32, 52,
    189
"On the Origin of the Work of Art"
    (Heidegger), 21, 32, 44n34, 46, 47, 134, 184
ontological difference, 12–13, 35–37, 85, 110, 149,
    178, 192

pain, 154–155, 157–159
Parmenides, 144–145
passion, 101
πέρασ (limit, closure), 143–144
performativity, 9, 38–42, 53–54, 67, 194n10
Petrarca, Francesco, 137
φύσις (nature), 25, 29, 43n27, 74–75, 132,
    143–146; *Entmachtung der* (disempowerment
    of), 74–75
plight, 10, 16, 22, 29–31, 34, 75, 148; *Not der
    Notlosigkeit* (plight of a lack of sense of
    plight), 10, 26, 30, 57, 125–126
poetry, 33, 46, 66, 120–123, 171; thinking and,
    123, 162–164, 176. *See also* Hölderlin,
    Friedrich
Pöggeler, Otto, 20
poietic writings (*seynsgeschichtliche
    Abhandlungen*): description of, ix–xi, 1–2;
    questions for interpretation of, 11–17
poverty. See *Armut*
power, 67–72, 95–96, 120, 130–131; in a positive
    sense, 74–75; will to power (*see* Nietzsche,
    Friedrich, will to power). See also *das
    Machtlose*
presencing, 4–5, 74, 127n8, 143. *See also* ἀλήθεια
presentiment. See *Ahnung*
projection, 3, 77, 117, 152
properness. See *Eigentlichkeit*
propriation. See *Ver-eignung*

questioning, 41, 78–79, 87, 141, 158–159, 163–164,
    186–187; the question-worthy, 83, 164

Rede (speech, discourse), 9, 162, 183. See also
    Sagen
refusal, 22, 30–32, 34–35, 37–38, 51, 72, 82; in
    Saying, 162; *zögerndes Sichversagen*
    (hesitating self-refusal), 34, 37
releasement. See *Gelassenheit*
religion, 176–177, 190, 193
representation. See *Vorstellen*
resonating. See *Anklang*
response. See *Anspruch und Antwort*

Sage (Saying), 116, 161–162; as distinct from
    Sagen, 159–160, 165n47, 183. See also *Sagen*
Sagen (saying), 28, 49, 85, 111–112, 116, 121–123,
    140, 173; philosophy's, 66. See also *Sage*
Scheu (diffidence, awe), 25, 28, 40, 157
Scott, Charles, 103n13, 135
seclusion. See *Abgeschiedenheit*
sedimentation, 50, 191
Seiendheit (beingness), 36, 68, 81, 111
Sein (being): and plurality, 52, 55, 193–194
    (*see also* singularity); as presencing, 4–5, 29,
    36, 54, 74, 188. *See also* being and beings;
    Seiendheit; *Seyn*
Seinlose (beingless), 14, 107–108, 112–115, 119,
    134–138, 149–150, 160, 168–170, 179, 183,
    185–186, 187
Seinlosigkeit (beinglessness), 112–115, 149–150,
    178
Seinsermächtigung (empowering being), 74–75.
    See also power
Seinsverlassenheit (abandonment of beings), 7,
    22, 26, 29–30, 35, 37, 51, 73, 82, 94, 111–112,
    113–114, 134, 147–149
Sein und Zeit (Heidegger). See *Being and Time*
Selbstbesinnung der Philosophie (philosophy
    meditating on itself), 65–66
Seyn (beyng), 66, 72, 78, 81, 108, 122, 188;
    "beyng" vs "being," 1, 113, 127n8, 127n11,
    193–194; beyond, 104, 113; call (*Zuruf*) of, x, 5,
    10, 22, 138, 161, 182; clearing of (*see Lichtung*);
    as Da-seyn, 156; word of (*see* word, of being).
    See also being and beings; *Sein*
seynsgeschichtlich (beyng-historical), 1–2, 6–7,
    18n13, 92–94, 121, 131, 157. *See also* thinking,
    beyng-historical
die Schaffenden (the creative ones), 10, 102
sheltering, 13, 35–38, 44n34, 47–49, 56–57, 81,
    134, 183–185, 191
shock. See *Erschrecken*
Sich-fügen (complying), 152

silence, x, 9–10, 15, 28, 40, 153, 176; *Erschweigen* (bearing silence) and *Verschweigung* (keeping silence), 28; Heidegger's, 97–98; silent voice of beyng, 119, 170–174; silent word of beyng, 153, 171–172
simultaneity. *See* being and beings, simultaneity of
singularity, 17, 24, 38, 55, 58, 96, 99, 122, 135, 154, 160, 171–172, 179–180, 180n4, 192–193. See also *Einzigkeit*
sounding, 146–147, 160, 170–172
sovereignty. See *Herrschaft*
space. *See* time-space
Sprung (leap), 22–23, 39, 46, 90n25, 141–142
staying. See *Bleiben*
staying away. See *Ausbleiben*
steadfastness. See *Inständigkeit*
stillness, 28, 57; of pure incipience, 116
Stimmung (attunement, disposition), 42, 58–60, 64, 75–76, 98, 102n7, 159, 170, 174; embodiment and, 49–50, 55, 94, 190–192; language and, 9–10, 118–120, 153, 183–184, 187–190; non-grounding attunements, 94, 97, 189–190; *stimmende Stimme* (disposing voice), 160, 170; translation of, 50, 194n9. See also *Grundstimmung*
strangeness, 95–96, 130, 135
Streit (strife). *See* strife of earth and world
strife of earth and world, 34, 43n32, 47–49, 66, 76–79, 85, 155, 184–185
structure: of *Contributions to Philosophy*, 20–22, 24, 141; of *The Event*, 14, 167–168; of *On Inception*, 105. See also *Gefüge*
style, 39–41

τέχνη (know-how, skill), 29, 74, 146
Temporalität. See temporality, primordial
temporality, 2–4, 37–38, 80, 134, 151; the body and, 50–51, 55; coming-in-between (see *Dazwischenkunft*); ecstatic (*Zeitlichkeit*), 27; linear, 123, 129–130; primordial (*Temporalität*), 27; temporal spacing (*see* time-space); timeless, 110
thanking, 158–159, 162–164
"Thing, The" (Heidegger), 193
things, 48, 169, 177–180, 181n16, 186, 193; dispositions toward, 94, 188–189, 191; no-thingness, 135; as objects (see *Gegenstand*)
thinking, 1, 47, 123, 157, 168–174, 184, 193; *anfängliches Denken* (inceptual thinking), 7,

28, 35, 40–41, 93–94, 109, 116–118, 133, 158–159, 183; of being, 2, 5, 24, 33, 66, 117; beyng-historical, 23–24, 83, 92–94, 97, 116–117, 158–159, 162, 190; cosmological, 178; creative, 13–14, 53–54, 79; foundational, 43n32, 47, 183–184, 186; going under, 104, 120, 131, 175, 185, 190; imageless, 163, 174–175; objectivity and, 1, 5, 7, 30, 41, 46, 54, 179; poetizing and (*see* poetry); sequential, 23, 33, 105, 125–126, 150; solitary, 169, 177–178, 185, 187; topological, 178; transitional, 21, 25, 85, 116–117
thrownness, 3, 77, 131, 152, 161, 182
time-space, 24, 27, 34, 37–38, 72, 118, 133–134. See also *Da-sein*; temporality
transcendence, 3–4, 32
transfiguration. *See* transformation
transformation, 136–138
transporting. See *entrückend*
Trawny, Peter, 102n6
truth, 5–6, 10, 21–24, 35–38, 54, 77, 79–80, 121–122, 145, 160; as correspondence, 29, 32, 69, 74, 146; errancy and, 59, 82–83, 189; inceptive occurrence of, 105–109, 121, 182–185; relation between truth of beyng and beyng of truth, 34–35, 151, 153, 156; sheltering in beings, 44n34, 46–49, 81, 134, 183–184. *See also* ἀλήθεια; unconcealing-concealing
turning. See *Kehre*
twisting free. See *Verwindung*
twisting out. See *Entwindung*

Übereignung (consignment), 34–35, 112, 153
überlassen (leaving), 114–115
Übermensch (overman), 70, 84
unconcealing-concealing, 13, 25, 27, 30, 34, 38, 47–48, 52, 74, 106–107, 109, 144, 156. See also ἀλήθεια
Unheimischen (unfamiliar), 163, 173
un-holy, 163, 176
uniqueness. See *Einzigkeit*; singularity
Unseienden (nonbeings), 112, 115
Unterschied (difference), 110–112, 149–150, 157, 159
Unterscheidung (differentiation), 81, 88, 89n15, 109, 110–112, 118, 149–150, 184–186

Vallega-Neu, Daniela, 42–43n15
values, 69, 99
Ver-eignung (propriation), 152, 165n27
Verhaltenheit (restraint), 25–28, 39–41, 43n19, 58, 67, 75, 93, 114

Verkehrung (distortion), 83–84, 164n10
verrückt (deranged, being unsettled, dislodged), 177
verwahren (preserve), 156
Verwindung (twisting free, overcoming), 115, 145, 147–148, 150–152, 164n3, 185
violence. See *Gewalt*
Vorbeigang (passing by), 147–149. *See also* letting pass by
Vorenthalt (withholding), 149
Vorstellen (representation), 2, 24, 32–33, 41, 49–50, 55–56, 69, 96, 120, 140, 154, 179, 184; history and, 123–124, 130; machination and, 29–30, 67; singularity and, 99, 126
vulnerability, 25, 131

die Wahr (attentiveness), 156. See also *Aufmerksamkeit*
Weg-sein (being-away), 35, 82–83
will: in a positive sense, 40, 43n19; as will to power (*see* Nietzsche, Friedrich, will to power)
Wirkliche (actual) and *Wirklichkeit* (efficacious), 73
Wissen (knowing), 41, 46, 98, 158–159; essential knowing, 66, 87
withdrawal: of being, 5, 7, 22, 24, 26, 29, 53; of beyng, 10, 26, 30, 32, 54–55, 69, 73, 80, 82, 111, 125, 149–150, 188; draft of being's, 86, 99, 108–109, 114, 136
withstanding. See *ausstehen*
Wonne (delight), 157
word, 15, 111–112, 121–123, 159–163, 170–174, 180n4, 188; of beyng, 15, 117, 153, 160, 165–166n48, 171, 173; *Gegenwort* (counterword), 153; image-words and imageless, 163; telling words, 168–169
work: of art, 40–41, 44n34, 46–48, 184; texts as, 21, 24, 39, 141–142, 186
world, 30, 32, 47–48, 95, 146, 181n17, 193. *See also* strife of earth and world
World War II, 15, 60, 64, 72, 84, 95–96, 100, 175, 190
wreath. See *der Kranz der Kehre*
writing, 13, 38–42, 67, 172–173. *See also* work, texts as
Würde (dignity, worthiness), 71, 75–76, 83, 115–116, 124, 177, 183. See also *Armut*

Zeitlichkeit. See temporality, ecstatic
Ziarek, Krysztof, 180n4
Zu-eignung (assignment), 153, 165n28
Zu-mutung (demand of courage, sending of mood), 119
Zuspiel (interplay), 22, 89n4. *See also* first and other beginning

DANIELA VALLEGA-NEU is associate professor of philosophy at the University of Oregon. She is translator (with Richard Rojcewicz) of *Contributions to Philosophy (Of the Event)* (Indiana University Press, 2012) and author of *Heidegger's* Contributions to Philosophy: *An Introduction* (Indiana University Press, 2003) and *The Bodily Dimension in Thinking* (SUNY Press, 2005).

CPSIA information can be obtained
at www.ICGtesting.com
Printed in the USA
BVHW04s0723040518
515311BV00001B/2/P